Understanding
BORIS PASTERNAK

UNDERSTANDING MODERN
EUROPEAN AND LATIN AMERICAN
LITERATURE

JAMES HARDIN, *Series Editor*

volumes on

Ingeborg Bachmann
Samuel Beckett
Thomas Bernhard
Johannes Bobrowski
Heinrich Böll
Italo Calvino
Albert Camus
Elias Canetti
Céline
José Donoso
Rainer Werner Fassbinder
Max Frisch
Federico García Lorca
Gabriel García Márquez
Juan Goytisolo

Günter Grass
Gerhart Hauptmann
Christoph Hein
Eugène Ionesco
Milan Kundera
Primo Levi
Boris Pasternak
Luigi Pirandello
Graciliano Ramos
Erich Maria Remarque
Jean-Paul Sartre
Claude Simon
Mario Vargas Llosa
Peter Weiss
Franz Werfel

UNDERSTANDING

BORIS
PASTERNAK

LARISSA RUDOVA

UNIVERSITY OF SOUTH CAROLINA PRESS

© 1997 University of South Carolina

Published in Columbia, South Carolina, by the
University of South Carolina Press

Manufactured in the United States of America

01 00 99 98 97 5 4 3 2 1

Library of Congress Cataloging-in-Publication Data

Rudova, Larissa, 1953–
   Understanding Boris Pasternak / Larissa Rudova.
       p.   cm. — (Understanding modern European and Latin
American literature)
   Includes bibliographical references and index.
   ISBN 1–57003–143–6
   1. Pasternak, Boris Leonidovich, 1890–1960. 2.
Authors, Russian—20th century—Biography.   I. Title.
II. Series.
PG3476.P27Z815 1997
  891.71'42—dc20
   [B]   96–45786

For Hans Jürg

CONTENTS

EDITOR'S PREFACE

Understanding Modern European and Latin American Literature has been planned as a series of guides for undergraduate and graduate students and non-academic readers. Like the volumes in its companion series Understanding Contemporary American Literature, these books provide introductions to the lives and writings of prominent modern authors and explicate their most important works.

Modern literature makes special demands, and this is particularly true of foreign literature, in which the reader must contend not only with unfamiliar, often arcane artistic conventions and philosophical concepts, but also with the handicap of reading the literature in translation. It is a truism that the nuances of one language can be rendered in another only imperfectly (and this problem is especially acute in fiction), but the fact that the works of European and Latin American writers are situated in a historical and cultural setting quite different from our own can be as great a hindrance to the understanding of these works as the linguistic barrier. For this reason the UMELL series emphasizes the sociological and historical background of the writers treated. The peculiar philosophical and cultural traditions of a given culture may be particularly important for an understanding of certain authors, and these are taken up in the introductory chapter and also in the discussion of those works to which this information is relevant. Beyond this, the books treat the specifically literary aspects of the author under discussion and attempt to explain the complexities of contemporary literature lucidly. The books are conceived as introductions to the authors covered, not as comprehensive analyses. They do not provide detailed summaries of plot because they are meant to be used in conjunction with the books they treat, not as a substitute for study of the original works. The purpose of the books is to provide information and judicious literary assessment of the major works in the most compact, readable form. It is our hope that the UMELL series will help increase knowledge and understanding of European and Latin American cultures and will serve to make the literature of those cultures more accessible.

J.H.

PREFACE

A volume on Boris Pasternak (1890–1960) in a series of studies on world authors may seem to require some justification, for it is clear both to the general reader and to literary specialists that Pasternak does not have the status of a Pushkin, a Tolstoy, or a Dostoevsky, to name but three great writers in the Russian literary canon. He did become famous when he was awarded the Nobel Prize after the publication of *Doctor Zhivago* (1957) in the West and became somewhat of a "cold war" celebrity as a result of the controversy over the award in Russia, but he is still not as widely read in the West as other major Russian writers. So why Pasternak? For an answer to this question several factors must be remembered. There is, first, a fundamental difference in Pasternak's reception in Russia itself and in the West. Outside Russia, and certainly among the reading public at large, he is almost exclusively known as the author of *Doctor Zhivago*—and as far as that goes, probably more through the successful film version than the book itself. *Doctor Zhivago,* however, is Pasternak's only novel, in fact his only major prose work, and it came almost at the end of his career as a writer. The Western view of Pasternak, therefore, is generally one-sided and inadequate.

In Russia on the other hand, Pasternak is primarily known as a poet; *Doctor Zhivago,* after all, was published there only in 1988. It is for his poetry that he arguably ranks among the greatest writers in twentieth-century Russian literature, together with the poets Mayakovsky, Mandelstam, Tsvetaeva, and Akhmatova. Pasternak's mixed appreciation is, then, primarily the result of the genre he predominantly worked in and certainly also a consequence of the difficulty of translating his poetic work. If this book contributes to a more balanced reception of Pasternak's literary achievements in the West it will have served one of its purposes.

There is another issue, however, that has overshadowed Pasternak's reception, both in Russia and abroad: it is the mystery of why and how he, in contrast to most other great poets of his time, survived the historical and political adversities of his epoch and his generation. How could an individual who survived the advent of socialist realist doctrine and its ruthless implementation, who made it through the political and cultural purges of the Stalin era and managed to publish throughout, possibly have remained untainted by the poisoned and poisoning cultural and political climate of his time? To put this bluntly: what compromises did Pasternak make with the political tsars of Soviet culture? This is, of course, very much an issue of Western moral idealism in the face of political adversity, an issue that few Western critics have had to face themselves. But the question itself is legitimate as to how Pasternak made it through those years, specifically the 1930s and 1940s.

Let us not forget: Pasternak's generation lived through two world wars and three revolutions in Russia; they lived through some of the most inhuman times in history and into a new, "socialist reality" that became increasingly less promising and more depressing as time went on. Survivors of Pasternak's generation, like himself, saw their families killed, their friends sent to prison camps, and their whole cultural, artistic, and intellectual world destroyed all around them—and still, somehow, Pasternak endured. How exactly this came about is the intriguing and still largely unanswered question surrounding Pasternak. No researcher of Pasternak has been able to provide a precise answer, and the reader should not expect a full clarification of these issues here either. Pasternak was too private and always reluctant in private matters to have left a broad trail of personal documents. If this book succeeds in at least addressing the issues and hinting at some answers, it will have served its second purpose.

The third, in fact the major goal of this study, however, is to present the reader with an introductory overview of Pasternak's work, and in so doing to create a fuller understanding of Pasternak the poet and Pasternak the author of *Doctor Zhivago,* Pasternak the avant-garde artist of the second decade of the twentieth century as well as Pasternak the writer of the midcentury's quintessentially "Russian" grand epic work on the joys and sufferings of the individual, on the everyday hopes and defeats of humans in the face of historical changes, and on the fervent affirmation of life in times of hardship and toil. The integration of and mediation between the two diverse yet, upon closer consideration, not really divergent or mutually exclusive aspects of Pasternak's oeuvre are the central tasks of this book.

A NOTE ON TRANSLITERATION
AND ON QUOTATIONS

This book uses a modified U.S. Library of Congress transliteration system for Russian script for the convenience of the general reader. Well-known Russian names are transliterated in their more familiar forms (for example, Mayakovsky, Dostoevsky, Sinyavsky). For the notes and select bibliography, however, I have used the original form of transliteration chosen by each translator.

All quotations from Pasternak's works are in my own translation. Although I tried to be faithful to the original, sometimes my rendering of Pasternak was guided by the goal of clarifying stylistically complex passages. Many quotations, therefore, appear in a plainer language than in the original. For quotations, unless otherwise indicated, I used the most recent collection of Pasternak's works, *Sobranie sochinenii v piati tomakh* [*Collected Works in Five Volumes*], edited by E. V. Pasternak and K. M. Polivanov (Moscow: Khudozhestvennaia literatura, 1989–1992). References in parentheses throughout are from this edition; the first numeral in parenthesis indicates the volume number, and the following numeral indicates page numbers.

CHRONOLOGY

1890	Born February 10 in Moscow, the first of four children of painter Leonid Pasternak (1862–1945) and pianist Rosaliia Pasternak (née Kaufman, 1867–1939).
1900	First encounter with the German poet Rainer Maria Rilke.
1901	Begins attending Moscow Fifth Gymnasium (High School).
1903	Meets the composer Aleksandr Scriabin. Begins serious six year studies of music. Discovers Rilke's *Mir zur Feier*.
1906	The Pasternaks spend a year in Germany.
1907	Serious interest in Rilke's poetry. Joins the symbolist group Serdarda.
1908	Graduation from gymnasium with gold medal. Admitted to Moscow University to study law.
1909	Decides to give up music and takes serious interest in literature. Transfers to historical-philological faculty to study philosophy on Scriabin's advice.
1910	Reads paper "Symbolism and Immortality" to members of the symbolist group Musagetes.
1911	Joins the moderate futurist group Centrifuge.
1912	Studies philosophy for a semester at the University of Marburg. Takes a trip to Italy.
1913	Graduates from Moscow University in philosophy. Writes poetry.
1914	Meets the futurist Vladimir Mayakovsky. Russia enters WW I. Pasternak is exempt from military service because of a leg injury suffered in 1903. Works as a private tutor. Translates Heinrich von Kleist. Publishes his first collection of poetry, *Twin in the Clouds*.
1915	Travels to the Urals. Begins work on his second collection of poetry, *Over the Barriers*.
1916	Back in Moscow. Works as a tutor for Moritz Phillip, a German manufacturer. Poems appear in the second collection of Centrifuge. In the winter he travels back to the Urals.

	Works in chemical factories until the news of the February revolution of 1917 reaches him.
1917	Returns to Moscow. The Bolsheviks take power as the result of the October revolution. Publishes the collection *Over the Barriers.*
1918	Works as a librarian at the Commissariat of Education. The Soviet government signs the peace treaty of Brest-Litovsk with Germany. Beginning of the civil war.
1921	Family immigrates to Germany. Stays in Moscow with brother Aleksandr. End of the civil war.
1922	Marriage to painter Evgeniia Lur'e. A trip to Berlin and Marburg. Third collection of poems, *My Sister-Life,* establishes him as a major Russian poet. "Liuvers's Childhood" is published.
1923	Son Evgenii is born. The fourth collection of poems, *Themes and Variations,* is published in Berlin.
1924	Publishes the short story "Aerial Ways" and fragments of the poem *Sublime Malady.* Works on the novel in verse *Spektorskii.* Death of Lenin.
1926	Publication of the epic poem *Lieutenant Schmidt.* Death of Rilke.
1927	The epic poem *The Year Nineteen-Five* is published.
1928	*Sublime Malady* is published.
1929	Publication of "The Tale" and *Safe Conduct,* part 1.
1930	Mayakovsky's suicide.
1931	Separation from wife. Visits Georgia with Zinaida Neigauz and her two sons. Develops strong connections with Georgian poets. Publication of *Safe Conduct* and *Spektorskii* in book form.
1932	Publication of *Second Birth.* The Union of Soviet Writers is created. Visits the Urals with delegation of Soviet writers.
1933	Second trip to Georgia. Begins serious work on translations.
1934	Marries Zinaida Neigauz. Telephone conversation with Stalin. Pasternak is asked about his opinion of Mandelstam. The concept of socialist realism is formulated at the First Congress of Soviet Writers. Trip to Georgia.

1935	Suffers from depression. Sent by the Soviet government to the International Congress of Writers for the Defense of Culture in Paris. Meets with Tsvetaeva in Meudon. Publication of *Poets of Georgia,* translated by Pasternak and Nikolai Tikhonov.
1936	Delivers a speech at the Minsk Plenary Session of the Board of the Union of Writers. Criticizes the bureaucratization of literature. A visit to Georgia. The beginning of Stalin's terror (1936–1938), known as the "purge." Receives a country house in Peredelkino, near Moscow, from the government.
1937	Refuses to sign a letter condemning a group of army generals accused of conspiracy. Son Leonid is born.
1938	Mandelstam dies in a prison camp.
1939	Death of Pasternak's mother in London. Tsvetaeva's return from emigration. Beginning of WW II.
1940	Pasternak's translations are published (Becher, Byron, Keats, Kleist, Petöfi, Raleigh, Hans Sachs, Shakespeare).
1941	Completes his translation of *Hamlet.* Hitler attacks the Soviet Union. Pasternak evacuates to the Urals with family. Tsvetaeva's suicide. Continues work on translations.
1942	Works on a new collection of verse, *On Early Trains.*
1943	Returns to Moscow with his family. *On Early Trains* is published. Visits the front near Orel with other writers. Describes his experience in a documentary story, "A Trip to the Front."
1944	Soviet army frees the occupied territory.
1945	Father dies in Oxford. End of WW II. Publishes a collection of poetry, *Spacious Earth.* Begins work on *Doctor Zhivago.*
1946	The government campaign against "cosmopolitanism" in the arts, known as "Zhdanovshina." Pasternak is attacked by critics and government ideologues. Meets Olga Ivinskaia; the relationship continues until the end of his life.
1947	Begins translation of Goethe's *Faust.*
1948	Continues work on translations.
1949	Arrest of Ivinskaia.
1950	Suffers two heart attacks in one year.

1952	Another heart attack.
1953	Fourth heart attack. Devotes most of his time to *Doctor Zhivago*. His translation of *Faust* is published. Ivinskaia's return from concentration camp. Death of Stalin.
1954	Ten poems from *Doctor Zhivago* are published.
1955	Completes *Doctor Zhivago*. Begins writing poetry that will be included in the book *When the Weather Clears*.
1956	Soviet publishers refuse to publish *Doctor Zhivago*. Offers the manuscript to the Italian publisher Feltrinelli.
1957	Publication of *Doctor Zhivago* in translation in Italy.
1958	*Doctor Zhivago* is translated and published in many countries. Awarded the Nobel Prize. Slanderous ideological campaign against Pasternak. Fearing expulsion from the Soviet Union, he renounces the prize. "People and Situations: An Autobiographical Sketch" is published in France and Italy.
1959	*When the Weather Clears* is published abroad. Feltrinelli publishes *Doctor Zhivago* in Russian. Last visit to Georgia.
1960	May 30: Dies of lung cancer in Peredelkino.
1988	First publication of *Doctor Zhivago* in the Soviet Union.
1989–1992	Five-volume collection of Pasternak's works published in Russia.

Understanding
BORIS PASTERNAK

Introduction

Boris Pasternak's place (1890–1960) in Russian literature has been compared to Johann Wolfgang von Goethe's in Germany (de Mallac 1981, xvii). Among his literary contemporaries, Pasternak is the only one who achieved international stature and in 1958 was awarded the Nobel Prize for his "important achievement both in contemporary lyric poetry and in the field of the great Russian tradition" (Conquest 1961, 85). Pasternak's work reflects the complexities of Russian historical realities more vividly than the work of most other representatives of his generation, including such prominent poets as Osip Mandelstam (1891–1938), Anna Akhmatova (1889–1966), Vladimir Mayakovsky (1893–1930), and Marina Tsvetaeva (1892–1941). Of these four only Akhmatova survived Pasternak, but her work was suppressed by the Soviet authorities and hardly published in the 1930s and 1940s. Both Mayakovsky and Tsvetaeva committed suicide, and Mandelstam perished in prison. Pasternak was the only one in this group who miraculously survived the purges of the Soviet cultural elite of his generation; even in the hardest years of political repression, unleashed by the dictator Joseph Stalin (1879–1953) in the 1930s and continuing until Stalin's death, Pasternak remained intellectually and professionally active, and most of his works were published throughout his career. This book will follow Pasternak's artistic development in the context of Russian cultural-political reality and point to the latter's effect on his work, hopefully making clear how this reality is reflected in his poetry and prose.

Although Pasternak's first complete collection of works was published in Russia only in 1989–1992 and consists of a mere five volumes, his work is truly multifaceted: he wrote poetry as well as prose, translated works of world literature, made himself a name as a literary critic, and attempted to write a drama.[1] Russian readers had known him well, although mostly as a poet, until his novel *Doktor Zhivago* (*Doctor Zhivago;* first published in Italian in 1957) was published in the Soviet Union for the first time in 1988. The West only took notice of him after publication of his novel. And it was only after this that Western readers became interested in his poetry. But even now Pasternak's poems are still not widely known by the educated reading public in the West, partly because a comprehensive and annotated study of his poetry is still to be written for the general Western reader. The several good biographies that appeared during the last decade only partially make up for this lack.

During his lifetime Pasternak authored nine cycles of poems demonstrating his enormous range of stylistic talent, from early technical virtuosity to the restrained simplicity of his late years. His fiction consists of a number of short stories—and his only novel, *Doctor Zhivago.* Also important among Pasternak's works are two autobiographies, *Okhrannaia gramota* (*Safe Conduct,* 1931) and "Liudi i polozheniia: Avtobiograficheskii ocherk" (literally translated as "People and Situations: An Autobiographical Sketch" but also known in English under the title "I Remember: Sketch for an Autobiography," 1956). Both autobiographies reflect Pasternak's views on art and shed light on his development as a poet, as well as describing the artistic and political climate that surrounded him. In addition to his collections of poems and fiction, Pasternak's writings include numerous critical essays and translations. Pasternak was among the most accomplished translators of William Shakespeare (1564–1616); Goethe (1749–1832); George Gordon, Lord Byron (1788–1824); Paul Verlaine (1844–1896), and other western European poets into Russian. He was also one of the best translators of contemporary Georgian poets into Russian.

A substantial part of Pasternak's literary-biographical heritage consists of his correspondence, which totals 345 letters in the most recent edition (1989–1992) of his collected works. This might not be an impressive number if compared to the voluminous correspondence left by such great Russian writers as Lev Tolstoy (1828–1910) or Fyodor Dostoevsky (1821–1881), but since Pasternak did not keep diaries or notebooks, these letters become a most valuable source for understanding his personal experiences and views. Because of the scandal caused by the publication in the West of the banned novel *Doctor Zhivago,* Pasternak's works were suppressed in the Soviet Union, and even after his posthumous rehabilitation in the 1960s, only selected works were published and no serious efforts were made to organize and publish his archives. It was only twenty-eight years after Pasternak's death that *Doctor Zhivago* was finally published in his own country for the first time in the journal *Novyi mir* (*New World*)[2] thanks to the new liberal policies introduced by the Soviet leader Mikhail Gorbachev. But a complete biographical study of Pasternak's life and work has yet to be written in Russia. It is not surprising, then, that the most impressive scholarship on Pasternak has been produced abroad, above all in England and the United States. The works of such scholars as Christopher Barnes, Lazar Fleishman, Henry Gifford, Ronald Hingley, Olga Hughes, Angela

Livingstone, and Guy de Mallac have greatly enriched our understanding of Pasternak's life and literary heritage.

Pasternak's works have been translated into many languages, and *Doctor Zhivago* is one of the most widely read Russian novels abroad today. It was made popular, of course, through its Hollywood screen version of 1965. In fact, this slightly schmaltzy movie is probably the only acquaintance most non-Russians have with Pasternak. For Russians, however, Pasternak is as much a poet as a novelist, and it is only due to unfortunate political circumstances surrounding the publishing of *Doctor Zhivago* that the novel was singled out for a special and exclusive reception by Western critics. Although this situation has since changed in favor of a more global view of his works, the difficulty of presenting Pasternak's poetry in all its brilliance will always remain insuperable. The main reason is, of course, that Pasternak is virtually an untranslatable poet and short fiction writer. Although there exist a good number of translations of his poems into English, no two of them sound similar, as most translators try to preserve one aspect of the original thereby inevitably losing others. The most prominent and complete collection of Pasternak's verse in English is by Eugene M. Kayden. While this translator's work is impressive in many ways, he takes liberty with Pasternak's imagery, metrical patterns, and stanzaic breaks.

As any great poet, Pasternak was deeply connected with his age, his literary talent firmly rooted in and shaped by his cultural and political environment and his work carrying the deep imprint of his age. Pasternak was born when Russia was still struggling with its feudal past after the emancipation of the serfs in 1861 and was slowly entering capitalism. He was a young man when the czar was overthrown and the Bolsheviks established their power in 1917. During the nightmare of political repression under Stalin, Pasternak was subject to continuous political attacks, but he survived and lived to see the dictator's death. But despite the relative liberalization in literature during the post-Stalin years, known as "the Thaw," Pasternak fell victim to ideological obscurantism after the publication of his novel abroad. In the words of one critic, Pasternak "lived to tell the tale, to proclaim, indeed to exemplify, the resilience of the poetic imagination. A 'hostage to eternity,' he sprang the bonds of time."[3]

In order to understand Pasternak's works and how they were affected by the turbulent times he lived in, it is necessary to take a close look at his personal background and the creative sources that nourished him to artistic maturity. A discussion of the origins of Pasternak's work will also enable us to understand the still-ambivalent status he occupies in Russian literature and his unresolved struggle to find a balance between the world of his prerevolutionary past and the world of Soviet Russia.

Origins and the Cultural Milieu; Scriabin and Rilke

Russia during Pasternak's childhood and youth was a land of "glaring extremes and contradictions."[4] By the time World War I broke out in 1914, the Russian Empire was still largely a poor agrarian country with two-thirds of the population occupied in agriculture. If one considers that Germany, itself slow to begin the industrial process, was down to some 50 percent of its population involved in agriculture as early as the 1860s, it is not hard to imagine the economic gap between Russia and the West. Although Russia's industry was ranked fifth in the world, industrialization affected only selected geographical regions, and many industrial sectors were still poorly developed. The living conditions of peasants and workers were dismal and presented a shocking contrast to the comfortable life of the small section of the nobility, professionals, and industrialists. Much also remained to be done in the area of education since the vast majority of the Russian population was illiterate. Yet at the turn of the twentieth century, Russia was far from being culturally backward, and its small cultural elite produced a remarkable constellation of authentic talents in all branches of knowledge and the arts.

Pasternak was born into a highly cultured Jewish family in Moscow on 10 February 1890. Later in life he played down his Jewish origin and was inclined more toward Christianity than Judaism. His seeming lack of interest in things Jewish was largely due to the secular atmosphere in the family and the completely russified surroundings in which he grew up (Barnes 1989, 27–28). According to Fleishman, Pasternak became concerned with the Jewish question only at the end of the 1920s when he became aware of the predominance of Jews in the Soviet government apparatus and the party in the early postrevolutionary years. After that time he associated the Jewish question with the revolution (Fleishman 1990, 263–64). But not until *Doctor Zhivago* did Pasternak directly express his views on the condition of the Jews in Russia.[5]

Pasternak's father, Leonid Osipovich Pasternak (1862–1945), was a famous painter working primarily in the impressionistic manner and a professor at the Moscow School of Painting. His work was a fresh breath in Russian painting, dominated by the *Peredvizhniki* (Itinerants), a group of realist painters who became active in the early 1870s and whose major concern was social criticism. Pasternak's mother, Rosaliia Isidorovna (née Kaufman, 1867–1939), was a brilliant pianist and a protégée of the composer and great pianist Anton Rubinstein. Before her marriage to Leonid Pasternak she toured extensively in Russia and abroad and played with many famous performers, among them the

4

brilliant Spanish violinist Pablo Sarasate. The cultural atmosphere at home played an important role in shaping young Boris Pasternak's interests. As a child he met many famous Russian and Western cultural figures. Tolstoy, the German poet Rainer Maria Rilke (1875–1926), and the Russian composer Aleksandr Scriabin (1871–1915) were among Leonid Pasternak's acquaintances and visited his home on various occasions. The significance of some of these personalities, especially Scriabin and Rilke, for Boris Pasternak's life is hard to overestimate.

Music and the personality of Scriabin were the first important influences on the artistic development of the young Pasternak. He received systematic musical training from 1903 to 1909 and planned a career in music. When he began to compose, Scriabin's work became his model (Barnes 1977, 17). Scriabin's music appealed to him through its innovative sound patterns and its new language that connected to spiritual as well as emotional receptors ("Autobiographical Sketch," 4:307–8). Pasternak was especially enthusiastic about Scriabin's *The Poem of Ecstasy,* and many years after he had abandoned his musical career he still recalled the overpowering effect of *The Poem* in his autobiography *Safe Conduct.*

So strong was Scriabin's impact on the young Pasternak that, in spite of the disappointment with the composer's later work, Pasternak never really renounced the "non-musical aspect of Scriabin's legacy" (Barnes 1989, 89). According to Barnes, Pasternak absorbed many of the composer's eclectic views on art and history that were shared by the symbolists even before he came in contact with them as a university student. Like Scriabin, and partially through him, Pasternak became deeply indebted to Russian symbolist culture and revealed interests similar to the composer's, particularly in his concern with originality and innovation in art. Scriabin's quest for new forms had emerged naturally out of his philosophy of music. He was drawn to mysticism and became an eager student of theosophy, a doctrine that teaches that man can know spiritual reality through meditation, mystical experience, or philosophical speculation. The composer believed in the superior status of music among the arts and its power to reach spiritual dimensions. Like symbolist poets, Scriabin saw himself as a priest whose task was to reveal spiritual truths to the world. And like the symbolists, Scriabin was inspired to find new forms to convey these truths.

Although Pasternak worshipped Scriabin and successfully composed music in a Scriabinesque manner, he eventually decided to abandon his own musical career because he did not have perfect pitch. Pasternak knew well that Scriabin himself did not have it, yet he firmly believed in the futility of composing music without it and treated his "defect" as a sign of fate. After Scriabin failed to persuade his young admirer to continue his pursuit of music, he encouraged him to turn to the study of philosophy at the University of Moscow.

Even after music was no longer Pasternak's vocation, Scriabin's heritage played an important role in shaping his future artistic sensibilities and manifested itself above all in a new artistic spirit marked by experimentation and a great ambition to create a new language in art. That language was oriented toward abstraction (in Scriabin's case, abstraction translated into experiments with "lush and mellifluous assonance" [Barnes 1977, 15]), breaking the old forms, and focusing on artistic devices. Perhaps Scriabin's preoccupation with combining different art media, for example, color and music, also affected Pasternak's first literary efforts. Despite his criticism of Scriabin's experiments in mixing media, Pasternak's own work, after a closer examination of synaesthetic principles, moved in the same direction as the composer's, and Pasternak's early style displays an affinity with Russian Cubo-Futurist painting and its fragmented imagery and elements of collage. As late as 1958 Pasternak admitted Scriabin's lasting influence on him: "I despised everything that was not creative. . . . The seeds of his views . . . fell on grateful soil" ("Autobiographical Sketch," 306).

When Pasternak abandoned music his interest in innovation in the arts did not subside. It was at that time, after Pasternak's first trip abroad in 1906, that another great personality, the German poet Rainer Maria Rilke, entered his life. The force, magnetism, and spirituality of Rilke's writing attracted Pasternak's attention and held it for the rest of his life. Now increasingly a verbal artist, Pasternak developed a much closer affinity with Rilke's art than he had with Scriabin's. In his 1926 letter to the great poet, Pasternak wrote: "I am indebted to you for basic aspects of my character and the very kind of my spiritual existence. They are your creations."[6] Pasternak believed that throughout his artistic life he "translated and varied" Rilke's motifs (Barnes 1972, 65). Having discovered Rilke's poetry in his adolescence, Pasternak's fascination with Rilke's personality and poetry grew even stronger when he realized that he had met Rilke on a train while traveling with his father in the summer of 1900. Pasternak's admiration of Rilke was so great that he dedicated his 1931 autobiography *Safe Conduct* to his beloved poet's memory.

Pasternak's fascination with Rilke's poetry is not difficult to understand, for Rilke, like Scriabin, had his roots in symbolism, went beyond it, and carried on the spirit of modernism. More specifically, Rilke was preoccupied with the synthesis of the arts as much as Scriabin was. The language of Rilke's poetry and prose, besides being highly musical at times and filled with musical imagery, also contains strong elements of the visual arts. Rilke was a great admirer of the French sculptor Auguste Rodin (1840–1917), whose secretary and biographer he was in the early years of the new century, and the French painter Paul Cézanne (1839–1906), a figure instrumental in transition of modern art from impressionism to abstraction; Rilke attempted to produce in his own verbal medium the effects of their respective arts. He was especially drawn to Rodin's and Cézanne's violation of the traditional forms and the gravitation of their art toward the abstract. Fragmentation, blurring of the borders between objects, and dislocation and rearrangement of the represented world were some of the devices Rilke learned from the two masters. His own works, especially the 1910 short novel *Die Aufzeichnungen des Malte Laurids Brigge* (*The Notebooks of Malte Laurids Brigge*), are a tribute to his preoccupation with painterly imagery. By assimilating the artistic principles of another art medium, Rilke underlined one of the central traits of his aesthetics—and of modern art in general—namely the push toward creating a mixture of forms, a total work of art or a *Gesamtkunstwerk*. From studying Rilke's poetry, Pasternak, in turn, learned a great deal about integrating artistic principles of different arts into his own poetry, and the spirit of musical and painterly imagery penetrates his early writing. Rilke's poetic principles, like Scriabin's earlier on, contributed profoundly to Pasternak's choice of representational techniques, stimulated his interest in symbolist culture, and defined the lines along which his own art would develop over the next two decades.

The Symbolists

Although symbolism emerged as a response to realism and naturalism and the effects of positivistic science, it also owed a great deal to the atmosphere of disillusionment and instability in contemporary Russian society and foreshadowed a disruption in the political and social spheres. In the larger picture of modernism, at whose beginning it stood, symbolism rebelled against the limitation of artistic forms and signaled their reshaping. By the turn of the twentieth century Russian culture was undergoing extensive changes, and most art forms were marked by a strong spirit of experimentation. After decades dominated by realist novels and socially oriented literary criticism, Russian literature began to explore new aesthetic territories, so that the impressionistic short stories and nostalgic plays by Anton Chekhov (1860–1904), as well as symbolist poetry and theater, felt refreshing. They were a sign of a new trend in culture focusing on intangibles: impressions, dreams, memories, associations, and other forms of experience marked by subjectivity and ambivalence. Realism, with its roots in mimesis and verisimilitude, seemed to be increasingly incapable of reproducing these subtle depths of human experience, and it fell to symbolism to devise means of representing them, largely through the replacement of mimetic representation by more elusive forms of evocation.

Whereas symbolism was accepted almost everywhere in Europe by 1885, in Russia it was not recognized as a movement until 1893 when in his seminal lecture "O prichinakh upadka i novykh tendentsiiakh v sovremennoi russkoi literature" ("About the Reasons for Decline and New Tendencies in Contemporary Russian Literature") the writer Dmitrii Merezhkovskii (1866–1941) raised questions about the way Russian art was developing. Merezhkovskii declared symbolism the leading art of the time and invested in it his hope for the spiritual revival of Russia. The symbolists aspired to reach new spiritual depths and understand the essence of reality with the help of art. It was exclusively art, not science, that the symbolists viewed as the primary means of cognition. Valerii Briusov, for instance, declared in his manifesto, "Kliuchi tain" ("The Keys to the Mysteries," 1904), that the doors to eternity could be opened only through art because art alone was capable of conveying the illuminating moments of communication between the soul and the invisible spiritual world. According to Briusov, symbolism had a liberating impact on art by going "beyond rational forms, beyond causal thinking."[7] Another great Russian symbolist, Andrei Bely, celebrated tearing off and breaking down the "old petrified mask of the classical art" and instead welcomed artistic expansions that clarified "the depths of the spirit."[8]

To the young Pasternak symbolism meant the transition to a literary career. In 1908 he joined Serdarda, one of the numerous artistic groups with a symbolist bent that mushroomed in Moscow and Saint Petersburg at the time. Initially he attended Serdarda's meetings as a musician, but encouraged by his friend Sergei Durylin, he shifted his artistic endeavors to poetry. The palette of Pasternak's acquaintances and interests at that time is of astonishing variety. He was still playing the piano, had begun to write poetry, had translated Rilke,[9] was interested in philosophy, and even lectured on symbolism. He was also associated with another symbolist circle called Musagetes that was not only a symbolist publishing house but also "a sort of an academy" ("Autobiographical Sketch," 4:319). During their meetings prominent Russian symbolists taught "sympathetic young people rhythmics, the history of German Romanticism, Russian lyrical poetry, the aesthetics of Goethe and Wagner, Baudelaire and the French Symbolists, as well as ancient Greek pre-Socratic philosophy" ("Autobiographical Sketch," 319). There were three major sections in Musagetes: the philosophical, the rhythmical, and the third devoted to the study of symbolism. Pasternak appeared in Bely's rhythmical section and attended the studies of symbolism. Initially Bely's section was appealing to Pasternak because of its attention to Russian classical iambics, which eventually proved to be important in the development of formalist analysis of poetry, but Pasternak's attendance at the seminar turned out to be short-lived and sporadic because he disagreed with Bely's idea that "verbal music is . . . an acoustic phenomenon" consisting in the euphony of consonants and vowels. Instead, he held that it resided "in the relationship of the sound of speech to its meaning" ("Autobiographical Sketch," 319). Yet Pasternak could not resist the appeal of Bely's approach to the study of rhythm. His own rhythmic experiments in poetry, starting with his first collection of poems, *Bliznets v tuchakh* (*Twin in the Clouds,* 1914), was a sign of his indebtedness to Bely's work. Pasternak introduced Bely's ternary meters with missing stress on the metrically strong syllables into his work, and his innovative use of the ternary classical meter was as pioneering as Bely's reform of iambic tetrameter.[10] In rejecting Bely's ideas about musical composition, Pasternak unconsciously stuck to an idea of Scriabin's, who was known to believe that each musical note contained its own meaning.

In the symbolist section of Musagetes, Pasternak attempted to work out some theoretical generalizations and gave a lecture entitled "Simvolizm i bessmertie" ("Symbolism and Immortality"). The lecture explored the symbolic and subjective nature of art; it had mystical overtones and demonstrated "much common ground" with "the general fund of Symbolist theory" (Barnes 1989, 151). The theses of the lecture were written in a vague symbolist style and alluded to the transcendental dimension of immortality.[11] According to Pasternak, the poet was endowed with a special form of consciousness that granted him immortality and connected him with the transcendental dimension or, as he called it, "free subjectivity" ("Symbolism and Immortality," 116). Pasternak's idea of "free subjectivity" developed in this lecture was similar to some of Bely's views on the nature of the subject-object relationship, in which the "'I' ceased to be the subject of individual perceptions and became an all-embracing poetic extension of the Kantian 'transcendental subject'" (Barnes 1989, 151). Along the same symbolist lines, Pasternak's notion of a special form of consciousness showed a resemblance to the "supra-individual form of consciousness," developed by two religious philosophers popular with the symbolists, Nikolai Berdiaev (1874–1948) and Semen Frank (1877–1950) (Barnes 1989, 151). In his lecture Pasternak discussed poetry as "madness without a madman" ("Symbolism and Immortality," 116), a concept closely related to the "Dionysian ecstasy" identified by one of the major Russian symbolists, Viacheslav Ivanov, as an "organic principle of art" (Barnes 1989, 151). On the whole, the points Pasternak makes in "Symbolism and Immortality" demonstrate his full familiarity with the symbolist agenda, as well as a symbolist bent in his own early thinking.

Serdarda and Musagetes were episodes in Pasternak's artistic biography, but taken in the context of his early development, they show him following the direction already charted by Scriabin and Rilke. Although symbolism was becoming an amorphous academic movement when Pasternak became its student and soon fell short of his artistic expectations, both Serdarda and Musagetes provided experiences that reinforced Pasternak's path toward nontraditional, even antitraditional art forms. Like the symbolists, he valued subjective expression in art, and he shared their view that art possesses a transcendental unifying power. These views survived in his work even decades later and reappeared in *Doctor Zhivago*. The symbolists held further appeal for Pasternak because they were concerned, as were Scriabin and Rilke, with the strict mastery of the medium—language—and strongly leaned toward fusion of the arts and toward abstraction.

The Futurists

By 1910, when Pasternak was a university student in Moscow, symbolism ceased to play a central role on the Russian literary scene. The newly emerging futurists were much more radical than their symbolist predecessors had been, driving further the abstraction of form and the synthesis of the arts. Despite their repudiation of symbolism, they pursued the symbolists' quest to go beyond the surface of reality and express its meaning in art. But unlike the symbolists, the futurists did not believe in a spiritual reality and were firmly grounded in the physical world, trying to understand it through its internal cohesion. Whenever the futurists turned to the representation of physical objects, it acquired a fragmented shape because they wanted to reveal both its spatial and temporal cohesion and realms of essence. The more the futurists destroyed familiar forms and complicated new ones, the more they made art into a self-contained entity, a thing-in-itself. Once their poetry proclaimed itself a thing, rather than a system of meaning, it distanced itself from logical comprehension.

In search of the ultimate abstract forms, the poets of the Russian futurist group Hylaea experimented with writing poetry in nonsense language that they called *zaum'*, or "transrational language." The first futurist experiments with the poetic word were confined to the creation of neologisms and the new "self-oriented word" and extended from there to the large-scale linguistic abstraction represented by *zaum'*. The term *zaum'* was invented by the futurist poet Aleksei Kruchenykh and described a mode of poetic expression that transcended rules of grammar as well as common sense and was meant to be completely nonreferential. *Zaum'* was an artificial and pure linguistic abstraction, incomprehensible to the reader.[12] Like Russian cubo-futurist painting, which owed to cubism in painting and futurism in poetry, *zaum'* sought to eliminate the possibility of reference to existing familiar forms. Later on, the futurists went so far as to create poetry using only punctuation marks. The central aim of transrational poetry was the invention of new linguistic forms, deliberately illogical and incoherent.

The new poetic spirit of futurism was closer to Pasternak's artistic needs than symbolism had been, and in 1914 he joined a moderate futurist group, Tsentrifuga (Centrifuge). Centrifuge was formed at the end of 1913 and represented something like the educated and cultured "aristocracy" in comparison with the more democratic and largely self-educated membership of Hylaea or the Mezzanine of Poetry (an ego-futurist group). Pasternak seems to have been very active in Centrifuge, and his name appeared under the group's manifesto, *Gramota,* together with the names of three other poets. In addition, Pasternak's "futurist" articles, entitled "Vassermanova reaktsiia" ("Wassermann's Reaction," 1914) and "Chernyi bokal" ("The Black Goblet," 1916), appeared in the group's publications *Rukonog* (translated into English by Vladimir Markov as *Brachiopod*) and *The Second Collection of Centrifuge.*

Centrifuge fits smoothly into the pattern of Pasternak's artistic-intellectual attractions described so far. It had a European orientation and strong ties with contemporary avant-garde painting.[13] The group also provided a direct continuity of the young writer's short symbolist past: despite its commitment to poetic innovation in the futurist vein, Centrifuge, especially at the beginning, had a symbolist bent and was dominated by the former Serdarda member and pupil of Bely in versification, Sergei Bobrov. Bobrov strongly supported Pasternak's first poetic experiments and became a figure crucial for the launching of his literary career.

Pasternak's initial enthusiasm for Centrifuge did not last, however. Within a year he became disappointed with the group's increasing involvement in the more outrageous futurist debates. Centrifuge was seriously concerned about its artistic status among other futurist groups and spent a lot of energy defending its own agenda by attacking other futurist groups. Pasternak, however, was more interested in pursuing his own poetic ambitions and felt distracted by the group's politics. Another serious problem for him was that Centrifuge, despite

Bobrov's efforts to strengthen its futurist reputation, was never able to over-come the lyricism of its symbolist past and match the poetic innovations of the cubo-futurists. In the meantime Pasternak, especially after his meeting with the cubo-futurist Vladimir Mayakovsky in 1914, was increasingly leaning toward cubo-futurist poetic experiments. His collection of poems *Twin in the Clouds* and his early experiments in fiction (1911–1913) were marked by complex imagery, anthropomorphism, and a convoluted syntax reminiscent of cubo-fu-turist poetry. Pasternak's *Poverkh bar'erov* (*Above the Barriers,* 1916), his only collection of verse published under the auspices of Centrifuge (in 1917), has been characterized by Markov as containing an "abundance of violence and anti-aestheticism in imagery [that] would suffice to put him [Pasternak] next to Kruchenykh and Burliuk," two of the most radical cubo-futurist poets (Markov 1968, 270). Pasternak himself commented on his poetic affinity with Mayakovsky in *Safe Conduct.* In spite of his intention to dissociate his writing from Mayakovsky's influence, Pasternak's *Above the Barriers* shows obvious similarities with Mayakovsky's poetry. The kinship reveals itself, above all, in the violent, fragmented imagery. And even though it would be hard to demon-strate that the fragmented and displaced imagery in the early Pasternak was inspired solely by Mayakovsky, it is undeniable that the young Pasternak was greatly influenced by Mayakovsky's ideas, themselves inspired by cubism.

Especially important among the new poetic principles was the synthesis of poetry and painting, arts that had never come as close to each other in Russia as they did during the period of the cubo-futurist movement. Most cubo-futurist poets were also, in fact, painters, among them Mayakovsky and Kruchenykh. An important concern of cubo-futurism was with theoretical-technical prob-lems in poetry and painting. Many cubo-futurists wrote about art, and their declarations and manifestos suggest their infatuation with the synthesis of po-etry and painting.[14] As early as 1912 Mayakovsky gave a lecture entitled "O noveishei russkoi poezii i zhivopisi" (About the Newest Russian Poetry and Painting) in which he addressed analogies between developments in poetry and painting.[15] The first line of Kruchenykh's and Velemir Khlebnikov's cubo-fu-turist manifesto, "Slovo kak takovoe" (The Word as Such, 1913) proclaimed: "Let it [word] be heard and seen in a blink of an eye!"[16] And in another 1913 manifesto, "Novye puti slova" (New Paths of the Word), Kruchenykh discussed the parallel developments of the principles of composition in avant-garde lit-erature and painting. Pasternak doubtlessly absorbed some of the cubo-futurist ideas about "painting with the word," as cubo-futurists described the process of poetical composition based on principles of painting. He must have heard of David Burliuk's artistic experiments from his father, who was Burliuk's teacher, and his own futurist environment and personal contact with cubo-futurists could have also drawn his attention to the problems of transposing the methods of one art onto another. It comes as no surprise, then, that his own poetry of that period reflects his tendency toward a synthesis of the arts.

This section has attempted to show that Pasternak came in contact with different literary movements and ideas of leading figures in modern art. What is important in this discussion of his cultural environment is that in spite of their differences, all the artistic groups and personalities blended rather smoothly into a common artistic orientation, thanks to their interest in synaesthetic issues, and as part of their creative aspiration to find a new artistic idiom—the modernist one. Pasternak always retained his individuality, and his own art belonged to no one; but during the early years of his artistic biography he was an integral and integrated part of this cultural environment and drew his inspiration from it. That cannot be said for his later phases.

CHAPTER ONE

Early Poetry

To bring the poet Pasternak to the English-speaking world is not an easy matter, especially where his early poetry, known for its stylistic complexity, is concerned. The Russian poetic system as such does not lend itself easily to an accurate rendering in English, and within this system Pasternak is notoriously difficult to translate. In order to illustrate the difficulties of translating Russian poetry into English, the Russian and English systems of versification will briefly be compared. Both are syllabo-tonic, that is, they take into account the number of syllables as well as the number of accents in a line. The stressed and unstressed syllables regularly alternate in a line and create the so-called meter or metrical scheme. The choice of meter naturally determines rhythm. In Russian words tend to be longer than in English and have only one stress regardless of their length; therefore, more stresses are omitted in rhythmical patterns in Russian than in English. In a Russian poem, unlike in an English one, a fully stressed line is not so common. This peculiarity accounts for different rhythms even if an English and a Russian poem have the same metrical scheme. Another difference is that Russian has more polysyllabic endings than English, which makes rhythmical possibilities more varied but rhyming more difficult. Whereas English poetry is characterized mostly by masculine rhymes, that is, rhymes with the stress on the last syllable, Russian poetry has a more even balance between masculine and feminine rhymes, the latter stressed on the penultimate syllable. Because of these differences, the lines translated from Pasternak's poems in this book can aim, at best, only to provide an approximation of the original imagery and meaning. It is for this reason also that discussion about Pasternak's prosodic innovations will be brief and concentrate mostly on the thematics, structure, and imagery of his poetry.

Twin in the Clouds

In 1909 after Pasternak abandoned music, he began to study philosophy at the University of Moscow. In the summer of 1912 he undertook a trip to Marburg,

Germany, to study Immanuel Kant under the famous neo-Kantian philosophers Hermann Cohen and Paul Natorp. His brief and unsuccessful courtship of his Moscow friend and former private student, Ida Vysotskaia, who, on the way from Belgium to Berlin with her sister, visited Pasternak at the end of his summer semester in Marburg, together with Pasternak's realization that a career in philosophy was not for him prompted his departure from Marburg. Not only did the young Pasternak suffer emotionally, he seemed to have lost his motivation to pursue the study of philosophy and felt a strong urge to write. He began to write poetry while completing his university degree in philosophy at Moscow University and after graduation devoted himself entirely to writing. The first volume of poems, entitled *Bliznets v tuchakh* (*Twin in the Clouds*), was published by the symbolist group and publishing house Lirika in 1914. In 1929 Pasternak revised eleven of the twenty-one poems of this volume for a new collection published under the title of his 1917 cycle, *Poverkh bar'erov* (*Above the Barriers*). More than forty years later in his "Autobiographical Sketch" Pasternak called the title of his first collection "stupidly pretentious" and admitted that it was chosen "in imitation of the cosmological profundities that distinguished book titles of the symbolists and the names of their publishing houses" (4:326). Pasternak also admitted that writing those poems had been a creative necessity for him and had given him great pleasure at that time. However, preparing the collection for a later edition brought him dissatisfaction. In a 1928 letter to Mandelstam, he complained that *Twin in the Clouds* could no longer be published in its original form because it was written in the spirit of the time when one could feel its "sympathetic drift . . . and accompaniment."[1] With the radical change in the Russian political climate at the end of the 1920s when the government imposed explicit restrictions on artistic freedom, Pasternak found it difficult to relate to the spirit that permeated his first volume and thought that its poems contained nothing but a "bare . . . movement of the theme brought to the level of nonsense."[2] By the time Pasternak made these critical remarks, he was already a recognized poet who saw his earlier collection as a failed experiment. In 1914, however, when *Twin in the Clouds* appeared, he was still trying to find his own poetic voice. The critical reception of these first poems at the time had not been enthusiastic and ranged from a lukewarm welcome to outright disregard, and more recent criticism of this collection has remained rather reserved. Characteristically abstaining from praising *Twin in the Clouds,* one sympathetic modern critic nevertheless tactfully observed that in it Pasternak demonstrates a "peculiar ability to engage the reader in the poetry as process, activity" (Plank 1966, 10).

The existing English-language translations of *Twin in the Clouds* are incomplete, and few collections of Pasternak's translated poetry include them. But even the few available translations can provide the curious reader with a good example of the obscurity and heavy symbolist overtones of Pasternak's early poetic style. The mood of many poems is melancholy and melodramatic. The title itself points to the connection with symbolism and its fascination with astrological signs, not to mention the clouds themselves, which, together with fog and mist, shroud the typical symbolist landscape. Other imagery betrays the symbolist sources as well. In "Venetsiia" ("Venice," 1913), one of the poems of the cycle that Pasternak later reworked, the whole atmosphere is programmatically symbolist: here are "Scorpio's stars" and "the lands of the zodiac," the window pane is predictably "murky," and fog is mentioned in two stanzas (1:435). Other symbolist elements include "the mystery of life," "glimmering shadows," a sad lonely tune, as well as dreams and dreamy states. The image of Venice is extremely abstract and does not contain any details that could point to the actual city. The same is true for "The Railway Station," whose model was presumably the Belorussian-Baltic station in Moscow. The image of the station does not contain any recognizable physical details and has an aura of mystery and vagueness, resembling early poetry of the great Russian symbolist poet Aleksandr Blok (1880–1921). In Pasternak's own words, his only concern in the two poems "Venice" and "Vokzal" ("Railway Station") had been to capture the spirit of these places: "I needed nothing from myself, from the readers, or from the theory of art. I needed only that one poem contained the city of Venice, and the other the Brest, now the Belorussian-Baltic, station" (*Safe Conduct,* 4:326).

Already these early poems display a semantic tension in the unusual connections between objects. Special mention should be made of such aspects as metonymy, a rhetorical device that substitutes a part for the whole, and anthropomorphism, which assigns human characteristics to inanimate objects. In *Twin in the Clouds* clouds shed tears; a nerve is in contortions from love; the day cannot wake up; the candles are dozing; and stanzas are sobbing. The coupling of animate and inanimate elements was not a pure linguistic exercise limited to *Twin in the Clouds:* anthropomorphism was to remain a prominent stylistic characteristic of Pasternak's poetry for at least another decade, and so was the complexity of imagery gravitating toward the abstract. Although *Twin in the Clouds* was a work that relied heavily on symbolist tenets, its significance in Pasternak's career should not be diminished: it celebrates his joy of writing poetry, as well as the intellectual motivation to search for his own poetic voice. Like his idol, Rilke, Pasternak was committed to perfecting his poetic craft, and, like Rilke, he had to achieve restraint in expressing the outpour of his emotions.

Above the Barriers

Shortly after the publication of *Twin in the Clouds* Pasternak became interested in futurist poetry. *Above the Barriers* (1917), his disorganized collection of forty-nine poems written between 1914 and 1916, marks his departure from symbolism and his turn toward futurist, especially Mayakovskian, poetics. Later in his career Pasternak often reworked his lyrics, and when he edited a selection of poems from *Above the Barriers* in 1929 and republished them under the same title, the new edition was dedicated to Vladimir Mayakovsky, the great cubo-futurist poet, whom he had met in the summer of 1914. After Scriabin and Rilke, Mayakovsky came to be the third determining influence on Pasternak's writing. In *Safe Conduct* he writes that he was "crazy about Mayakovsky" (4:218), and in fact his admiration went so far that he would talk about Mayakovsky when asked to say something about himself (4:221). In spite of Pasternak's great respect for Mayakovsky and the irresistible appeal of his art, it would be a mistake to consider Pasternak's poetry of that period a mere imitation of Mayakovsky's. Because not many of Pasternak's verses of that period survive, a textual comparison between Mayakovsky's and Pasternak's poetry is inconclusive and establishing the full extent of Pasternak's poetic debt to the futurist poet almost impossible (Barnes 1989, 188). Generally it seems that Mayakovsky's influence on Pasternak has been exaggerated because critics attributed too much significance to Pasternak's eulogizing remarks. Although there are noticeable similarities in their poetry of that period, both poets were prompted by the general artistic drift away from traditional realism toward impressionism and abstraction and by their interest in incorporating principles of cubist art in their own work. Both indulged in grotesque imagery, unusual rhymes, and a tendency for hyperbolization. When Pasternak noticed similarities between Mayakovsky's and his own poetry, he tried to overcome them: "I understood that if I did not do something, they would become more frequent. I had to save him [Mayakovsky] from their vulgarity. . . . I renounced the romantic manner. This is how the nonromantic poetry of *Above the Barriers* came about" (*Safe Conduct*, 4:227). Besides Mayakovsky's "romantic manner," Pasternak could not accept his idol's obvious inclination toward politicization and the aggrandizement of the poet as the center of the universe. Pasternak also came to reject Mayakovsky's loud and eccentric public behavior as incompatible with his preferred image of the poet as inconspicuous both in poetry and in public life. Neither was Mayakovsky's group psychology akin to his. Throughout his life Pasternak remained an individualist and tried to stay outside organized movements and groups.

Above the Barriers has no organizing principle. Its chronology is chaotic, and it lacks the unifying narrative movement found in *My Sister-Life;* rather, the themes are kaleidoscopic, and the poet's mood changes from poem to poem. The themes range from the poet's melancholy and nostalgia about the past to historical events and nature. Commenting on the variety of poems in the collection, one critic calls it "a testimonial document which reveals to us through the torments and passions of the poet, a poetic history of the mind of those who experienced, felt, and therefore lived, in the years between 1905 and 1917" (Dyck 1972, 62). There is some truth to this statement. It was a time of significant historical and political events in Russia. In 1905 the country was shaken by a wave of strikes, peasant uprisings, and national unrest, and there were even instances of rebellion in the army and the navy. But although the revolution of 1905 made Russia into a constitutional monarchy, the expansion of the civil liberties the people actually achieved was largely cosmetic. The radicals fighting for a constituent assembly lost the struggle, and the extreme Right joined the army and the police, giving birth to the protofascist groups called "Black Hundreds" who waged war against Jews, intellectuals, and revolutionaries. Political and social instability persisted in Russia after the 1905 Revolution, was aggravated by World War I (which Russia entered in the summer of 1914), and continued until the collapse of the imperial regime in 1917.

Although Pasternak never immediately reacted to political or historical events through his art, and his response to the 1905 Revolution and World War I was "neither prompt nor prolific" (Barnes 1989, 179), these events nevertheless figure in several poems of *Above the Barriers.* The second poem of the collection, for instance, called "Durnoi son" ("Bad Dream," 1914; revised in 1928), conveys the poet's reaction to the atrocities of war. It is a war poem in which nature partakes in the suffering of the people. The winter landscape devastated by war is portrayed through rich metaphors and an all-pervasive anthropomorphism. The images of death, decay, and destruction include "holes in the fences without nails," teeth fallen out of the jaw, and sounds of rattling bones. Pasternak uses metonymy to intensify the expressiveness of his death imagery. The macabre landscape is saturated with images of the decapitated bodies of dead soldiers: "Stick your hand into the biting whirls of the snow storm / And he will fall from a crack out into your hand / Like a meaty stump, like a useless muscle / Shot-off and dangling by a sinew" (1:63). The howl of the winter storm is saturated with the sounds of the artillery and the screeching of the brakes of medical trains carrying the wounded.

Particularly curious appears the image of God—who is ironically called "the heavenly faster"—as the one who has this bad dream. God sleeps through the nightmare of war and thus lets the bloodshed continue. The poem sounds like a reproach against an indifferent and nonintervening God at a time when his help is needed most to reinstate justice on earth. Per-Arne Bodin writes that Pasternak in "Bad Dream" "takes up the existential question of the relation between God and man with an almost Dostoevskyan frenzy. The answer which is given is a negative one" (Bodin 1987, 95). Pasternak held Christian beliefs throughout his life, but of a rather personal and unorthodox character and changing over time. Thus his early preoccupation with God's indifference toward the evil in the world later shifted to general issues of Christianity, questions relating to life and death, resurrection, morality, and self-sacrifice, among others.[3] In Bodin's opinion, "Bad Dream" expresses Pasternak's nonacceptance of official Christian attitudes held by the Russian Church during World War I, which were a "cocktail of religion and cheap nationalism" (Bodin 1990, 383).

Another poem, "Desiatilet'e Presni" ("The Tenth Anniversary of Presnia," 1915), alludes to an actual historical event. Presnia, a suburb of Moscow, was known for its political meetings and the bloody fighting between the revolutionaries and the gendarmes that occurred there during the 1905 Revolution. Again, as in "Bad Dream," the revolutionary unrest is portrayed metonymically through fragmented, rapidly changing imagery that evokes the violence of the events: the reader hears the "repressed calls for help" and sees the "shining of the uniform pants" of the gendarmes and "windows without lights late at night" (1:66–67). Strong metaphorical and anthropomorphic language, typical of cubo-futurist poetry, is used for the description of tension in Presnia: "The old scar of November clouds is on the old spot / The familiar sky, barely alive from fear / Pressed its finger to its lips. . . . / The sounds of shooting liked to fondle the snow / And the streets, as usual, / Were innocent as a prayer / And as holiness they were untouchable" (1:67). The poet leaves no doubt where his sympathies lie and describes the revolutionaries as "heroes" (1:67). "Bad Dream" and "The Tenth Anniversary of Presnia," however, are exceptional among the poems in the collection because they mention concrete places and events. But even in these two examples the historical events acquire an aura of abstraction as they are portrayed through nature imagery, "as it impinges, fleetingly but indelibly, on [Pasternak's] consciousness" (Hingley 1983, 46). The portrayal of people is also metonymic and contributes to the abstract fabric of the cycle. Through metonymy Pasternak establishes connections among the most incompatible objects, and their new interaction brings a fresh appearance to his poetry.

Pasternak's landscape in *Above the Barriers* no longer has the melancholy static quality of *Twin in the Clouds*. Rather its snowstorms, blizzards, and unsettling sounds convey the dynamism of real nature that will characterize his poetry from now on. "Posle dozhdia" ("After the Rain," 1915; reworked in 1928) may serve as an example of Pasternak's brilliant animated poetic landscapes that bear unmistakably cubo-futurist features: "There is a crush behind the windows, the foliage is crowding up / And the fallen sky is not picked up from the roads. . . . / From the window panes of the balconies, as from the hips and backs / Of cold bathers sweat is dripping. . . . / Here is a ray of the sun that fell down from a spider web and is hiding / In the nettles, even if not for long" (1:92). Bold metaphors are scattered throughout the poem and connect the "scattered parts of reality, embodying the great unity of the world, the interaction and interpenetration of phenomena" (Sinyavsky 1978, 69). Everything is connected in Pasternak's world and permeated with a sense of change and transition.

The last poem of the collection, "Marburg," was generally praised by the critics. Inspired by the unhappy love experience with Ida Vysotskaia in 1912, "Marburg" captures events of Pasternak's life in the old German university town, where he spent the summer semester. The poem, originally written in 1915, resonated throughout Pasternak's career. In 1928 he revised it for another publication, and he made additional changes in 1956. He also elaborated on his Marburg experience in his autobiography *Safe Conduct*. Despite its biographical origin, "Marburg" reflects Pasternak's reluctant nonacceptance of traditional autobiography, expressed more fully in *Safe Conduct* (4:159). Indeed, actual autobiographical facts are veiled in "Marburg." The only concrete event appears in the opening lines and describes his proposal of marriage to Vysotskaia. The swift rejection overwhelms the young man, as is reflected in the emotional intensity of the poem's first lines: "I quivered. I flared up, and then burned out. / I shook. I had made a proposal— / But too late. I got scared, and she had refused me. / I pity her tears. I am more blessed than a saint" (1:106).

The blow of the rejection, however, does not sadden the narrator for a long time. On the contrary, it has a liberating effect on his creative potential and makes him feel as though reborn. The second stanza introduces the theme of the second birth, that is, the birth of the poet, and rapidly leads the reader away from the triviality of autobiographical data, moving the world of the poet's feelings into the foreground. As in other poems of the collection, these feelings are largely portrayed through nature. Nature is the poet's friend and confidante who helps him overcome the unavoidable banality of the rejected man's suffering. There is a gradual transition between the heightened passion of the first stanzas and the more restrained emotional state reached at the end of the poem. Pasternak achieves this transition by turning his attention from the lyrical "I" at the beginning of the poem to "the impersonality of pure receptiveness at which he has arrived" (Gifford 1977, 43). In this his "I" differs profoundly from the futurists', and especially Mayakovsky's, central positioning of the "I." In Andrey Sinyavsky's words, Pasternak "prefers to let the world speak for him and instead of him" (Sinyavsky 1978, 78). Although Pasternak's lyrical hero could sometimes be associated with the author himself, it would be a mistake to identify the two. Pasternak always maintains a distance between his own person and his lyrical "I" and, unlike Mayakovsky, never speaks directly of himself in his poetry.

Characteristically, the hero's initial emotional confusion is portrayed anthropomorphically through the dazzling images of nature transformed by the poet's perception: " . . . the forehead of the street / Was dark and scowled up at the sky . . . / The roof tiles swam, and the day looked / At the tiled roof without blinking. . . . / The sand showed yellow, devouring the clouds. / The storm played in the eyebrows of the bushes. / And the sky stopped bleeding after falling down on a piece / Of the styptic sprig" (1:106–7). Subsequently the emotional recovery manifests itself in the playful insomniac interaction between the poet and the night: "The night sits down to play chess / With me on the moonlit parquet, / It smells of acacia and the windows are open, / And passion, my witness, is getting gray in the corner. / The poplar is king. I play with insomnia. / The queen is a nightingale. / I reach for the nightingale. / And the night wins. / The pieces make way / For the recognizable white face of the morning" (1:108). The outcome of the rejection is no longer tragic; passion has already abated ("a gray witness"), and the poet rejoices at the melodious sounds of the nightingale's tune, welcoming the coming morning. The poem's closing turns into a celebration of life, nature, and creativity, themes that will carry into Pasternak's next cycle, *My Sister-Life.*

Above the Barriers is a definite step forward in Pasternak's development of his poetic idiom, which turned him from an experimenting young poet trying to find his own voice into a major poetic talent. He himself recognized the superiority of *Above the Barriers* over *Twin in the Clouds.* In a 1929 letter to his friend V. S. Pozner, Pasternak talks about *Above the Barriers* positively, stressing its conversational style: "The book is reworked with the faith in the reader, it talks to him simply, almost spitting at art . . ." (5:282–83). In this letter Pasternak also plays down his connections with futurism and symbolism. Although at the time of the letter Pasternak was ready to deny his symbolist and futurist past, *Above the Barriers,* even in its reworked version, is saturated with this past. While this second volume goes a long way to overcoming the stiffness of the young poet's symbolist-colored imagery so explicit in *Twin in the Clouds,* there are still occasional obscurities in *Above the Barriers* that are clearly reminiscent of the first collection. And futurist elements figure quite prominently in *Above the Barriers*. Futurism's appeal rested not only on its liberation of poetic language from the fetters of conventionality and making it colloquial and bold, but also because it allowed a new vision of the world by creating eccentric imagery inspired by the new experiments in visual art. Futurists tried to create in art "a synthesis of the organs of perception" and to express this synthesis in a language that would integrate everything around them.[4] Futurists, therefore, searched for a linguistic equivalent of the devices of contemporary painting, especially cubism, which was set firmly on the road toward abstraction. Particularly fascinating for these artists was the rearrangement of space. Dislocations, fragmentation, blurry and dissolving borders, arbitrary dimensions, abolishment of one-point perspective, and other features marked the appearance of the new art. For the futurist poets the principles of linguistic incorrectness, complex—not to say tortured—syntax, and esoteric vocabulary were the equivalents of the technical experiments of modern art. Pasternak's early poetry shows all these trademarks of futurism, and *Above the Barriers* provides this. While the futurist touches in *Above the Barriers* do not make Pasternak a futurist, they signify his departure from symbolism and his increasing proclivity for modernity, expressed in the tendency toward abstraction, linguistic intensity, concision, and deliberate obscurity of meaning. "Marburg" marks the end of Pasternak's search for his individual voice in poetry, a significant step toward his first true poetic masterpiece and one of the major achievements in Russian poetry, the cycle *My Sister-Life*.

My Sister-Life

The cycle *Sestra moia-zhizn'* (*My Sister-Life,* published in 1922) bears the subtitle "Summer of 1917," the year when most of its poems were written. There is no doubt that this cycle will always rank among the greatest achievements in Russian poetry. Two events of that year were particularly significant and inspiring for the writing of this third volume of Pasternak's poetry. The first was his infatuation with Elena Vinograd, with whom he had become friends in 1909. Pasternak's courtship of Vinograd began in the spring of 1917 and triggered two visits to see her in July and September of the same year in the Saratov Province, several hundred miles southeast of Moscow, where she did social work for the local authorities. His relationship with Vinograd was short—as had been the one with Vysotskaia. It remained platonic and one-sided and had already ended by the fall of 1917 (Barnes 1989, 230). The second significant event of that year was the February Revolution that brought about the fall of the Russian monarchy and the transition of power to the liberal Provisional Government until 7 November, when the Socialist Revolution brought it down.

Pasternak was in the Urals when news about the February Revolution reached him, and he immediately rushed back to Moscow. Although he had never been a revolutionary, he was enthusiastic about the changing political climate in Russia and felt an urge to write about it. Upon his arrival Pasternak discovered that life in Moscow was filled with a novel revolutionary spirit and a sense of far-reaching future changes. The Provisional Government was weak and slow to react to Russia's most pressing problems: industrial production continued to decline; transportation was in terrible shape; and the badly needed land reform demanded by the peasantry was far from being implemented. Moreover, the Provisional Government was committed to continuing the highly unpopular war with Germany despite incredible losses and the profound demoralization of the army. To make matters even more complicated, the Provisional Government also had to deal with the powerful Petrograd Soviet of Workers' and Soldiers' Deputies that came into being in March. Originally dominated by moderate socialists, it gradually became radicalized and increasingly determined to take power from the "bourgeoisie." The political crisis and unrest in Russia culminated in the so-called "July days" when the radical elements, including the Bolsheviks, tried to seize power in the capital. Although the attempt failed, it greatly undermined the authority of the Provisional Government and gave the socialists further advantages. The subsequent mistakes made by the government alienated both the Right and the Left and eventually led to its collapse during the successful Bolshevik-led revolution on 7 November and the subsequent establishment of the Soviet regime.

In the summer of 1917, however, Pasternak was intoxicated by the spirit of freedom and a new poetic inspiration. He wrote in the afterword to *Safe Conduct*: "The summer I saw on the earth seemed not to recognize itself. It was natural and prehistoric as in a revelation. I have written a book about it. In this book I expressed everything that one can learn about the revolution that was most unprecedented and elusive" (1:651). That book was *My Sister-Life*. Not all its poems, however, were written in 1917; some of them were added as late as the winter of 1922 when Pasternak had long lost his initial enthusiasm for the revolution. Neither is *My Sister-Life* a book about the revolution, although the drift of the revolutionary time permeates it. Whereas the revolutionary events create but a vague background for the poet's journey, the book is saturated with the sense of freedom that these events carry with them. The poems of the cycle succeed in recording "with the most delicate needle the atmospherics of the time" (Gifford 1977, 49). What the book seems to celebrate above all is the poet's realization of his poetic freedom and individuality, and his final triumph in the search for his own voice.

My Sister-Life is linguistically a brilliant book, but according to Lazar Fleishman, it makes tremendous demands on the reader because of the "unconventional treatment of idioms and syntactical units, dismantling them and placing them (or parts of them) in unexpected contexts, eliminating or transposing their components." Fleishman notes that it is not the quantity of tropes that presents a problem for the reader but the way in which these tropes are used. Pasternak does everything possible to "blur the distinction between a trope and a nontrope" thus creating ambiguity and multiplicity of interpretations (Fleishman 1990, 106). Each poem of this volume seems to be elusive, yet read in the general context of the cycle, it acquires meaning and reveals initially invisible connections in the text. The cycle reads as a poetic narrative and could be compared to a novel in verse. It has a unifying structure and two characters, the poet and his beloved, and the narrative progress follows the development of their relationship. But this story is not the poet's main goal. His focus is on nature, which becomes a true lyrical hero in *My Sister-Life*. It will become clear how the union between poet and nature manifests itself in the cycle as it is followed section by section.

Structurally *My Sister-Life* consists of ten sections, each under its own heading: "Ne vremia l' ptitsam pet'" ("Isn't It Time for the Birds To Sing?"), "Kniga stepi" ("The Book of the Steppe"), "Razvlechen'ia liubimoi" ("Diversions for the Beloved"), "Zaniat'e filosofiei" ("Studies in Philosophy"), "Pesni v pis'makh, chtoby ne skuchala" "("Songs in Letters That She Would Not Be Lonely"), "Romanovka" ("Romanovka"), "Popytka dushu rasluchit'" ("The Attempt To Separate the Soul"), "Vozvrashenie" ("The Return"), "Elene" ("To Elena"), and "Posleslov'e" ("Afterword"). Despite the diverse section headings, there are many connections among individual poems of the cycle, as shall be clarified.

My Sister-Life is dedicated to the Russian Romantic poet Mikhail Lermontov (1814–1841), who died in a duel at the age of twenty-seven. In a letter to his American translator Eugene Kayden, Pasternak explained the meaning of his dedicating the book to Lermontov: "I dedicated *My Sister-Life* not to the memory of Lermontov but to the poet himself as though he were living in our midst—to his spirit still effectual in our literature. What was he to me, you ask, in the summer of 1917?—The personification of creative adventure and discovery, the principle of everyday free poetical statement."[5] Pasternak was attracted not only to Lermontov's free spirit but equally by his conception of "personal biographical realism and the foreshadowing of our modern poetry and prose." The affinity between the two poets carries even further: like Lermontov, Pasternak was profoundly interested in writing prose, and like Lermontov, he would write only one novel toward the end of his life.

The opening poem of *My Sister-Life* is saturated with Lermontov's imagery. Here Pasternak introduces one of Lermontov's most famous romantic characters, the Demon, who is grieving in solitude after the death of his beloved, the Georgian princess Tamara. The majestic mountainous Caucasian landscape creates a melancholy background for his despair and grief. In one critic's opinion, there is a connection between this poem and the rest of *My Sister-Life,* for Pasternak celebrates "his passion through the medium of nature, in his case, the rolling steppe, with its blistering heat and its summer storms" (O'Connor 1988, 23), like the Demon's passion is celebrated through the beauty of the Caucasus.

My Sister-Life also bears an epigraph taken from the Austrian poet Nikolaus Lenau, a melancholy late Romantic, and quoted by Pasternak in its German original: "The forest roars / And thunder flights of storm / Are rushing through the sky / Into this weather, I, oh, girl / Am painting your features." The epigraph suggests nature's animated, even diabolical qualities; it does not simply serve as a passive background but becomes itself a source of the creative process. The meaning of the epigraph is magnified by the whole cycle, which "rings like a poetic manifesto" (Sinyavsky 1978, 79) because it reveals the poet's unity with nature and life.

"Isn't It Time for the Birds To Sing?"

In this opening section the relationship between the poet and Life is addressed even before he mentions his beloved. Whereas she appears only as a vague image in the poem that gives the cycle its title, Life receives a striking and rich description. While the beloved is asleep and looks like a "fata morgana" in her sleep, Life overwhelms the poet with its omnipresence: "My sister-Life today floods over / And bursts on everyone in spring rain . . ." (1:112). Life is everything in nature: the spring rain, the night, the steppe, the sun, and the stars that share the poet's feelings and become his companions during his train journey to his beloved: "and the sun, setting, condoles me" (1:112). The poet forms a close relationship with life, free from anxiety and expectation, which seem to characterize the relationship with his beloved. Pasternak "strips the noun *life* of its abstractness and impersonality and transforms it into the poet's intimate relation and sibling" (O'Connor 1988, 45).

In "Plachushii sad" ("Weeping Garden") the poet's sad feelings and tears are shared by the garden. The garden, one of Pasternak's favorite images, is animated through and through and appears as the poet's companion in his sorrow. The parallel between the wet garden and the crying poet is carried through the poem so skillfully that it becomes difficult to distinguish who is whose witness in crying, sighing, and loneliness. Sinyavsky observes that "the usual parallelism— 'the garden and I'—turns into an equation, 'I am the garden'" (Sinyavsky 1978, 76). This fusion is especially perceptible in the last stanza when splashing, sighs, and tears interrupt the silence and could be attributed to both the poet and the garden (1:113). The garden is at the center of another poem, "The Mirror." This time, however, it is seen by the poet indirectly, as a reflection in the pier glass: "The huge garden bustles about in the room, / In the pier glass, but does not break the glass" (1:114). The poet animates the reflection through his poetic medium and thus gives the garden a second life. The garden is not merely a static mirrored reflection but a living being animated in the poetic transformation. Pasternak suggests that the poet himself become a mirror that captures the life of nature.

The last poem of the first section, called "Dozhd'" ("Rain"), reintroduces the love theme and the presence of the poet's beloved who was mentioned only as a mirage before. Not untypical for the early Pasternak, he barely mentions his beloved in the first stanza and then lets her disappear altogether after the declaration "She is with me" (1:119) and instead calls on the rain to celebrate his reunion with his beloved. As in "Weeping Garden," Pasternak reaches out into nature as a friend with whom to share his feelings. In this union Pasternak manages to "re-create the all-encompassing atmosphere of existence, and to communicate the feeling of intimacy with the universe which gripped the poet" (Sinyavsky 1978, 77). Nature's moods never seem to be tranquil in Pasternak's world, however, echoing the poet's elemental joy or sadness. Rain, wind, snowstorms, and other natural phenomena take center stage from the beginning of *My Sister-Life* and push any human characters into the background.

"The Book of the Steppe"

This section focuses on the poet's love affair and the emotions it triggers. Pasternak associates his moods with the seasons and the changes in nature. From the depression and horror of winter in the absence of his beloved in the poem "Do vsego etogo byla zima" ("Before All This There Was Winter") the mood shifts to the excitement and passion of spring in "Iz suever'ia" ("From Superstition"), when the beloved appears in the poet's "small den." Pasternak avoids explicit descriptions of either the poet or his beloved and instead portrays the two and their affair metonymically through sounds, gestures, movements, colors, and nature. In "Balashov" (the name of a small town) the overwhelming passion of the poet is expressed through the exuberant imagery of the clouds singing in the voice of the beloved and this song then rushing out into the train car in which the poet rides toward Balashov, where she lives: "And anyway, the chest was bursting / And the clouds' song was, 'I'm yours, I'm yours!' / And poured into the heat / into the train car, onto the luggage" (1:124).

"Diversions for the Beloved"

This section takes the woman's perspective. The poet introduces the reader to her world, but the trip could be misleading if Pasternak is expected to catalog in precise terms the "diversions" his beloved chooses for herself. As has been clear from the beginning of the cycle, the clues to the world of the characters are scattered throughout the poems, and as the reader collects them, he or she is free to put them together in whatever way the imagination allows. Among the beloved's favorite pastimes is participation in strikes and demonstrations—although it is not clear how serious she is about them—English literature, and, above all, her own love life, portrayed in close connection and association with nature. The beloved woman appears drawn in impressionistic tones vague and abstract by a poet who is obviously more interested in her as an excuse for exercising his poetic gift than treating her as the center of his universe. The overall impression this poem produces is that the poet's love for the linguistic exuberance is stronger than his love for the beloved.

Indeed, the poem "Slozha vesla" ("With the Oars at Rest") demonstrates precisely the privileged position of language in the poet's life. When he and his beloved are in the boat with the oars at rest, it is not the poet himself who kisses the beloved but rather the willows "bending low to kiss the collarbones, / Elbows and oarlocks"; "Oh, wait," he continues, "This could happen to anyone" (1:129). The hero and his beloved remain pure abstractions as their embrace continues. The physical closeness of the lovers is rendered purely metonymically. According to Barnes, this "springs from a 'melting of boundaries': moving beyond pathetic fallacy of self-dramatization through nature, [it] is the discovery of a mutual interaction of all elements in the landscape on the poet's behalf: in it subjects, objects and qualities are realigned through acoustics and contiguity—as in some Cubist or Expressionist painting . . ." (Barnes 1989, 233–34). As would a cubist painting, the poem only suggests the content, but its main focus is on the connection of things and how the exposure of these connections defamiliarizes the world.

"Studies in Philosophy"

Pasternak opens this section with an attempt to explain his own concept of poetry. "Opredelenie poezii" ("Definition of Poetry") is often considered a programmatic statement by Pasternak, a kind of poetics: "[Poetry is] a whistle sounding tight, / It's a cracking of crushed ice, / It's the night frosting the leaves, / It's two nightingales' dueling. / It's sweet peas that became quiet, / It's the tears of the universe in pea pods . . ." (1:134). If the first quatrain emphasizes poetry as sound, the second evokes the already familiar identification of poetry with nature and life that surround us. "Definition of Poetry" also provides an elucidation of Pasternak's statements on art and poetry in *Safe Conduct*. For Pasternak art is a record of displacement of reality by feeling; art imitates this as a displacement from nature: "How is nature displaced? Details gain in brilliance and lose their independent meaning. Each can be replaced by another, and each is precious. Any one you choose is a good evidence of a condition that envelops the whole of displaced reality" (4:187–88). What Pasternak asserts here is that art, freed from mimetic representation, relies on the associative capacity of the artist's imagination and thus allows an arbitrary repositioning and re-placement, or interchangeability, of objects and details. Indeed, in "Definition of Poetry" each detail stands out as a part of the great whole and each can be replaced by another.

The poem "Opredelenie dushi" ("Definition of the Soul") describes the inseparable ties between the poet's soul and his poetry and compares these ties with those of a ripe pear to its leaf. There is also an allusion to the revolutionary events ("The storm burned our native land," 1:135) that acquires a near apocalyptic tone in the next poem, "Bolezni zemli" ("Diseases of the Earth"). Images of a rainstorm, sharp wind, and thunder create a gloomy and hostile picture of the outside world as the poet relates his sympathy for the earth: "One should be delirious / To consent to be the earth" (1:136). The reader has already observed that Pasternak has a strong penchant for imagery of rain, hail, dew, and other liquid elements as tropes for the essence of life, and for the most part those images are life-affirming. In this poem, however, rain and the wet earth carry with them the fear of disease and death because they are filled with bacteria and "staphylococcus clouds" (1:136). Pasternak's morbid portrayal of the diseased earth strongly resonates with his negative attitude toward war in the poem "Bad Dream" from the cycle *Above the Barriers*.

After "Diseases of the Earth" the poet's mood lightens as he turns toward a contemplation of art and creativity. "Opredelenie tvorchestva" ("Definition of Creativity") contains programmatic lines for understanding Pasternak's ideas on creativity: "And gardens, and ponds, and fences, / And creation . . . / Are only the eruptions of our passion / Accumulated by the human heart" (1:137). Creation emerges from "the eruptions of . . . passion" that apply to the creation of the universe as well as the creation of a work of art. Pasternak's perception of the creative process is reminiscent of the Romantics', for whom spontaneity and feelings are vital aspects of writing. Allusions to Beethoven as well as Tristan and Isolde reinforce the conception of creativity as inseparable from the forces of passion. Pasternak repeats this understanding of creativity in one of his digressions on art in *Safe Conduct*: "When we imagine that in Tristan, Romeo and Juliet, and other monuments a powerful passion is expressed, we underestimate their content. Their theme is more fundamental than this topic, however powerful. Their theme is the theme of power. From this theme art is born" (4:187). The gist of Pasternak's definition of creativity is splendidly expressed in Dale L. Plank's study of the poem: "it is most of all the poetic act displacing its own result, the poetic impulse becoming thematic, that demonstrates the power of the single theme of creativity" (Plank 1966, 55).

The remaining two poems of the section, "Nasha groza" ("Our Thunderstorm") and "Zamestitel'nitsa" ("The Substitute"), are devoted, respectively, to the poet's conversation with his beloved and the beloved herself as the poet looks at her photo. In "Our Thunderstorm" the poet pledges his love but at the same time confesses his inability to separate it from his love of poetry: "What can I do with my joy? / Put it into my poems or ruled notebooks? / But their lips are chapped / From the poisons of writing paper. / At war with the alphabet, / [My poems] blush on your cheeks" (1:139).

In the context of the whole cycle, the poems of the section "Studies in Philosophy" discussed above occupy an important position as they define Pasternak's aesthetic principles and philosophical attitudes toward poetry and the creative act. In the course of this section the reader also learns that despite the poet's undoubted passion for his beloved, he never lets her take the place of his unconditional love and devotion to art and creativity. The beloved is only one among the many wonders that overwhelm the poet in his life. One critic also detects a "whimsical note of masculine superiority" in Pasternak's differentiation between the seriousness of his "studies in philosophy" and the lightness and intellectual noncommitment of his beloved's "diversions" (O'Connor 1988, 93).

"Songs in Letters That She Would Not Be Lonely"

The themes of love, life, and nature in this section coexist with a serious, almost melancholy digression about time in the poem with the German title, "Mein Liebchen, Was Willst Du Noch Mehr?" ("My Love, What Else Do You

Want?"). Pasternak borrowed this line from Heinrich Heine's poem "Du hast Diamanten und Perlen" ("You Have Diamonds and Pearls"). Read together with Heine's line, the question by Pasternak's lyrical subject "What else do you want?" (1:143) expresses his frustration with the mundane side of his relationship with the beloved. It is understandable, therefore, that he turns to a meditation about the two contrasting kinds of time: personal and historical. Personal time appears as fleeting, filled with tedium, squabble, household chores, and superstitions. The banality of personal time is emphasized in the association of its passage with the crawling of cockroaches ("an hour crawls like a cockroach" v. 1; p. 143). Historical time, on the other hand, is colored in a tangibly tragic mood: "The year was burnt on kerosene . . . / Old, frightening in its pity, / It peers into the window. / The pillow is wet / From the year's burying its tears" (1:143). The reference here is once again to the revolution and its far-reaching destructive impact on personal life. The two perspectives on time intertwine in this poem and make the poet question his personal interests in the face of historical reality.

"Romanovka"

In this section the poet conveys further impressions of the war and the revolution as he recognizes their effects on a train journey through the Povolzh'e region in central Russia, where Romanovka, a small village, is located. The poem "Dushnaia noch'" ("Sultry Night") intensifies the oppressive picture of historical time that the poet began to draw in Moscow: "In the orphaned, sleepless, / damp universal vastness, / Groans fled their posts. . . . / Raindrops were blindly fleeing after them. / Beside the fence, wet branches / Were quarreling with the wind. / I became still: it was about me!" (1:148). Less philosophical and more personal than "Mein Liebchen . . . ," this poem introduces personal fear, loneliness, and anxiety that lead to insomnia. There is a touch of paranoia in the poet's new and cautious awareness of his environment: even nature becomes hostile in its quarreling about the poet.

Impressions of the war and the revolution reach almost cosmic proportions in the poem "Eshe bolee dushnyi rassvet" ("An Even More Sultry Dawn"). In the first stanza nature is depicted in somber imagery. No longer comforting and luxurious, nature becomes gray and unattractive: tree branches are dying; rain clouds look dusty; the dawn is gray "like prisoners' talk" (1:149). There are also references to the new conscripts' procession to the front, allusions to Austrian prisoners of war, and the suffering of the wounded. This recurring theme of the devastating effect of war is intensified in the gloomy description of the surrounding world, and the reality of the revolutionary time acquires more serious overtones as the narrative progresses.

"The Attempt to Separate the Soul"

Historical and personal dimensions come together again in this section. The first poem, "Muchkap" (a station on the way to the poet's destination), metaphorically refers to the revolutionary times of trouble. Although the poet describes a distant restless fishing village filled with gray sails and boats and the unpleasant smell of fish, it is not clear whether he actually sees the village or whether it is a product of his imagination. This depressing landscape, as it turns out, provides an appropriate background for his meeting with his beloved. The poet's premonition of a breakup with her is conveyed in the association of his apathy while waiting for her with the "darkness before stormy weather" (1:151). In "Muchkap" the poet's vision of his relationship is clearly no longer as romantic and all-absorbing as it was at the beginning of *My Sister-Life*. Like his initial perception of the revolution, it undergoes a tormenting scrutiny at this stage of his trip.

"Dik priem byl, dik prikhod" ("Wild Was Your Welcome, Wild Was My Arrival") confirms the poet's worst fears about the meeting with his beloved. Yet the unusually concrete and straightforward description of their meeting, sustained in a dense fast rhythm, does not come as a shock. The attentive reader has been prepared for it by the poet's earlier apprehensions of the future: "Wild was your welcome, wild was my arrival, / I could barely drag my feet. / You did not utter a word / And glued your eyes to the ceiling" (1:154). After being thus rejected, the poet self-indulgently withdraws into the memories of his beloved and his trip. These images, now touched by time, again evoke some blissful memories, but their main effect is to push the poet to writing.

"The Return," "Back Home," and "To Elena"

For a while, however, art and memories remain helpless in the face of nostalgia and lost love. The sections "The Return" and "Back Home" are devoted to the poet's pain of separation from his beloved and his feeling of oppression. A break in this mood comes in the form of bitter irony about the beloved and the cleansing tears of grief in the penultimate section "To Elena." For the first time the woman's name is mentioned and is immediately associated with several Elenas: Elena Vinograd, the queen of Sparta, and Helen of Troy. The image of Elena thus becomes complex and contradictory in the poet's perception: she is simultaneously an object of his fascination and a "cold and manipulative seductress," like Helen in Troy from the myth of Paris (O'Connor 1988, 143). The choice of adjectives expresses the poet's resentment of the cold and vile nature of his beloved in the following stanza: "I thought Troy would have loved / To kiss her twisted bitter lips for ages. / Her majestic eyelids were / Royal and plaster-cast" (1:162). In these lines Elena appears as an embodiment of the irrational female power over male rationality, and, like a sphinx, she remains fascinating and enigmatic yet threatening at the same time. The image of Pasternak's Elena in this poem is curiously close to the decadent image of the female as a devouress of males. The poet, however, is not willing to accept her maliciousness and philosophically decides to leave it for the future to judge her true nature: "Let fate decide / whether she was a good mother or a wicked witch" (1:162). Finally, at the end of the section, the poet reconciles with his fate and relegates the summer of 1917 and his unrequited love to his memory. The spectacular photographic imagery of the poem "Groza, momental'naia na vek" ("An Instantaneous Eternal Thunderstorm") alludes to the affair as past, as a picture illuminated by memory.

"Afterword"

This last section of the cycle shows the poet in a contemplative philosophical mood as he generalizes and summarizes his experience. In the opening poem of the section, "Liubimaia—zhut'! Kogda liubit poet" ("Darling, It's Awful When the Poet Is in Love"), he meditates on the nature of his love and realizes that he can love only romantically and is therefore unable to commit himself to mundane practical things. He thinks he appears to women as anachronistic as a mammoth and as a sentimentalist with "tons of fog" in his eyes that makes him "pour tears" generously (1:166). For him marriage trivializes the experience of romantic love, and he is horrified by the vulgarity of the wedding ceremony with ritual drinking and sobering up in the morning ("He sees how people wed, / Get drunk and sleep it off . . ." [1:166]), as well as by the thought of a future life in comfort with his beloved. Although this poem is addressed to her, it reads like a poet's attempt at self-analysis. What he concludes from his failed love experience is that he needs the primordial chaos of romantic love (1:166), untouched by marriage.

The second poem of the section, "Davai roniat' slova" ("Let's Scatter the Words"), is structured as a dialogue between the poet and the beloved, but the woman now represents the other, the crowd, to whom the poet explains his desire to go beyond the obvious and trivial and present life in the richness of "its myriad *fine* details that are never *trivial*" (O'Connor 1988, 162). Although the poem sounds like a rational affirmation of his role as a creative artist who finds inspiration in life but is ultimately committed to art only, his attempt at a dispassionate meditation about the past events is interrupted by outbursts of bitterness and anger and the gnawing pain of hurt feelings after he has been rejected. His emotional instability surfaces again in the last poem of the cycle, symbolically called "Konets" ("The End"). Now the poet's mood swings from despair ("Oh, like you, autumn, I am sick of living" [1:174]) to the longing for another, more comforting and understanding love.

Thus, with the feeling of anxiety and discontent, ends the cycle *My Sister-Life*. Now that the poet's beloved is gone, like the Demon's Tamara in the introductory poem, he finds himself alone with his faithful sister-Life whose overwhelming complexity and wonder will never stop surprising him. The poet also seems eager to put the distracting and dramatic personal and historical events behind him and stop wasting words on them ("But with the bitter after-taste, with the numbness, and lumps in the throat, / But with the sadness of so many words you get tired of this friendship" [1:175]). The time is ripe for a new poetic pursuit. After closing this fascinating volume of poetry, the reader may still wonder who the poet is and what his relationship to life, creativity, and love is: nothing in *My Sister-Life* is formulated in precise terms and therefore everything remains elusive. It has been mentioned before that the cycle was inspired by Pasternak's own experiences in the summer of 1917, and these biographical events are indeed mentioned in the poems. Pasternak is especially meticulous in recording the names of the train stations his hero passes on his way to his beloved. Beyond these geographical indicators, however, the objective outside world is largely nonexistent for the nameless poet who can be identified as Pasternak's persona only remotely. To the reader, the poet's world opens up through his art rather than concrete biographical data of his creator. Pasternak redirects external events into the poet's inner states and makes his hero's perceptions the key to understanding the cycle. The poet is a unique individual, and it is *his* life that is opened up for us. But it is also Life as the "phenomenal world" (Gifford 1977, 52) that becomes his companion and whom he treasures above all. The poem seems to indicate a kind of relationship of two peers, the poet and Life, free and independent. The poet's relationship with Life is more meaningful than his relationship with a woman because it is free and devoid of resentment. Whereas the poet's love of Life brings him joy and freedom, the love of his beloved is enslaving; it threatens to burn him up—with obligations, jealousy, dependence, hatred, suspicion, fear of abandonment, and family life. Of the two relationships—one with Life, the other with his beloved—he chooses the former. The poet's defiance of love for a woman in the cycle is strictly spiritual and validated by his devotion to art, for which he would readily give up any other reality. Thus in *My Sister-Life* the poet's relationship with life is "creatural," that is, "his celebration of life is also a celebration of the creative principle which has made his mind what it is, and enabled it to discover its likeness in the world he observes" (Gifford 1977, 53). The end result of the poet's journey is his recognition that not for a moment can he cease to exist as an artist. The whole cycle therefore can be read as an allegory of the artist's existence in his communion with life, love, and art in a prosaic world.

When *My Sister-Life* was published, it was received as a poetic break-through by many critics, although utilitarian Marxist criticism was generally hostile (Barnes 1989, 286). But such great Russian poets as Mandelstam, Mayakovsky, and Tsvetaeva were enthusiastic about the cycle. The critics especially noted the "modernity" and "contemporaneity" of *My Sister-Life* (Barnes 1989, 285). As we have seen, Pasternak's modernism is most clearly in evidence in his use of language and imagery that demonstrates his affinity with cubo-futurist painting. Yet in the area of versification, Pasternak rejects radical experiments and remains faithful to the classical tradition. As Yury Tynyanov observed in 1924, Pasternak was that poet who "reached a new tier of poetic culture to use the nineteenth century as material without construing it as a norm but without being ashamed, either, of kinship with one's fathers."[6] Efim Etkind, who studied Pasternak's innovations in poetic speech, came to the conclusion that one of the poet's major contributions to Russian prosody consists in a fresh use of some old metrical forms, the revival of the old French ballad, and unusual rhymes.[7] According to Etkind, Pasternak also enriches the poetic vocabulary by introducing professional jargon and combining lexical elements previously considered incompatible (134–40). Pasternak's dazzling imagery and the unusual variety of poetic forms in *My Sister-Life* place him in the vanguard of Russian poetry at the beginning of the 1920s. Despite the changing political climate that affected his life and literary tastes, as well as everybody else's, the flourishing of his talent, so evident in *My Sister-Life,* continues in his next collection, *Themes and Variations,* as well as in his short fiction.

Themes and Variations

The time that followed the October Revolution brought even more suffering to the Russian people than the prerevolutionary years. Although the Bolsheviks easily seized power, it took them years to consolidate it. They first gained the public's approval by concluding the Soviet-German Treaty of Brest-Litovsk in March 1918. But the price of this peace was high for Russia as it lost substantial territories that it formerly controlled: the Ukraine, Poland, Finland, Lithuania, Estonia, and Latvia became independent. Even though there were other conditions, including a tremendous war indemnity, that were as outrageous as they were humiliating for Russia, the peace treaty seemed necessary, as the war's heavy burden on the government's budget continued to impoverish the people among whom the war was extremely unpopular. The new communist government led by Lenin desperately needed some stability, and the peace treaty with Germany was one of the first steps in that direction. Domestically, the new rulers tried to penetrate all sectors of Russian society as quickly and efficiently as possible. Private property was abolished, and the upper and middle classes lost all that they owned; industry, banks, foreign trade, housing, and all land were nationalized. In addition, the church was separated from the state and its property confiscated. The new communist propaganda and education of the masses quickly kicked into high gear. As early as 1918 compulsory labor was introduced and the government began to ration food and basic necessities of life.

As the communist government continued its reforms, discontent and resistance grew throughout the country. It was not only the upper and the middle classes that were dissatisfied with the results of the revolution; the peasants equally felt themselves to be victims of the new regime when it forced them to turn over their entire food supplies to cities and the Red Army when the civil war began in 1918. The civil war was fought between the Bolsheviks, often called the Reds, and the counterrevolutionary forces, known as the Whites. The Whites consisted mainly of former czarist army officers, Cossacks, educated young people, representatives of the middle class, and political groups opposing communism. Although it ended in 1920 with the Red victory, military suppression of anti-Soviet resistance continued until 1926, ending only with the establishment of Soviet control over the Transcaucasian republics, the Crimea, and central Asia.

The revolution and postrevolutionary events unquestionably affected the standard of living and the emotional state of the cultural intelligentsia. Those who did not emigrate immediately after the revolution had to face many hardships, including hunger (even starvation), epidemics, the lack of basic life necessities, and appalling housing shortages (for example, the poets Blok and Khlebnikov died of disease and general exhaustion, in 1921 and 1922 respectively). Like most other Russians of his class, Pasternak experienced a dramatic change in his living standard and had to divide time between his writing and taking care of the family household. In the winter he stoked their Dutch stove, and when fuel supplies ended he went, like other Muscovites, around town with his brother stealing fencing and other wooden objects that could be used as fuel (Barnes 1989, 244). He also did some cooking for the family. Summers were easier, as the family managed to grow some vegetables in a friend's garden. The housing conditions had also gotten worse for the Pasternaks. They had lost a part of their apartment to other tenants, and Boris himself had to share apartments with friends until he moved to his own in 1921. In 1921 the government introduced the so-called New Economic Policy (NEP), a slight loosening of state control, in order to save the country from starvation and total economic disaster: private enterprise was legalized once again and the economic situation in Russia drastically improved within a year. The NEP also brought some liberalization and revival to the cultural scene after four years of silence.

Temy i variatsii (*Themes and Variations*) was published in 1923 in Berlin, where Pasternak stayed for seven months beginning in August 1922. At that time Berlin, together with Moscow and Petrograd (renamed Leningrad after Lenin's death and renamed Saint Petersburg recently after the fall of communism in the Soviet Union), was one of the main centers of Russian culture, and Pasternak was interested in exploring it. The reviews of his new book were generally favorable, and it was enthusiastically received by the young artistic intelligentsia. Although most poems from *Themes and Variations* were originally written for *My Sister-Life* but then withdrawn from publication by the author at that point, by no means should the former be considered as an extension of the latter. But since most poems of *Themes and Variations* were written at the same time as *My Sister-Life,* biographical and thematic affinities between the two collections are unmistakable.

Themes and Variations preserves the same division into sections as *My Sister-Life*. The poems of this cycle are not united by one narrative line, although Pasternak returns to the events and emotional states already familiar to the reader from *My Sister-Life*. In *Themes and Variations* Pasternak reaches the pinnacle of his technical virtuosity, equaled only by the most dazzling lines in *My Sister-Life*. In Barnes's words, the book's very title suggests "a preoccupation with matters of structure and technique" (Barnes 1989, 265). Gifford compares Pasternak's technical endeavor in *Themes and Variations* to that of "the extemporizing pianist elated by his audience. This virtuosity plays with syntax and form, with conceits caught in midair, with splendidly improvised rhymes, and with many changes of tone, from the colloquial or proverbial to an urgent complexity in which language, while not divorced from the speaking voice, enters into unprecedented relations" (Gifford 1977, 70). It is these characteristics that make *Themes and Variations* barely translatable, and no translator has attempted to translate all sixty-two poems of the cycle into English. Because a complete English version of *Themes and Variations* is unavailable and many of the poems carry on the poetic and emotional spirit of *My Sister-Life,* this section will examine only selected poems of the cycle for reasons of their content and message.

Section I: "Five Tales"

"Piat' povestei" ("Five Tales") opens with the poem "Vdokhnovenie" ("Inspiration"), which brings back the memories of the familiar love affair between the poet and his beloved in the summer of 1917 and reads like a variation on the themes from *My Sister-Life.* But already this first poem overwhelms the reader with its startling technical escapades. The imagery is daring in its intermingling of animate and inanimate elements: "Gun-ports run across the fences, / Breaches appear in the wall, / When the night is disturbed by the wagon / Of tales unknown to spring" (1:176). As in *My Sister-Life,* life, poetry, and history blend when the poet describes his experiences of the war and time of the revolution. In "Vstrecha" ("Encounter"), one of the more distinct "pictorial" poems whose imagery is strikingly cubo-futurist, Pasternak portrays the poet and a March Night walking home together from a meeting. The very idea of this union is reminiscent of Mayakovsky's 1920 poem "Neobychainoe prikliuchenie, byvshee s Vladimirom Maiakovskim letom na dache" ("The Unusual Adventure That Happened to Vladimir Mayakovsky at His Country House One Summer), in which the poet and the Sun sit at the table and talk to each other. But this unusual coupling of the poet and Night personified is only one of the allusions to cubo-futurism; in fact the entire poem could be read as a tribute to it. Gifford calls the poem "difficult" because of its cubist imagery and Pasternak's "highly-wrought idiom" which requires an especially careful reading (Gifford 1977, 74). Pasternak presents the poet as a part of the night's landscape, which in its turn seems to be painted: "And the March night and the author / Went fast, glancing from time to time / At the ghost that seemed to be real / And then suddenly disappeared. / That was the dawn. And like an amphitheater / That showed up at the harbinger's call, / Tomorrow rushed toward them /As if uttered on a staircase" (1:178). In the following stanza, according to Plank, who discussed this poem in terms of its pictorial allusions, "the poetic 'I' has now stepped across the frame, through the looking-glass, and is on the stage. It is now literally in the landscape. We are made to look through the eyes of the lyrical 'I' out into darkness over the edge of the stage" (Plank 1966, 95). The displaced urban landscape becomes a demonstration of Pasternak's ability to assimilate poetic and pictorial techniques. The painterly effect of displaced imagery in the "Encounter" reveals Pasternak's strong indebtedness to modernist and abstract culture, with which his whole art of the period is saturated.

"Margarita" and "Mephistopheles," two further poems of the section, despite their allusion to Faust, have little in common with Goethe's masterpiece and instead celebrate youth, love, and the joy of spring. In the last poem of the section, "Shakespeare," Pasternak alludes to another classic of world literature in the title and subsequently anthropomorphizes the Sonnet, who then wittily and rebelliously argues with its creator, Shakespeare, about the discrepancy between the refined form and language of which it consists and the uncouth atmosphere of the tavern in which it was written.

Section II: "Theme with Variations"

"Tema s variatsiiami" ("Theme with Variations"), itself a slight variation of the title of the whole collection, is devoted entirely to themes from Aleksandr Pushkin's poetry. Pushkin (1799–1837), perhaps the most venerated Russian poet, wrote unforgettable lyrics, and every Russian knows at least a few lines of his by heart. Pasternak's variations are on three Pushkin poems, "Mednyi vsadnik" ("The Bronze Horseman"), "Prorok" ("The Prophet"), and "Tsygane" ("The Gypsies"). The first variation, entitled "Tema" ("The Theme"), begins like the prologue of the "The Bronze Horseman," in which the Russian czar Peter the Great looks at the Neva River and envisions the splendid city he will build on its banks to protect his country from the "Northern neighbor," Sweden. After the introductory line, Pasternak improvises on the theme rather like a jazz musician, playing with it and trying out his modern rhythms and intonations. It is no longer Peter the Great who stands on the bank of the Neva but Pushkin himself who sees the elemental beauty of nature before his eyes. The witty and absolutely stunning imagery includes "beer pouring down in delirium from the mustaches of the ravines, capes, rocks, spits, shoals, and miles"; "the salty taste of fogs on the sphinx's lips"; and "sand covered with the damp kisses of medusas" (1:183). The poem reads like a parody, a modernist subversion of Pushkin's classical theme. Gifford offers a comparison between this poem and "Picasso's game of parody and subversion with, for instance, a canvas by Velazquez" (Gifford 1977, 71). The second poem of the section is in fact called "Variatsii" and includes six parts. All the variations develop Pushkin's themes in a burlesque and technically dazzling manner that, like the first poem of this section, "The Theme," evokes strong pictorial associations. One of these parts,

"Imitation," begins with a direct quotation from Pushkin and develops into another variation on "The Bronze Horseman."

Section III: "Sickness"

"Bolezn'" ("Sickness," 1918–1919) consists of seven poems that reflect both the hardships of the postrevolutionary time and Pasternak's unresolved relationship with Elena Vinograd, the poet's lover in *My Sister-Life*. The Russian population at that time suffered greatly from epidemics and malnutrition, and Pasternak himself had a serious flu in 1918 and for several days was in a delirious state.

The imagery of the whole section is dominated by winter and night. The fear of death and diminishing physical strength is intensified by predominantly nocturnal snowy landscape, blizzards, wind, ice, and frost. In a characteristically anthropomorphic image, the surrounding world becomes a barometer of the poet's state: "Christmas eve was perspiring"; "the house has an inflammation"; "chandeliers have pleurisy"; and "the swollen shrub was as white as fear" (1:191). These images of suffering associated with the poet's home contribute to his melancholy and sense of loneliness and alienation. The monotony of the harsh winter landscape also further adds to the poet's tangible preoccupation with his unfortunate love experience of the previous summer. In the last two poems of the section the theme of physical suffering interweaves with the theme of emotional pain, death, and suicide. In desperation the poet identifies love as the source of his misery and confesses his inability to deal with it: "Alas, oh, love! This should be confessed! / With what can I replace you? With castor oil? With bromide? / With a slanting feverish glance, / I fear a great insomnia is coming" (1:194).

Section IV: "The Break"

"Razryv" ("The Break") clarifies all earlier references to the previous summer's love. The nine short poems of "The Break" deal with the poet's confused and passionate feelings for his deceitful beloved. The fluctuation of moods in this cycle is swift and dramatic and finds its expression in a variety of rhythms. Pain and bitterness over his faithless beloved are constantly renewed by his fascination with her, against his own will. The unusually adventurous metrical structure of "The Break" has attracted considerable critical attention for its dramatic emotional intensity and has been called "a compelling and breathless act of poetic indictment, differing in style from almost all Pasternak's earlier work" (Barnes 1989, 249).

Section V: "I Could Forget Them"

In "Ia ikh mog pozabyt'" ("I Could Forget Them") Pasternak addresses a variety of themes, all at least vaguely autobiographical, reaching from the poet's memories of childhood to his joy of writing poetry. The tone of the first poem, "Klevetnikam" ("To Slanderers"), is restrained. Although the first three quatrains convey some elevating emotionalism expressed in seven exclamatory sentences, they are free from nostalgia. The poet calls his childhood "a scoop of the soul's depth" and "my inspirer and choirmaster" (1:199). The innocence and excitement of childhood are then juxtaposed to the corruption and triviality of a more mature age (1:199). The next four poems of this short section were written between 1921 and 1922 and could be read as Pasternak's self-analysis during those complex years of adjustment to the Soviet regime. Characteristic of this mood is his continuous and tormenting self-scrutiny and uncertainty about where he stands in relation to official Soviet literature. In the penultimate poem of the section, "Nas malo" ("We Are Few"), Pasternak surprisingly ranks himself among the three chosen poets of the epoch: "We are few. / We are maybe three. . . . / Once we were people. / Now we are epochs . . ." (1:203). This poem as preserved in its original in the Central Literary Archives of Russia, has the title "Poety" ("Poets") and is supposedly addressed to Nikolai Aseev and Mayakovsky, two poets actively supporting the revolution. That Pasternak included himself among the company of the two poets so different from him in their poetic temperament and attitude to literature points to his vacillation between the desire to be in step with the revolutionary epoch and a commitment to his poetic ideals, which by that time had become mutually exclusive.

Section VI: "Neskuchnyi Garden"

The poem called "Poeziia" ("Poetry," 1922) in this final section, "Neskuchnyi sad" ("Neskuchnyi Garden"—literally, "nonboring garden"—a large popular park in Moscow, later renamed Gorky Park), clarifies what these ideals are at this time. Whereas in *My Sister-Life* Pasternak identified poetry mostly with the vastness of the universe and the richness of nature, in *Themes and Variations* his definition of poetry is brought closer to real life. The poet is no longer an excited romantic celebrating the beauty of nature, but rather finds his inspiration in the busy life of the city and its suburbs: "Poetry, I will swear / By you and end up groaning out: / You are not the posture of a sweet singer, / You are summer with a seat in the third class car, / You are a suburb, not a refrain. / You are hot as Iamskaia street in May, / As Shevardino redoubt at night, / Where the clouds utter moans, / And scamper out quickly when they are allowed to" (1:220). In the context of the time, however, these lines could also be read as a commitment to the representation of life as free and untouched by any political agenda. Pasternak was not willing to follow the path of Aseev and Mayakovsky, who made revolution the central issue of their poetry, and turn his own poems into "a refrain" easy to read and recite. In this respect, his poetic declaration in "Poetry" remains faithful to his earlier beliefs: poetry is above all free; and although the poet is now less removed from everyday life than he was in his youth, he has no intention of becoming a voice in the glorification of the achievements of the new Soviet state.

This last section is also significant because it reveals Pasternak's interest in writing fiction. In one of the last poems he writes: "I will say good-bye to verses, my mania, / I have arranged a meeting with you in a novel. / As usual, far from parody, / We will find ourselves close to nature" (1:224). This statement, written in 1917, signals a change in Pasternak's attitude toward his creative work. Poetry no longer allowed him to convey the complex impressions of the time he lived in, and the challenge to write a novel that would encompass his personal experience and the turbulence of his age became increasingly appealing to him. Although it only fully materialized with *Doctor Zhivago* some three decades later, Pasternak was beginning imperceptibly to move toward the novel by writing short fiction and epic poems. Ending on this note of foreshadowing, the cycle *Themes and Variations* thus indicates Pasternak's awareness that a change in his work was imminent. Although—or perhaps precisely because—politically uncommitted, he certainly felt pressure to conform to the literary politics of the early 1920s and define his position. The literary climate of the time—although still far from the official call for "socialist realism" of the 1930s when this method was virtually required, favored works based on factual life rather than on fantasy. Lyrical poetry was viewed as bourgeois and a thing of the past. Social themes were clearly preferred over personal lyrics and clarity over the avant-garde obscurities and ambiguities. In 1917 when many of the poems of the cycle were written, Pasternak still officially belonged to Centrifuge, and his name was associated with it until its dissolution in 1922. He also kept close ties with the cubo-futurists, especially with Mayakovsky, despite the differences in their attitudes toward the realities of Soviet life and Pasternak's rejection of Mayakovsky's proposal to work together on posters for the Windows of ROSTA (the Russian telegraph agency) because of their political content (Fleishman 1990, 114). In 1922 Pasternak had a meeting with Leon Trotsky (1879–1940), one of the masterminds of the October Revolution and at that time the most prominent leader of the Soviet state after Lenin. Trotsky, who was sympathetic to the prerevolutionary artistic intelligentsia, wanted to know why Pasternak shunned social themes. In response to Trotsky's question, Pasternak defended his right to individual expression as an "integral part of every new 'social organism'" and stressed his intention to be faithful to his principles in the future (Fleishman 1990, 118).

Pasternak indeed did remain faithful to this pledge of the individuality of the creative artist. Yet his path in poetry was to change after *Themes and Variations.* Never again would he demonstrate such an array of technical brilliance, and never again would his membership in the poetic avant-garde be as pronounced as in this cycle. Although avant-garde movements survived until the end of the 1920s, their spirit was fading rapidly in Soviet Russia due to the intensifying party control over the arts. All avant-garde groups were effectively brought to heel with the establishment of the monolithic writers' organization, the Union of Soviet Writers, in 1932.

CHAPTER TWO

Early Prose

It seems that Pasternak had meant to write a novel for a long time, and his short fiction, composed mostly between 1911 and 1931, appears, in retrospect, as a preparation for such a project. The textured innovative language of Pasternak's short stories marks Pasternak's talent as a prose writer. In his prose, as in his poetry, he explored potentialities that go far beyond realism. His short fiction is, not surprising, far more cubo-futurist than realist. His interest in the nuances of perception and their extension into and transformations through memory define his artistic goals. Although never complete, his abstraction is a way for Pasternak to convey his relationship to the world. He abstracts in order to extend the culture he is abstracting from. The social scene is almost always present in his short fiction, which thus never allows the reader's total withdrawal into nonrepresentational realms. Pasternak's formal avant-gardeism does not annihilate his ties with the Russian literary heritage, and ethical considerations always figure in his stories. But the central focus of Pasternak's early prose is on language and its ability to extract the unusual from the quotidian and draw attention from the commonplace to the extraordinary.

Pasternak started composing prose and poetry simultaneously in the summer of 1910. His first prose sketches survived, and most of them have been published with critical commentaries in the five-volume Russian edition of his collected works.[1] His first published story, "Apellesova cherta" ("The Apelles Mark," 1915; also known as "Il tratto di Apelle," after its 1925 edition), was followed by "Pis'ma iz Tuly" ("Letters from Tula," 1918) and "Detstvo Liuvers" ("Liuvers's Childhood," 1917–1918; also known in English as "The Childhood of Liuvers"), published in 1922. The latter was conceived as the beginning of a novel, tentatively entitled *Tri imeni* (*Three Names*). Beyond that, Pasternak published "Vozdushnye puti" ("Aerial Ways," 1924) and "Povest'" ("The Tale," 1929). From his letters we know that he considered "The Tale" to be yet another beginning for a novel. And finally, there is his autobiography "Okhrannaia gramota" (*Safe Conduct,* 1929–1931), which became the last significant piece of fiction he wrote before *Doctor Zhivago.* Pasternak's short stories were not published collectively during his lifetime, although some of them appeared in two volumes, *Short Stories* (*Rasskazy,* 1925) and *Aerial Ways* (*Vozdushnye puti,* 1933).

Pasternak also left a few unfinished pieces of fiction, which have been published in the five-volume collection of his works. A short sketch, "Byl strannyi god" ("It Was a Strange Year," 1916), describes World War I and has a strong similarity to the writer's commentary on the war in *Doctor Zhivago* (4:860). A longer piece, "Istoriia odnoi kontroktavy" ("The History of a Contraoctave," 1916–1917), reflects Pasternak's interest in music and impressions from his trips to Germany in 1906 and 1912. This story is one of his first attempts to define the relationship between art and artist, the destructive power of art for human love and the artist's moral responsibility before human life. "Peterburg" ("Petersburg") was probably written in 1916 as part of a novella and is based on Pasternak's recollection of his relationship with the professional revolutionaries whom he met during his stay in the Urals. A piece entitled "Dialog" ("Dialogue," 1917) was written under the influence of the February Revolution and reflects Pasternak's hope in the revolution's positive impact on the fate of Russia as well as presenting his idealistic vision of the country's future. Included among his other unfinished works are "Bezliub'e" ("Without Love," 1918), a sketch based on his return to Moscow from the suburbs in February 1917; "Tri glavy iz povesti" ("Three Chapters from a Tale," 1922), connected with his later novel in verse, *Spektorskii*; and a few pieces from the late 1930s, regarded by him as preparation for *Doctor Zhivago*. The longest among them is "Zapiski Patrika" ("The Notes of Patrick"), published in 1936 under the title "Nachalo prozy 1936 goda" ("The Beginning of Prose in 1936"), which Pasternak planned to continue and treated as part of yet another novel.

The reception of Pasternak's fiction among his contemporary critics was generally favorable, although it was frequently referred to as the "prose of a poet" (Fleishman 1980, 174–75). However, if Pasternak's short fiction is placed in the context of the literary developments of his time, it appears that its stylistic peculiarities were strongly shaped by changes in the language of European culture during the first decades of the century and reflect Pasternak's response to these changes. Pasternak's formative years coincided with the blossoming of modernism; he absorbed some of its features, and his innovations in poetry and prose bear strong signs of the modernist paradigms. Wladimir Weidlé called him "the boldest and most complete exponent of Russian modernism" who stood out in his "most radical and closest connection with Western modernism."[2] But Pasternak's modernism was unique. Henry Gifford argues that it consists mainly in his urban sensibility and complexity of style (Gifford 1990,

305, 308–9). Gifford also emphasizes Pasternak's modernist stance in his conviction that "the world's best productions . . . actually tell about their own birth" (Gifford 1990, 313). Such works are about writing itself. Apart from the basic commonalities, such as of style and themes, however, Pasternak's early poetry and fiction stand outside Western European modernism, not lastly in the fact that life "never appears in his own writings as absurd and meaningless" (Gifford 1989, 26). And although Pasternak admired the works of Marcel Proust, Thomas Mann, and James Joyce, other prominent figures of European modernism such as Franz Kafka and Jean-Paul Sartre remained alien to him (Gifford 1989, 26–28).

When Pasternak began writing, he treated prose and poetry as two inseparable poles.[3] Christopher Barnes observes that "not only did his [Pasternak's] early manuscripts show a free ebb and flow between verse and prose, but his bewildering poise between music, philosophy and literature caused a further blurring of boundaries between belletristic and other writing" (Barnes 1989, 110). In "Some Propositions" Pasternak wrote that prose and poetry each come face to face with life in their own way: "poetry searches for the melody of nature in the noise of a dictionary . . . and artistic prose looks for and discovers man in the category of speech" (4:369). In his speech at the First Congress of Writers in 1934, Pasternak identified "pure prose" as poetry (4:631). It is therefore important to remember that Pasternak's prose, in Elliott Mossman's words, "was an alternative to, but not diversion from verse" (Mossman 1972, 280). And indeed, some critics have recognized that Pasternak's early prose was no less accomplished than his verse and was even more satisfying (Gifford 1977, 85).

For all these reasons it is appropriate to treat Pasternak's prose fiction not just as a poet's experiment but as a creative accomplishment in its own right. However tempting it is to ascribe the complicated syntax and imagery of Pasternak's early prose to his poetic achievements, this would only be partially accurate, and it is necessary to acknowledge that the peculiarities of his style, while an expression of his poetic diction, were equally dependent on and reflective of the innovative trends in the arts of the time. So strong was his response to the unfolding of new idioms in the arts that his affinity with avant-garde painting attracted the immediate attention of the critics. This fact was originally emphasized by Roman Jakobson in his seminal essay of 1935, "Marginal Notes on the Prose of the Poet Pasternak" (Jakobson 1987, 311).[4] On closer scrutiny one discovers that Pasternak's early prose style was in line with the literary experiments of such European modernists as Joyce and Proust, who responded to the new theories in psychology and philosophy with innovative modes of writing. Like them, Pasternak was interested in these new theories that moved toward understanding the structure of consciousness.

One philosopher who was particularly influential with modern writers in both Russia and the West was Henri Bergson (1859–1941). Pasternak was familiar with his writings through his studies of philosophy, and Bergson influenced his perception of time.[5] Pasternak's only philosophical essay, "O predmete i metode psikhologii" ("About the Object and Method of Psychology," 1913),[6] points in the direction of Bergson. The essay was inspired by a book written by one of Pasternak's neo-Kantian teachers at Marburg, Paul Natorp, titled *General Psychology through Critical Method.* Pasternak's essay discusses the complex structure of consciousness and its subjectivity as well as the connection between being and consciousness, issues that are also central to Bergson's philosophy. Bergson attempted to redefine consciousness and temporality and claimed that consciousness has a layered structure and that only nonsequential time, which he called *durée,* was capable of describing psychical processes. In *durée* present, past, and future interacted in a free flow. Bergson was not the only one attempting to redefine consciousness and temporality. Such phenomena as dreams, memories, and the subjective experience of time and space were also very much at the center of attention of the artistic vanguard. Many Russian writers and artists were preoccupied with the new theories of time and space.[7] All these ideas were exciting as ideas, but in order to translate them into aesthetic form it was necessary to develop a new mode of discourse capable of reflecting these redefined notions of time, space, and consciousness. One response to this need was the emergence of new principles of representation that were to define the modern movement in both art and literature. The language of Pasternak's prose was firmly in step with the development of the new modernist prose discourse that was becoming ever more poeticized in the density of its tropes and idiosyncratic syntax.

"The Apelles Mark"

Submitting "The Apelles Mark" for publication in *The Third Collection of Centrifuge* in December of 1916, Pasternak wrote to its editor Bobrov: "You will find a lot of nonsense there. But this piece was written with engagement and enthusiasm. . . . after I wrote 'Apelles,' I made more than one attempt to write prose, with an inclination toward technicalities" (4:805). Indeed, this first published short story by Pasternak is full of difficult stylistic escapades in the cubo-futurist manner that were also characteristic of his poetry of the same time. Like other Pasternak stories, this one is "a startling mixture of fact and poetry" (Payne 1963, 87). "The Apelles Mark" is also a labyrinth of complex relationships and unbelievable coincidences. Scattered throughout the narrative are examples of the most exquisite poetic prose, with a tangible rhythm, alliteration, and assonance and distinguished by its metaphors. The sources of "The Apelles Mark" are both biographical and literary. For example, the lush descriptions of the sultry Pisa night, the smell of Tuscan laurel leaves, and the scents of the Ferrara air reflect Pasternak's impressions from his trip to Italy in 1912, which was also the source of his Italian pages in *Safe Conduct*. The story bears another reference to Pasternak's biography. The relationship between the two poets in "The Apelles Mark" begs to be compared to Pasternak's relationship with Mayakovsky. Although Pasternak was a great admirer of Mayakovsky's poetry, he saw traces of romanticism in it and considered Mayakovsky's understanding of life romantic too.[8] The character of Relinquimini bears a strong resemblance to Mayakovsky in displaying the same romantic inclinations and theatrical elements as the great futurist poet.

A literary source of "The Apelles Mark" is Heinrich Heine's story "Florentine Nights" (Mossman 1972, 288), but Pasternak's character Heine has nothing in common with the great German romantic poet Heine (1797–1856), who stood at the end of the romantic movement. Rather, Heine points to Pasternak himself. Another source that inspired Pasternak's story is the opening paragraph of Heinrich von Kleist's (1777–1811) scandalous story, "Die Marquise von O" ("The Marquess of O") (Payne 1963, 91). There are still other literary sources for "The Apelles Mark," however, and Relinquimini's name is not mentioned in any of them; it is simply derived from a form of the Latin verb "to remain" (4:806). As a beginning poet Pasternak had used this name to sign his first poems. The story narrated in the epigraph of "The Apelles Mark" is a parable with a purely fictional basis since no mention of a meeting between the two Greek artists Apelles (fourth century B.C.) and Zeuxis (end of fifth century B.C. / beginning of fourth century B.C.) is made in any classical sources nor about any rivalry between them. The concept of the Apelles mark, however, is explained by the Roman scholar Pliny the Elder (23–79 B.C.) as a symbol of mastery or an authentic poetic "signature."[9] According to Pliny, Apelles' sign of mastery consisted in a single brush stroke that produced an exquisitely thin line. In the epigraph Apelles draws a line on Zeuxis's house wall. When Zeuxis sees the line, he immediately guesses the identity of his visitor; in the absence of Apelles, he leaves his own "sign" on the wall of Apelles' house, which becomes a "byword for mastery" (4:7).

"The Apelles Mark" is about a complex relationship between art, life, and the artist. It develops in analogy to the story in the epigraph and deals with a contest between Heine and Relinquimini. One August night in Ferrara the romantic Ferraran poet Emilio Relinquimini, author of the celebrated poem "Il Sangue" ("Blood"), pays Heine, a Westphalian poet, a visit. Unable to find him in his hotel room, Relinquimini leaves him a card with a spot of blood on it. When Heine receives the card, he immediately recognizes its author since it reminds him of the anonymous arrogant letter left for him (Heine) a few days earlier. In that letter a stranger had challenged him to demonstrate his "signature of Apelles" and promised to come back in three days to see it. Heine decides to respond to the challenge of his rival and immediately departs from Pisa to Ferrara, leaving behind an envelope for Relinquimini. The envelope contains a small piece of paper with a line cut out from some manuscript: "but Rondolfina and Enrico, having discarded their former names, managed to exchange them for hitherto imaginary ones. He shouted wildly: 'Rondolfina!' She cried out: 'Enrico!'" (4:8) In Ferrara, Heine checks into a hotel and places an announcement in the newspaper *Il Voce* about his wish to find a manuscript by Emilio Relinquimini and asking the author or his confidants to contact him at the hotel. Since Relinquimini is not in Ferrara, his mistress Camilla Ardenze comes to the hotel to pick up the manuscript. Heine, fascinated by Camilla's beauty and charm, seduces her by reenacting a relationship between the fictitious characters Rondolfina and Enrico. But soon Heine realizes that he has become trapped in the game himself for his fictional love for Camilla has become real. Thus art becomes real life for Heine as his true love for Camilla turns out to be the "signature of Apelles," a response to the real blood spot left by the author of the poem "Blood."

At the time he wrote this story Pasternak was still in search of his poetic identity, and his new friendship with Mayakovsky was of major importance to him. Pasternak's admiration of Mayakovsky, however, was mixed with doubt. Pasternak was fascinated by his poetry, but when he noticed some similarities with it, he actively tried to overcome them. Moreover, certain traits of Mayakovsky's character, as fascinating as they must have been for many people, did not agree with Pasternak's conception of a true poet. It is the false aspect of the poet's identity that "The Apelles Mark" argues against. Like Mayakovsky, Relinquimini seems to be preoccupied with his image of a true poet, which he carefully constructs. Like Mayakovsky's, his behavior is affected and theatrical. Later, in his pages on Mayakovsky in *Safe Conduct,* Pasternak observes that Mayakovsky, to a higher degree than other people, was "a manifestation" of his own being and assuming a pose: "Behind his bearing there was something akin to a decision which had been realized and whose consequences could not be revoked. . . . he chose the pose of exterior integrity. . . . He sustained this pose with such perfection that now it is almost impossible to characterize what lay behind it" (4:216–17). Pasternak was divided in his attitude toward Mayakovsky's constructed image. Like Mayakovsky, Pasternak initially believed in "a conception of life as the life of a poet," which for both of them was the heritage of symbolism borrowed from the romantics (4:227). But Pasternak eventually became critical of this attitude and tried to avoid the romantic excesses both in his poetry and in constructing his image as a poet. His skepticism toward romanticism relates him to the historical persona of Heine, who represented the most rational and skeptical trend of the romantic movement. In "The Apelles Mark" Pasternak identifies with Heine, and Heine's response to Relinquimini can be interpreted as Pasternak's response to Mayakovsky's poetics and behavior. Whereas Relinquimini's blood-stained card remains a theatrical gesture of a romantic poet, Heine's Apelles mark breaks the boundaries of romantic conventions and asserts true love and life themselves.

Apart from the romantic story line in "The Apelles Mark," its style approaches the cubo-futurist imagery already familiar to readers from Pasternak's early poetry. Most of the story's descriptive passages represent the world through displacement, through arbitrary repositioning and replacement of objects or details. Pasternak's linguistic puzzles, largely based on anthropomorphism and metonymy, can be solved only with the help of associative thinking as seen in the following passage describing Heine's train trip to Ferrara: "Rocks and precipices, neighbors shattered by sleep, stench of the carriages, and a tongue of gas flames in the lamp. It licks off the rustling and shadows from the ceiling, it licks its own lips, and it gets short of breath when the rocks and the precipices are followed by a tunnel. Rumbling, the mountain crawls down the carriage roof and spreads the engine smoke flat, driving it into the windows, clinging to the coat hooks and baggage nets" (4:10). In this passage Pasternak intentionally draws the readers' attention to the linguistic rearrangement of reality.

The gravitation of Pasternak's style toward the displacement of logical connections by artistic devices does not, however, violate his faith in artistic representation. In his early essay "Chernyi bokal" ("The Black Goblet," 1916) Pasternak addresses the question of how reality could and ought to be rendered. Pasternak declares that realism for him, as for the futurists, means subjectivity, originality, and innovation (4:357). He sees two existing powers in reality: irrationality and objectivity. Irrationality was fundamental to lyricism, whereas objectivity laid the foundation for history. Lyricism rebelled against history and strove to achieve *extemporale,* that is, eternity (4:358). According to Pasternak, futurist lyricism was superior to other kinds of lyricism because it avoided "packaging" reality into symbolist and impressionist "landscapes, real and fictitious," into "tales real and illusory . . . into myths and metaphors," but rather filled art with an essence as "lively and adventurous" as life itself (4:357). The futurist poet succeeded because he grasped the "limitational moment" during which the ephemeral and temporary transformed themselves into the eternal (4:357). It is this transformation that represented for Pasternak true art whose symbol was the Apelles mark.

"Letters from Tula"

The theme of the Apelles mark continues in Pasternak's next short story, "Letters from Tula," written for a collection of works on the nature of art in 1918 (published in 1922). As in "The Apelles Mark," in this story Pasternak explores the relationship between art and life, together with the connection between the projected image of the artist and his true self. Should the poet juxtapose himself to the "crowd," to "non-poets"? Should he carry on the legendary aura of exclusivity or should he shed the romantic pose? Years later, in *Safe Conduct,* Pasternak elucidates his attitude toward the romantic understanding of the poet's life in the following line: "[the romantic poet] is not a living being absorbed by his ethical perception, but rather is a visual-biographical emblem which requires a background for his visual outline" (4:228). In contrast to Mayakovsky, whom he mentions as the epitome of a poet with a romantic aura, Pasternak freed himself from this romantic model because he was afraid of "any kind of poetization that would put [him] into a false or inappropriate position" (4:228). There is a distinct aura of morality in Pasternak's attitude toward the poet as a poseur. Although not a moralist in the sense that Tolstoy was, Pasternak retains a recognizable element of the great writer's concerns in his own thinking. This is particularly evident in his commitment to truth and authenticity, as well as in his intolerance of any kind of affectation in life and art.

"Letters from Tula" is Pasternak's quest to deromanticize the image of the artist not only through the choice of characters but also through the setting itself. Gone are the foreign names and the alluring romantic atmosphere of "The Apelles Mark" and of earlier prose sketches. The action of this story takes place in the provincial Russian town of Tula, only a few miles away from Iasnaia Poliana, the place where Tolstoy lived and wrote most of his works. It is not surprising, therefore, that the spirit of Tolstoy defines to a certain extent the atmosphere of the story. One of the two main characters shows full awareness of Tolstoy's spiritual presence in this location and, influenced by the aura of the place, tests his own moral composure as an artist: "But this is Tula! And this night is a night in Tula. Night in a place of Tolstoy's biography. Is it surprising that compass needles start dancing here? This event is in the nature of this place. This is an occurrence on the *territory of conscience,* on its gravitational, ore-bearing sector" (4:30). Although "Letters from Tula" pays tribute to the great Russian novelist, Pasternak's attitude toward him was generally ambivalent (Fleishman 1990, 94). He sympathized with Tolstoy's view that the individual can find the truth through moral self-perfection but found it impossible to accept Tolstoy's hostility toward modern art or any art that was foreign to his sensibilities. Also Pasternak, unlike Tolstoy, was unable to give a clear-cut account of the moral function of art despite his own demanding attitude toward the moral self of the artist. *Safe Conduct* confirms his understanding of art as a record of the displacement of reality by feeling (4:187), a formula completely incompatible with Tolstoy's principle of realistic representation of life.

"Letters from Tula" is divided into two unrelated parts narrated by two different characters. There is also a third-person omniscient narrator in both parts. But because the narrative is nonsequential and consists mostly of letters, thoughts, and memories, it is hard to understand whether there is any connection at all between the two narrative voices represented by the two main characters. Their namelessness further makes it difficult to establish such a connection, although the theme of artificiality and vulgarity versus truth and authenticity in art appears in both parts of the story. The first narrator is a young poet who observes a movie crew that shoots a film entitled *The Time of Trouble,* about a peasant uprising in seventeenth-century Russia. The behavior of the crew members repulses him by its theatricality, affectation, and vulgarity so much that he calls the whole group "the worst type of bohemians" (1:29). The actors' loud behavior also provokes the poet's most critical attitude toward himself. His self-criticism is merciless when he recognizes himself in their use of vocabulary and pattern of behavior: "This is a display of the ideals of our age. . . . It is the stench of ignorance and the most unfavorable impudence. It is my own self. . . . This is their vocabulary: genius, poet, ennui, verses, mediocrity, philistinism, tragedy, woman, I and she" (4:29). The moral self of the poet suffers when one of the actors identifies him as one of his bohemian kin and addresses him as a "colleague." The poet's moral torment reaches hyperbolic proportions as the voice of the omniscient narrator declares that "the night lay spread on the whole extent of the wet Russian conscience" (4:31). Here in Tula, in the shadow of Tolstoy, the poet "thought of his art and of how to find the right path" (4:31). The moral conflict within the poet points once again to Pasternak's own anxiety at the time to rid himself of any association with Mayakovsky and his entourage, whom the story's movie crew resembles so vividly. In fact, Pasternak's criticism seems to be directed not only at Mayakovsky but at the whole modern movement in Russia, from the 1890s to the moment of the narration: "For thirty years now, all these unusual men both young and old have lived like this, dampening their shame. And now it has spread to the world of the men unknown" (1:29). Here the narrator directs his sarcasm at the art that, in his view, failed to fulfill its moral function.

In the second part of the story the main character is an old actor who, like the young poet, experiences dissatisfaction and alienation at the sight of the mediocre film production. But unlike the young man, he turns to creativity and the transforming power of great art for consolation and performs a scene from his own life of some twenty-five years before. The old man brings back the voice of his long-deceased wife and is so overwhelmed by the authenticity of revived experience that he bursts into tears.

"Letters from Tula" is doubtless associated with Tolstoy's moralistic sentiment; but on the narrative level this story represents an example of precisely that modern art that Tolstoy condemned. The language and structure of the story are difficult to follow as Pasternak presents his characters through their own thought processes. Thus the style of the poet's first letter to his beloved reflects his distracted state; his narrative is incoherent and its fragments are dispersed:

Ah, my dear, they are all strangers around me. There was one man, but he [the general] has gone. And there is still one more, the magistrate—but they do not recognize him. Nonentities! Why, they think it is their sun that they sip with milk from the saucer. They think their flies stick neither in your sun, or ours. The kitchen boys' saucepans clash, seltzer water spatters, and, as if clicking their tongues, coins clatter noisily on the marble tabletops. I will go and look around the town. It has remained somewhere aside. There is the cabby, but it isn't worth it. They say it is about forty minutes on foot. I have found the receipt. You were quite right. I will hardly have time tomorrow. I must catch up on my sleep. The day after tomorrow. Don't worry. It's a pawnshop. It isn't urgent. (4:28)

The poet's thought process lacks any logical development and pours further as a stream of consciousness. The fragmented quality of the passage illustrates the instability and anxiety in the character's psychological state. Since the poet's thoughts lack focus and wander from people he knows, to objects, to his beloved, and back to the objects and his beloved again, readers experience the breakdown of syntax. Sentences become abrupt, fragmentary, unfinished, and the word order seems to be whimsical.

The first part of the narrative of "Letters from Tula" is often interrupted by authorial parentheses: "crossed out"; "carefully crossed out"; "crossed out, left incomplete"; "heavily underscored with a line that tears through the paper in places" (28–29). The effect is the foregrounding of the device by laying it bare. Parentheses are the literary equivalent of the painterly "rough surface" that cubo-futurist artists advocated in their paintings. In the story parentheses not only accentuate gaps in logical thinking but also draw attention to how the work is made—in short, to the material, the texture, and the composition itself. The story is built as a futurist collage entirely made out of "parentheses," or disruptions and shifts of recognizable forms.

On the syntactical level, the collage consists of fragmented metonymic images that coexist in one sentence. Anthropomorphism and interpenetrating imagery are common here: "The skylarks in the open sang freely their song, and a suffocating sun was carried along on many striped benches in the train from Moscow. The sun was setting. The bridge with the inscription 'Upa' sailed across a hundred carriage windows. At that same instant the stoker flying along in the tender at the head of the train discovered the town away to one side of the track, and through the roar of his own hair and the fresh excitement of the evening he saw the town rushing toward him" (4:27). This description provides a vivid example of dislocation of space in the manner of collage. The story's rich pictorial texture in the vein of cubo-futurism is complemented by the liberal use of color: "Across the table sits an agriculturist or something of the kind. He has a ruddy face. He stirs his coffee with a green hand" (4:28).

The new stylistic strategies in "Letters from Tula" were for Pasternak a means of creating a new realism characterized by his strong desire to portray inwardness, mood, and sense impressions. Finding a narrative form that expressed these phenomena was Pasternak's great achievement. But the characteristic extravagance of his style is best understood in its relation to the contemporary avant-garde experiments in the visual arts. Describing the prose of Russian writers in search of this new realism, the Russian writer Evgenii Zamiatin noted that they did not "narrate" but rather "showed," and therefore it would be more appropriate to call their narratives "visuatives" rather than "stories."[10] This was certainly true for Pasternak's early fiction with its striving toward the notably pictorial.

"Liuvers's Childhood"

Pasternak wrote "Detstvo Liuvers" ("Liuvers's Childhood," 1918) as the beginning of a novel tentatively titled "Three Names." Upon its publication the story was praised by the critics for its refined portrayal of a child's inner world and ranked among the best works about childhood, such as those written by Tolstoy and Maksim Gorky (4:808). Despite the comparison, there is not much in common between "Liuvers's Childhood" and the works of the two masters of Russian literature, although Tolstoy's moral bent is perceptible in the story. Whereas Tolstoy in the famous trilogy *Detstvo,* (Childhood, 1852) *Otrochestvo,* (Adolescence, 1854), and *Iunost'* (Youth, 1857) focuses on his hero's moral development and Gorky's description of childhood in the trilogy *Moi universitety* (*My Universities*, 1922) is largely concerned with the character's growing social awareness, Pasternak chooses to explore Zhenia Liuvers's poetic apprehension of the world and her rich emotional experiences. Hers is a world of observation, association, and imagination, which give the story its impressionistic tinge. Moreover, in actual narrative volume, Zhenia's childhood in the small provincial town of Perm' in the Urals occupies barely a page and a half and ends with the narrator's abrupt announcement "Years passed."[11] Shortly after this temporal leap, which occurs early in the narrative, Zhenia discovers her first menstrual blood and realizes her transition into womanhood. Thus the story is more about an adolescent girl who preserves the freshness of the child's perceptions than about a child developing into an adolescent. Free from verbal high jinks, "Liuvers's Childhood" is written in a simpler, more straightforward style than Pasternak's two earlier published stories. But despite its relative simplicity, the language of "Liuvers's Childhood" is profoundly lyrical and perfectly suited to convey the complex psychological world of a young artistically inclined girl.

"Liuvers's Childhood" consists of two parts, "Dolgie dni" ("The Long Days") and "Postoronnii" ("The Stranger"). Although the two parts have unquestionable connections and share the main characters, "The Stranger" could almost be treated as a separate story with its own independent plot and an additional set of characters. "The Long Days" has a conventional beginning describing Zhenia's background. She was born in the town of Perm'. Her father was a business manager of the Lunev mines, and the family had a comfortable existence. The narrator provides minimum information about the family history and instead devotes the bulk of the story to Zhenia's poetic discovery of the world. Already at a young age, when she is perhaps three years old, Zhenia demonstrates an ability to endow her surroundings with mysterious qualities. Once she wakes up at night and sees something unusual on the other bank of the river: "This had no name, and no precise color or definite outline. And as it stirred it was familiar and dear . . . throwing fresh and flighty shadows on the russet beams of the gallery" (157). Zhenia is so overwhelmed by this mysterious picture that she begins to cry. Her father's brief explanation that the thing she sees is Motovilikha, the location of a factory, does not satisfy her. The name for Zhenia does not replace the world of magic that just opened itself to her. Whereas adult logic is satisfied with a matter-of-fact explanation of the phenomena, for Zhenia only seeing the world fresh in the richness of her experience provides satisfactory answers. That sets her apart from those who explain the world through ready-made formulas. When Zhenia reaches puberty, she has a much more difficult time understanding things in terms of their preconceived notions and labels than does her brother Serezha. For instance, when the family moves from Perm' to Ekaterinburg, Zhenia is disappointed that the border between Europe and Asia is marked only by some small and insignificant post with a sign on it, resembling a "tombstone," whereas "in her enchanted mind the 'frontier of Asia' arose like a phantasmagoric barrier—maybe like those iron bars that marked a strip of terrible-pitch-black, stinking danger between the public and the cage with the pumas" (169). Serezha, on the other hand, accepts the little "tombstone" as a simple sign, a label necessary for indicating a geographical border. The next morning they wake up with a different sense of the place: "Serezha in Ekaterinburg and Zhenia in Asia" (172). Ekaterinburg is a concrete geographical point; Asia represents the whole fantastic and magnificent universe of nature that Zhenia saw from the train window. The desire to find what lies behind the surface sets her apart from the world of adults and her brother and distinguishes her perceptions as uniquely poetic. Through the contrast between Zhenia's sensitivities and those of others, Pasternak explores the romantic theme of the affinity between the poet and the child.[12] The true world of wonder opens up only to those with a childlike vision unspoiled by "adult" conceptions. Romantic in its very essence, this idea is embodied in all of Pasternak's art. Late in his life he wrote in a letter—in English—to Stephen Spender: "I also from my earliest years have been struck by the observation that existence was more original, extraordinary, and inexplicable than any of its separate astonishing incidents and facts. I was attracted by the unusualness of the usual."[13] This "unusualness of the usual" was at the center of Pasternak's understanding of true artistic realism, which lay in subjectivity, originality, and innovation, as he defined it in the essay "Chopin" (4:404).

To convey Zhenia's original and rich perceptions, Pasternak uses verbal collage, already familiar from "Letters from Tula." When Zhenia sees the bustle of a railway station in a provincial town, the verbal projection of her perception of it is only an approximation of reality broken into fragments, rearranged, and defamiliarized, as in a cubo-futurist painting. The reality that Zhenia sees through relationships of things becomes a stream of images. The representation of

Zhenia's spatial apprehension in the following passage is highly pictorial: "Zhenia looked through the window. She saw not a street but another room, only more serious and gloomy than the one here in this decanter. Into that other room engines slowly came and stopped, spreading darkness. But when they left and cleared the room, it turned out not to be a room because there, behind the pillars, was the sky, and on the far side—a hill and wooden houses with people going away toward them. Perhaps the cockerels were crowing there right now, and the water-carrier had recently been and left a trail of sludge . . ." (167). A key to the understanding of this description is cubo-futurist or cubist painting, especially its intended simultaneities—that is, the projection of different objects onto one plane.

Everything in the story is oriented toward Zhenia's perceptions. In fact it is only through them that the reader can relate to other characters, no matter how mysterious her perceptions are. In "The Stranger" her unusual way of making connections between events is conveyed through the device of coincidence. It is coincidence that brings together and clarifies the impressionistically scattered events of the second part of the story. Coincidences are prominent in Pasternak's prose and therefore draw attention to themselves as a defining narrative strategy. Some critics have labeled them, especially those in *Doctor Zhivago,* as absurd and artificial; yet on closer look it will become apparent that coincidence fits in Pasternak's work as a device consistent with the general outlines of his narratives.[14] It is important to note that coincidences are seemingly free from causal constraints and are therefore a sign of resistance against the idea of predestination peculiar to naturalism. Embedded in them is, in Pasternak's own words, the spontaneity of life that he describes in the letter to Spender quoted above: "there is an effort . . . to represent the whole sequence of facts and beings and happenings like some moving entireness, like a developing, passing by, rolling and rushing inspiration, as if reality itself had freedom and choice and was composing itself out of numberless variants and versions . . . through this means [coincidences] I wanted to show the liberty of being, its verisimilitude touching, adjoining improbability" (5).

Pasternak's use of coincidence is similar to that of such modern writers as Joyce and Proust. Mossman, for example, considers Pasternak's use of coincidences as a device that convinces readers of a reality beyond the scope of their vision. This reality is created through an intricate system of spatial relations formed of various details: "This portrayal of reality as such through the coincidences in the daily rounds of people, analogous to Bloomsday and Dublin seen in the peregrinations of Leopold Bloom and Stephen Daedalus, is a major innovation in narrative fiction of the twentieth century" (Mossman 1972, 299). We can say, then, and this also follows from Pasternak's letter to Spender, that Pasternak uses coincidences to undermine the effect of naturalism. Coincidences are highlighted by modernism to draw attention to that which underlies the obvious.

Coincidences in the narrative always connect temporal perceptions with consciousness. In Pasternak's coincidences, temporal arrangements are in a way reversed because coincidences materialize only when the present and past collide in the realm of memory. In the narrative, then, we always have to retrace those puzzling details that later bring significance to the moment when the paths of the characters cross. As in Joyce and Proust, coincidences in Pasternak grow into a temporal system that does not exist outside of the pure time characteristic of interacting states of consciousness. And so in "Liuvers's Childhood" coincidences do not exist apart from Zhenia's consciousness. They grow out of a series of puzzles that revolve around a strange limping man who catches her attention. Somehow their paths repeatedly cross; the girl begins to see the limping stranger everywhere. Once she sees him with her tutor Dikikh but somehow fails to make a connection between the two men. It is only at the end of the story that her tutor's remark about the loss of a friend makes her realize, through instantaneous flashbacks, that the mysterious stranger was that very Tsvetkov who had been a friend of her family's Belgian friend Negaraat. It is from Negaraat that Zhenia had heard Tsvetkov's name for the first time. Once when she wakes up early at dawn and looks out the window, she sees a horse and then in a window across the street the limping stranger pacing around his room with a lamp in his hand. Later Zhenia establishes connections between Tsvetkov's death and her mother's illness; in fact, her mother had a miscarriage because of a nervous shock inflicted by a road accident on her way to the theater. The shock had occurred when the horse that pulled Mrs. Liuvers's carriage became wild and kicked to death a passerby, who happened to be Tsvetkov. What triggers the realization that all these episodes are coincidences is the word *theater,* which Zhenia's tutor pronounces as he tells her in a few words about his friend's death.

Instantly Zhenia also establishes the connections between her mother's miscarriage and Tsvetkov's death. It is then that the deaths, the figure of Negaraat, the lamp she saw in the stranger's hand early in the morning, the horse, Tsvetkov's very name, and other episodes crystallize in Zhenia's consciousness and shed light upon the present: "So many deaths—and all so sudden!" she sighed. But the tutor was just about to tell her the story of Tsvetkov's death when something quite inexplicable occurred. She suddenly changed her ideas about how many deaths there had been. Clearly forgetting the evidence she had seen by lamplight that morning, she stopped him: "'Wait. One time you were at the tobacconist's—when Negaraat was leaving—I saw you with someone. Was that him?' She was afraid to say 'Tsvetkov'" (206). Dikikh was dumbfounded by her discovery.

This is a moment in the story when Zhenia makes a moral discovery: she realizes that the abstract stranger who has been an object of her curiosity for so long was above all another human being: "It was the person the Commandments have in mind, addressing men with names and consciousness, when they say 'Thou shalt not kill,' 'Thou shalt not steal,' et cetera. . . . 'As a living human individual,' they say, 'you must not do to this featureless generalized man what you would not wish for yourself as a living individual'" (208). The thrill of following the stranger and fictionalizing his life is replaced by the realization of the Christian principle of love for the stranger. Overwhelmed by her discovery, Zhenia begins to cry, and her tutor Dikikh, although unable to understand the true nature of her tears, suddenly notices the dramatic change in his student: from a child she has become a woman with a complex inner world.

Barnes believes the message of this story is Tolstoyan because of Zhenia's moral revelations (Barnes 1989, 272), and Gifford points out that once again, after "Letters from Tula," Pasternak "found his way to 'the territory of conscience'" (Gifford 1977, 91). But despite the fact that most critics praise "Liuvers's Childhood" above all for its subtle psychological observations and nuances of Zhenia's maturation, the moral significance of the story in its historical context should not be overlooked. As Barnes points out, the story was written in the midst of the revolutionary terror in Russia when arrests and executions as well as "swallowing up of the individual by mass movements and statistics were a part of everyday life. It is because of these circumstances that "Liuvers's Childhood" "makes a powerful, if oblique statement on the sanctity of the individual and of human life," qualities ignored by the new rulers of Russia (Barnes 1989, 272, 273). Pasternak magnifies the theme of the value of individual life by placing it squarely in the historical context in his next story, "Aerial Ways."

"Aerial Ways"

"Aerial Ways" was first published in the journal *Russkii sovremennik* (*Russian Contemporary*) in 1924. The story's original version is unknown since the editorial board of the journal asked Pasternak to shorten the manuscript and eliminate its implicit nonacceptance of capital punishment. Since the original has not survived, it is hard to say how Pasternak changed it and what the original ending was. Regardless of its original form, however, "Aerial Ways" appears as an outline for *Doctor Zhivago*. Its themes clearly resonate in Pasternak's great novel, and its main characters, Larissa and Strelnikov, anticipate the story's characters Lelia and Polivanov.

"Aerial Ways" is marked by the same linguistic eccentricities as Pasternak's previous stories despite its more dramatic historical context, whose main theme is human destiny in the revolution. Divided into three parts, the story deals with two episodes from the lives of the characters Lelia and Polivanov. The first two parts describe the kidnapping and search for Lelia's son, Tosha. Lelia, her husband, and the naval officer Polivanov, presumably her lover, are unsuccessfully looking for Tosha, who is finally found by two students. In the third part, fifteen years later, fate brings Lelia and Polivanov together again. This time Lelia appeals to Polivanov, now a Red Army official, once again to save her son, who has been arrested by the Bolsheviks. As in the earlier episode, she claims that Polivanov is Tosha's father. Polivanov tries to prevent the execution of the young man but learns that it has already taken place.

From the beginning of the story the reader is aware of a new relationship between himself and the narrator. The narrator draws attention to the fictionality of the story by telling the reader what he is doing: "I will relate how, as the sun went down, the parents of the little kidnapped boy cleaned their white canvas shoes. . . . I am coming to the promised story. . . . Is it by reason of this dubious observation that the author has been concealing from his readers what he knows so very well?" (4:87–88, 91). The narrator's interpolations constantly point to the fact that the reality seen through his eyes is an artistic creation.

In the first two parts of "Aerial Ways" the narrator's vision of the world is profoundly poetic: "The storm-cloud cast a glance at the sun-scorched stubble fields. They stretched all the way to the horizon. The storm-cloud lightly reared up. The stubble fields stretched further still, even beyond the camps. The storm-cloud came down upon its forefeet and having smoothly crossed the road, noiselessly began to crawl along the fourth track of the railway siding" (4:87). The narrator humanizes what is not otherwise perceived as living by violating the borders between animate and inanimate objects: "His own footprints continued to live and quiver behind. They also wanted to sleep. The gravel, disturbed in its peace, sighed and turned from side to side . . ." (4:93). Everything is connected with everything else. The narrator also destroys the unity of the part and the whole. Bizarre shifts in the story create images that are vague and ambiguous and seem without a definite temporal placement. Lelia's walk home, together with her husband and the midshipman, is described metonymically:

> They would follow the path to the hedge, slam the wicket, and without a drop shaken from its ridges, cornices, and gutters by the tinkling of the ear-rings that danced in its ears, the iron planet would slowly begin to get in step with their approach. . . . But, a far flight from them, like linen torn by a gust of wind at daybreak and carried who knew where, on the farther edge of the fields three human shapes now appeared dimly for a moment, while on the opposite side eternally rolled and reverberated the evanescent murmur of the distant sea. These four persons were carried only from the past into the future, and were never brought back. (4:89–90)

Pasternak often uses a complex chain of metaphors to express the over-whelming variety of nature and the polyphony of voices with which it speaks:

> From under the trees, as if from under cowls pulled low over foreheads, were streaming the first beginnings of the not yet conscious morning. . . . Coming from no one knew where, a sickly sweet trembling that grew faster and faster ran across the tree-tops. One after another, having slapped the fence with their sweaty silver, the tree-tops fell back to a slumber rudely disturbed. Two rare diamonds separately and independently shimmered in the deep nests of this twilight paradise: a bird and its twittering. (4:91)

The narrator's intention constantly seems to subvert the reader's expecta-tions. At the beginning of the story the images are fragmented, these images are as strange as the language itself, and the reader is faced with only an approxi-mation of the familiar world. Like a cubo-futurist painting, Pasternak's story creates meaning by association, by establishing correspondences and connec-tions between things and phenomena inside the narrative, not between the nar-rative and "real" outside world. Even the characters are not fully described because, in Jakobson's words, Pasternak never uses "an actor" in his early fic-tion; rather, he prefers "a man's condition, or one of his remarks or attributes" as a kind of character-place holder (Jakobson 1987, 308). For example, a fe-male character in the story can be represented by a contralto and a man by a bass voice: "'What? What do you mean, not there? He's lost?' simultaneously cried out a bass voice, hoarse, like a slackened string, and a woman's contralto glistening with hysteria" (4:89). The fragmented surface of Pasternak's fiction is the result of his extensive use of metonymy, one of the two predominant modes of artistic expression, according to Jakobson. Jakobson, in his famous piece from 1935, characterizes metonymy as association by contiguity rather than by similarity or contrast, as in metaphor (Jakobson 1987, 306–7). Metonymy is so abundant in Pasternak that the reader is forced to follow the connections between things, whereas things as such fall out of the picture altogether.

In "Aerial Ways" the revolution and the Third International are depicted in an image of abstraction by means of metonymy. In the third part of the story Pasternak describes space as deformed and fragmented—a stratified construction in which aerial ways occupy the uppermost position. We can easily extend Jakobson's argument that in Pasternak "a realm of metonymy [is] awakened to independent life" (Jakobson 1987, 308) to the image of aerial ways. The aerial ways in the story are the revolutionary ideas reified. They are inflexible and allow movement only along a predetermined route, like the railway tracks with which they are associated. The image of aerial ways is endowed with physical characteristics that should leave no doubt as to their connection with the idea of "world revolution"; the aerial ways have an "oppressive enormousness," and they expand and set in motion the "rectilinear thoughts" of the Third International: "These were the aerial ways by which daily, like trains, the rectilinear thoughts of Liebknecht, Lenin and a handful of minds of their flight of thought left the station. Those were the routes established on a level adequate for the crossing of any frontiers, whatever their name" (4:94). A political idea thus acquires material characteristics and begins an independent existence. In Jakobson's words, "an abstraction becomes objectified" (Jakobson 1987, 309). Here space, metaphorically portrayed, communicates a vision of the revolution as an inflexible, inexorable, and gloomy force.

Spatial arrangements reflect the narrator's perception of events. In the first two parts of the story characters are of miniature stature in comparison with the immensity of the surrounding space. In the third part the space in which the action takes place shrinks to the size of a room, and the characters became central. From the vastness and poetic immensity and grandeur of the ahistorical world at the beginning of the story, the narrator takes the reader to the stark materiality of the revolutionary epoch, where images of people are brought to the foreground and the surrounding world of nature is used as a grim backdrop. The contrast in the representation of humans and nature directs attention away from nature in the first half of the story to the human drama in the second half. The change of spatial relations is achieved through changes in the imagery as the light and transparent colors of the first two parts of the story fade and darken. At the beginning the characters wear white clothes, the station is filled with "the bright splashing of skies and sails and sailor shirts" (4:88), the earth is covered by sparkling rain drops, the garden is washed by the white light, and the trees are painted white. In the third part, however, the palette is predominantly dark: "Outside, the light was falling, indoors it was dark" (4:93). The sky "frowned, speechless" (4:93–94). Lelia comes "straight from the station, filthy, long unwashed" (4:96). The town is "engulfed in utter darkness" (4:96). Darkness also surrounds the first moments of the meeting between Lelia and Polivanov, who is now a high-ranking official in the local Soviet. The deeper they go into the enclosed space, the darker it becomes: "In comparison with the vestibule, the office was pitch dark" (4:95). What happens is the translation of a psychological reality into an external progression toward darkness in which the sense of direction disappears and normal temporal and spatial perceptions become distorted and confused.

The light and color coding of the psychological climate of the story culminates in Polivanov's totally dark office, where Lelia becomes completely spatially and temporally disoriented. In this darkness her past comes back to her and she finds herself within restructured space and time: "Imagination had only just transported that room with pictures and furnished with bookcases, palms and bronzes, to one of the boulevards of old Petersburg and stood there, with a whole handful of lights in an outstretched hand to fling them over the whole length of the perspective . . ." (4:96). The image of Petersburg takes Lelia to the idealized world of the past where Polivanov and she were lovers. The temporal sequence is broken as the stream of Lelia's past perceptions penetrates the present. Time itself stops being an objective experience and turns into a flow; it becomes illogical and personal, reminiscent of Bergson's *durée*.

When suddenly the phone rings in Polivanov's office, however, the world of the past disappears for Lelia and she is brought back to the reality of Soviet Russia: "suddenly the telephone rang. Its gurgling jangle strongly redolent of fields or a god-forsaken village, was an instant reminder that the wire had felt its way here through the city engulfed in absolute darkness, and the action was taking place in the provinces, under the Bolsheviks" (4:96). This is also the moment when Polivanov recognizes Lelia. But this moment is not a moment of joy; on the contrary, it triggers alienation. Both Lelia and Polivanov realize that the old world has vanished forever and that they are total strangers to each other: "Suddenly it all vanished. . . . In the light of the oil-lamp her coming, . . . everything said by her before the light seemed to be a depressingly compelling truth . . ." (4:96).

As "Aerial Ways" moves toward its denouement, the spatial metaphor once again comes to play a key role for the reader's understanding of the story's meaning. Characters begin to lose their human identity and become objectlike. This metamorphosis seems to be natural if the reader recognizes its parallel unfolding with the spatial transformation. In parts 1 and 2 of "Aerial Ways" the aura of the images of space is lyrical and romantic. Nature is animated and presented in its immensity as subjective aesthetic abstraction. In the third part the image of space loses its vitality and begins to ossify. The texture of space thickens and becomes stratified, turning into the fixity of aerial routes and the dead landscape of a courtyard. The change in the texture of space from living to dead matter runs parallel to a change in the characters. Polivanov dissolves into a verbal stream, into commas and conjunctions: "Polivanov flared up and began to talk and talk and talk, quickly, without stopping. He spoke just as if he were writing an article with 'whiches' and commas" (4:97). Lelia, on the other hand, upon realizing that her son, lost and found fifteen years ago, has been killed by the Bolsheviks, faints and lies on the floor like an "enormous, unbroken doll" (4:98).

Thus ends "Aerial Ways." Although not a protest against the excesses of Bolshevik power, this story portrays a grim picture of it. "Aerial Ways" also appears as a reflection on Pasternak's old theme of lyricism and history that he developed in "The Black Goblet." He believed that futurist art was successful because it overcame the rationality of historical thinking by adopting the lyrical mode. Pasternak juxtaposed lyricism and history and clearly favored lyricism. But "Aerial Ways" seems to point to the contrary: lyricism cannot escape history because there is a direct connection between them. Moreover, history dominates lyricism, or as Pasternak put it through his character Vedeniapin in *Doctor Zhivago,* "man does not live in nature but in history" (3:14).

"The Tale"

Pasternak wrote "The Tale" in 1929. He treated it as the first part of a future novel and, according to his letters, had further plans about expanding the short story. The original manuscript of "The Tale" has not survived, but the first sketches of it introduced its main character, Sergei Spektorskii, and were presumably connected with an episode from Pasternak's civilian service that he did in lieu of military service in the Urals in 1914–1916, where he worked as a tutor at the home of a wealthy businessman. In addition to having eponymous main characters, "The Tale" is also thematically closely connected with Pasternak's novel in verse, *Spektorskii,* which he composed between 1925 and 1929 (discussed in the next chapter). The narrator of *Spektorskii* says that the story he is writing was conceived ten years earlier and that some of its completed parts were published "at the beginning of the revolution." He also adds that in a somewhat changed version the characters and events reappear in his novel *Spektorskii* (4:99). In reality Pasternak hoped that "The Tale" would help him shape one of the chapters of *Spektorskii* devoted to World War I. But this hope was never quite fulfilled, and the war events described in "The Tale" cover only the late summer of 1914.

The literary-historical atmosphere in which "The Tale" appeared was grim. After Lenin's death in 1924, the struggle for power between the Trotsky and Stalin camps began and ended only after the Fifteenth All-Union Congress of the Communist Party in 1927. Stalin was the winner, and Trotsky was expelled from the Soviet Union in 1929. The Fifteenth Party Congress also brought the end of the New Economic Policy and adopted the First Five-Year Plan (1928–1932), which was scheduled for completion in four years. The vast economic transformations in the Soviet Union were accompanied by massive social and ideological changes. This was the time when the party ended its so-called soft line toward the arts. Under this soft party line in the 1920s, diversity of artistic expression was tolerated and the creative intelligentsia was not actively harassed. However, in the spring of 1928 the party began to establish ideological control over the arts. The event that triggered the hard line policy toward the arts was the so-called Shakhty trial, when a large group of engineers and technicians from the coal-mining Donbass area was accused and eventually convicted of conspiracy and sabotage. This case allowed the party to question the loyalty of the bourgeois intelligentsia in general and unleash a class war against it. Writers, as much as other Soviet citizens, were expected to participate in the building of socialism and produce works that reflected the current events of Soviet history. To ensure its control over the arts, the party took the first steps toward censorship and virtually authorized the Russian Association of Proletarian Writers (RAPP), a literary group supportive of the party's literary policy, "to scourge and chastise [literature] in the name of the party."[15] The literary situation worsened in the summer of 1929 when RAPP unleashed an attack on those writers whose ideological positions were ambiguous or whose works did not portray a bright picture of the new Soviet state. The first blow was struck against the two talented and recognized writers Evgenii Zamiatin (1884–1937) and Boris Pilniak (1894–1937), and it did not take long until other distinguished men of letters were subjected to RAPP's hysterical campaign to purge the literary ranks of nonconformist elements.

Pasternak's initial reaction to the beginning of the ideological repression in the arts was to stop writing. When he resumed writing a few months later, he concentrated primarily on revisions of his early poetry as well as attempting to finish his incomplete projects. Fleishman suggests that at that time Pasternak was "driven by forebodings of the imminent end of all real literature, and envisioning an impending abandonment of literary activity" (Fleishman 1990, 154). Nevertheless, before literature was put under complete control of the party, Pasternak decided to continue writing in his usual manner without making any concessions to the outside pressure. In fact, in "The Tale" his modernism stands out most clearly. The story is pure narrated consciousness as the main character, Sergei, relives his life in retrospect. Because everything in the story is geared toward memory, spatial and temporal explorations become the story's most important characteristics and make it difficult for the reader to follow chronology.

"The Tale" begins as Sergei arrives in a small town in the Urals to visit his older sister Natasha. While he is at her place, somebody calls her on the phone. Sergei, tired and confused, overhears the conversation and thinks that Natasha is talking to a seamstress in the room next door rather than to someone on the phone. But, in fact, Natasha is talking to an operator who is also a seamstress. At this point the reader is thrown back to the moment when Sergei gets off the train, and another character, the sailor Fardybasov, is introduced. Fardybasov came to town on the same train as Sergei to visit his relative and a friend. It turns out that this relative is the seamstress, with whom Natasha talks on the phone. Then Fardybasov finds his friend Otrygan'ev. At this point Sergei, still at his sister's, tries to take a nap. He attempts to remember some summer afternoon in order to relax and fall asleep but does not succeed as the image he recalls triggers a flow of pure memory, which takes the reader from 1916 back to prewar 1913. The rest of the story consists almost exclusively of Sergei's memories, mostly of his love affairs and his romantic struggle to write a tale to earn money for himself and his beloved women. Only at the end of the story does Sergei escape his memory for a moment and reunite with other characters in the present. He converses with his sister's husband and with the engineer Lemokh, with whom Natasha had been talking on the phone before she spoke to the seamstress at the beginning of the story. From their conversation it follows that Sergei knows Lemokh's brother, who, at some point, appeared as a nameless person from somewhere in Sergei's past.

This summary of the story, however sketchy, is important because the frame of "real" reality, that is, the reality of the fictional physical world, and the reality of Sergei's memory are intertwined in such an elaborate, arabesque configuration that sometimes they are difficult to distinguish. When readers attempt to reconstruct the story, they become aware that Sergei does not really exist as a character. What exists instead is his memory, and when an attempt is made to take him outside of his stream of memory, it becomes apparent that his image is only vaguely sketched: it exists as a shadow and a voice. If his portrait is translated into pictorial language, what remains is a mere outline that borders on the abstract. His is a portrait made of randomly arranged lines, shapes, and colors rather than of full realistic details and gestures. The dissolution of the character results from the narrator's interest in his inwardness and could be compared in principle with the achievement of nonrepresentational painting.

Pasternak's narrative strategy in portraying psychical processes is also reminiscent of Bergson's suggestion of the possibility of a literary technique that amounts to "a direct quotation of the mind."[16] Such a technique is recognizably close to—although not quite identical with—the stream-of-consciousness narrative, whose classical illustration is James Joyce's *Ulysses*. Pasternak's representation of memory can also be compared to Proust's celebrated tour de force, *A la recherche du temps perdu* (*Remembrance of Things Past*). In one critic's opinion, Pasternak's "psychological probing, like that of Proust, 'deconstructs' our language and takes over its function in order to reconstitute our image of the world and our own self-awareness."[17] The comparison with Proust is relevant here because both writers demonstrate similar aesthetic sensibilities and philosophical inclinations. The similarity of their styles, though, is coincidental because Pasternak discovered the French author only in 1924–1925 while working as a researcher in the library of the People's Commissariat for Foreign Affairs, and his actual fragmentary acquaintance with Proust's work would not have occurred before 1925–1926. Yet when Pasternak did read Proust, according to Michel Aucouturier, he was deeply impressed by his writing and recognized his own affinity with it. Aucouturier maintains that both writers followed a "Bergsonian inspiration" in the treatment of their characters' psychology. He calls their poetics a "poetics of sensations which analytically 'deconstructs' the superficial layers of our psychology, and in doing so seeks to revive the real life experience which our convention-ridden language can only distort."[18] If the reader looks at Pasternak's "The Tale" through Proust's saga, it becomes clear that Pasternak's narrator is comparable with Proust's Marcel in spite of the difference in magnitude between the two works and thus the scope of the two characters. On the whole Proust's character dissolves almost as much in memories as does Pasternak's. This dissolution of characters in their memories becomes crucial to an understanding of the two works.

Because the flow of memory is characterized by a certain plasticity of the temporal sequence, a narrative that follows this flow correlates with the very nature of memory, manifest in shifts of time and space. Plasticity comes close to Bergson's nonchronological time, *durée,* reflecting inner space and time and allowing the intermingling and interpenetration of states of consciousness. With the narrative oriented toward expressing inwardness, the reader is bound to

experience unexpected temporal and spatial dislocations. One example is sufficient to demonstrate how the exploration of inwardness affects the development of the narrative and makes it "plastic." The following is an excerpt from
Sergei's flow of memory:

> He stood with his back turned to the table. . . . Suddenly for the first time in
> the past year he began to suspect that he actually helped Il'ina to clear out of
> the apartment. . . . Baltz is a bastard. . . . Here he felt with certainty that he
> guessed correctly. He felt a tug at his heart. . . . He was struck not by last
> year's rivalry, but by the fact that during his time with Anna he imbued her
> with a pitiful animation which was foreign to her nature. . . . He decided
> something and having turned around on his heels, surveyed the room and the
> table. . . . The dwindling rays of that crimson sunset were gathering them-
> selves into a final spasm. The air . . . was sawed from top to the bottom
> and from the ceiling to the floor hot sawdust was falling. . . . Serezha
> forgot with all this that Anna and he had an arrangement to go for a
> walk. "I am getting married," he wrote to Kovalenko, "And in my finan-
> cial situation I'd kill for a dime. I am reworking into a play the tale I
> have told you about." (4:133–34)

While the reader could try to set the events apart in this stream of Sergei's
consciousness and rearrange them according to chronology, Pasternak's modern sensibility demands that they remain in their subjective temporal order. As
memory and perceptions exist in nonchronological time, space seems to disin-
tegrate and breaks into illogically connected fragments. Spatial order is dream-
like, comparable to a collage whose features interpenetrate and include
anthropomorphic imagery, bizarre arrangements of objects and their parts, jux-
tapositions, and other features associated with cubist and cubo-futurist art. It is
these devices that caused one critic to call Pasternak a "creator of 'Cubist'
prose."[19]

But the major shift in time and space, according to Mossman, occurs in the
ambiguity of the story's title, which refers not only to the story of Sergei's life
but also to the story Sergei is trying to write (Mossman 1972, 299). The hero of
his story is a poet and pianist with a tentative algebraic name X. Driven by a
philanthropic obsession to raise a large sum of money and distribute it to the
people, he decides to sell himself at an auction and subject himself to any demand his future owner might make on him. When the public gathers for the
unusual event, the hero demonstrates his brilliance by performing beautiful music
and reciting his own poetry. At the end of the auction the hero is bought by a

famous philanthropist. A few days later the philanthropist sets the talented young man free, but unexpectedly the latter refuses to leave him. During their conversation they receive news that the money raised at the auction and distributed to the people in town has caused disorder and riots. Upon hearing this, the young hero realizes that his hope to change himself and others through his art has failed. Aware of his failure, he leaves his master to continue his life on his own.

Sergei's tale continues Pasternak's theme of the Apelles mark, that is, the theme of an authentic artistic act that would leave its "signature" on time. However, the artistic act, in Sergei's scenario, although original, has a negative result. The young hero does not foresee the unfortunate outcome of his performance because he is blinded by his creative passion and never questions what its moral implications might be. Pasternak thus continues to explore the theme of moral responsibility of the artist that he already touched upon in "Letters from Tula" and in his unfinished story from 1917, "The History of a Contraoctave."

On the structural level, the double perspective of "The Tale" (the story read and the story written by Sergei) contributes to the already complex web of temporal and spatial perspectives created by Sergei's memory. Pasternak will carry on the theme of memory in his next work, *Safe Conduct,* but thereafter his "Proustian" inclinations will not reappear in his work again. Like many Soviet writers of that time, he experienced pressure to return to a more traditional, "realistic" mode of writing with which the style of his early fiction was incompatible. Yet despite certain stylistic concessions, it is obvious that traces of Pasternak's early aesthetic tastes survived in his novel *Doctor Zhivago.* Boris Gasparov for one, recognizes in the very structure of *Doctor Zhivago* such conceptions of Bergson's philosophy as simultaneity, a nonlinear development of time, and the principle of temporal continuity (*durée*).[20]

Safe Conduct

Safe Conduct, Pasternak's autobiography from 1931, occupies a prominent place among his short fiction and marks the end of his early period. Pasternak began work on *Safe Conduct* in 1927 and finished it in 1931. Its intriguing title has a historical as well as biographical meaning. In old Russia a "safe conduct" was the term for a legal or business document allowing certain privileges to its bearer, but this meaning was anachronistic already in the late 1920s. "Gramota," the second word of the original title, was the title of a futurist manifesto of 1914 that Pasternak co-authored with three other poets. Most important, the title points to a period of the civil war when a "safe conduct" was issued to protect valuable art and book collections from vandalism or plundering by the revolutionary mobs. It also protected private citizens from widespread arrests and confiscation of their property. In view of the historical-political conditions under which Pasternak's autobiography was written, safe conduct could also symbolize art itself, especially its capacity to offer a private refuge; it offered a space free from the brainwashing doctrines—at least as long as the artist's work remained unpublished. In Fleishman's view, the title is related to Pasternak's idea that art "fabricates" reality (Fleishman 1981, 187) and thereby deceives those who want to manipulate the artist. At the end of the 1920s, when the party began to tighten the screws on the freedom of artistic expression, the only remaining escape for Pasternak was an artistic fabrication of reality that on the surface complied with the new policies but in fact was a protest against them. Pasternak must have realized that a safe conduct granted him by art would soon expire in the current political situation and used this last opportunity to define his views on art as well as crystallize the experiences of his past.

In any case, Pasternak's peculiar autobiography must be understood in relation to the literary policies of the Left Front of the Arts (LEF). This was a group of the left avant-garde, formed in 1922, that published a literary-critical journal by the same name, which largely served the purpose of party propaganda. Its publication began in 1923 and lasted for two years. LEF's members included, among others, the poets Vladimir Mayakovsky and Nikolai Aseev and the formalist critics Boris Eikhenbaum, Viktor Shklovsky, and Osip Brik. The proletarian wing of the group was represented by Nikolai Chuzhak, Boris Kushner, and Sergei Tret'iakov. Although Pasternak was a regular visitor of LEF's headquarters at the beginning of the group's work, his disagreement with its agenda soon became clear. In his answers to the questionnaire in the publication "Our Contemporaries" in 1928 Pasternak stated that his membership in LEF was only a favor to Mayakovsky and that he made numerous attempts to dissociate himself from LEF. Especially objectionable to Pasternak was LEF's popular concept of "literature of fact" (*literatura fakta*). LEF's theoreticians maintained that Soviet Russia needed factographic genres such as diary, reportage, memoirs, and travelogue, whereas imaginary writing was considered of secondary importance. For LEF the writer's true duty during that period was to serve revolutionary ideas and the goals of the young Soviet state. LEF combined a utilitarian approach to art with "blatant political instrumentalism."[21] Its agenda included de-aesthetization, propaganda, and a strict political functionalism of art. One of the leaders of LEF, Sergei Tret'iakov, wrote: "Lef is for working out the methods for a precise fixation of facts. Lef places the uninvented literature of fact above invented belle lettres, noting the growth in demand for memoirs and sketches among the active strata of readers."[22]

On the surface Pasternak seems to comply with LEF's program, and his work in the late 1920s and early 1930s is increasingly characterized by biographical themes, as in the short story "The Tale" and the novel in verse, *Spektorskii.* Yet, as Fleishman puts it, Pasternak "deliberately cast [*Safe Conduct*] so that the boundary between fact and fiction was blurred" (Fleishman 1990, 158). In Fleishman's view, *Safe Conduct* becomes Pasternak's polemical response to "literature of fact" and can be seen as a subversive aesthetic statement. Indeed, in it Pasternak seems to confirm his commitment to modernism and clearly goes against the grain of the LEF's and RAPP's austere political programs.

Safe Conduct has nothing of the traditional nineteenth-century autobiography that arranges events chronologically and places them in a defined social-historical atmosphere. Neither does Pasternak explicitly emphasize fact and experience, nor the stages of his own individual growth that lead him toward professional recognition as a writer. Almost none of these traditional documentary features survives in *Safe Conduct.* Instead, Pasternak prepares the ground for a different perception of the author's self, which no longer depends purely on facts alone.[23] It is because of this rethinking of the autobiographical genre that critics can no longer treat *Safe Conduct* as a reliable autobiography. The tension between fact and fiction in this work is so perceptible that the reliability of the author is called into question. *Safe Conduct* confirms Pasternak's defiance of factographic writing and his inclination toward the aestheticized discourse characteristic of modernism. Pasternak the autobiographer is incapable of telling "the truth" because "autobiographical truth is not fixed but an evolving content in an intricate process of self-creation."[24] The linguistic-narrative transformation that the autobiographer's self undergoes in the process of writing results in an illusion by its author rather than his/her truthful picture. The image of the author's self is caught in the "rhetorical structure of language" and is "reinscribed . . . in [its] prison-house" (Eakin 1994, 186).

In *Safe Conduct* Pasternak focuses on the process of writing and his own mental states as its raw materials rather than on fact and experience. He explicitly draws attention to the "literariness" of his work and to the lack of biographical information in it.[25] For Pasternak, "the world's finest works of art . . . in fact tell of their own birth" (4:186). This statement emphasizes the significance of the making of art, the creative process itself. To Pasternak's readers his autobiography is a literary collage of fragments of biographical events that often rest upon associations. Pasternak shifts the focus of his writing from "what" to "how" and intentionally excludes such elements as love affairs—only one youthful romantic infatuation is mentioned in *Safe Conduct*—details of marriage and divorce—in 1931 his first marriage had broken up—his family's immigration to Germany in 1921, his awareness of being a Jew, among other events that could fill his life story. Pasternak's intention is to defamiliarize the self.

Pasternak's shunning of the facts prompted Jakobson to call the narrator of *Safe Conduct* "a chronic bungler, because the actual successes of his original model, the historical Boris Leonidovich Pasternak, are of no use to Pasternak the poet" (Jakobson 1984, 195). Pasternak's self exists in the seams between fiction and reality and is not verifiable by biographical accounts:

> I am not writing my autobiography. I turn to it when someone else's [autobiography] requires me to. Together with its main character I believe that only the hero deserves a real biography, but the story of a poet is completely inconceivable in such form. It would have to be assembled from inessentials. . . . [The poet's life] cannot exist in the vertical axis of biography where we expect to meet it. It cannot be found under his own name and must be sought under someone else's, in the biographical column of his followers. The more a productive individuality is reserved, the more is its story . . . collective. . . . It is composed of everything that happens to his readers and of which he himself is unaware. (4:158–59)

What Pasternak suggests in this excerpt is that the poet's self is not a static category but rather an ongoing process. Whereas a great historical figure's self can be presented in a conventional autobiographical mode, the poet's transcends any concrete definition because it is constantly shaped and reshaped by inessentials, which may include anything from new encounters and events to visual impressions, to contemplations about art and history. The self thus introduced is not anomalous in any way; it is simply presented through the writer's subjective perceptions, which are often disengaged from the objectivity of external data.

In accordance with this understanding of self, the very structure of *Safe Conduct* is nothing but an illusion of a traditional life account. From the first glance, it has the promise of a strict chronological story line since it is logically defined by Pasternak's most significant sequential experiences: the first part is devoted to Scriabin and Pasternak's studies of music; the second part relates the story of his interest in philosophy and the trip to Marburg to study neo-Kantianism under Cohen; and the third tells of his first poetic experiences and his friendship with Mayakovsky. But whenever the reader expects facts and details of this life, Pasternak "bungles" and collapses his own story with his accounts of Rilke, Scriabin, Cohen, or Mayakovsky, personalities to whom he owes his artistic growth. He insists on the composite image of his self, "Whenever I was invited to say something about myself I started on about Mayakovsky. It was no mistake on my part. I worshipped him. I saw him as a personification of my spiritual horizon" (4:221). The narrator image related in this manner remains forever incomplete. But so does everybody else's since Pasternak consistently avoids realistic portrayal and provides his subjective account instead.

For example, *Safe Conduct* is dedicated to the memory of Rainer Maria Rilke and is thus bound to raise the reader's curiosity about the relationship between the two poets. Despite Pasternak's declaration of his profound indebtedness to Rilke, however, Rilke's portrait is barely outlined and referred to only twice. What remains of the German poet in the narrator's memory is a "silhouette among bodies, a fiction in the thick of reality" (4:149). Rilke's portrait is completely stripped of biographical concreteness as Pasternak transfigures him into an abstraction. Similarly, the portrait of Scriabin is replaced by the description of Pasternak's emotional and intellectual response to the composer's music. Pasternak's obsessive need to expand a fact beyond its structural limits vividly manifests itself in the following Scriabin episode characterized by heightened emotional intensity:

> The music was let loose. Multicolored, breaking into infinite fragments, multiplying like lightning, it leapt and scattered across the platform. It was tuned up and rushed with a feverish haste toward harmony. Suddenly reaching a roar of an unheard-of unity, it would break off, . . . die away entirely and straighten up along the footlights. It was man's first settlement in those worlds discovered by Richard Wagner for fictitious beings and mastodons. On this place was erected a fictitious lyrical dwelling, equal to the entire universe that had been ground down to make its bricks. The sun of Van Gogh burned above the fence of the symphony. Its windowsills were covered with the dusty archive of Chopin. Yet the residents did not poke their noses into the dust, but with their whole life style they fulfilled their forerunner's brightest behests. I could not hear it without tears. It had engraved itself on my memory before it settled on the zincographic plates of the first proofs. (153

Scriabin's significance for Pasternak's development is thus unveiled indirectly: through the substitution of "fact" by psychological states. The power of Scriabin's orchestral composition, *Poème de l'Extase,* brings the narrator into the dimension of nonreality, in which time is suspended as mythical thinking takes over. He sees the general in the particular and demonstrates how the composer's music resonates with the art of the past—and not only with music—with Wagner, Van Gogh, and Chopin. While an impression of Scriabin's music lingers, the image of the composer himself, just like Rilke's, remains immaterial.

The third part of *Safe Conduct* almost entirely focuses on Mayakovsky, whose friendship played a significant role in Pasternak's life. In spite of their different attitudes toward politics and diverging conceptions of the image of the poet and the role of poetry, Pasternak was attracted by Mayakovsky's intense personality and considered him a poetic genius. The news of Mayakovsky's suicide in 1930 was shocking to him, and he saw this death as an ominous sign of the terrible times to come. But when Pasternak turns to Mayakovsky's life in *Safe Conduct,* his narrative becomes oblique and dissolves into a metaphor: "'What was his personal life like?' . . . You will now be enlightened. The vast area of ultimate contradictions is drawn together, concentrates and made level, and suddenly, with a simultaneous shudder in every part in its structure, begins its physical existence. It opens its eyes, it sighs deeply and throws off the last traces of the pose which was given to him as a temporary aid" (4:232). Presented in this way, Mayakovsky's portrait appears as undefined as Pasternak's own. After describing their first meeting in a group of futurist poets in 1914, Pasternak moves away from facts, replacing them by fragments of historical reality and conveying them through his defamiliarizing, fictionalized discourse.

When he describes Mayakovsky's funeral, Pasternak is hardly interested in the attending mourners or the details of the physical surroundings. Rather he turns to Mayakovsky's life again, animates and objectifies it, and talks about it with passionate lyricism:

Suddenly down below the window I imagined I saw his [Mayakovsky's] life, belonging now entirely to the past. It moved away obliquely from the window like a quiet road planted with trees resembling Povarskaia Street. And the first thing on that road, right by the wall, was our State—our impossible, unprecedented State, bursting in upon the centuries and accepted by them for ever after. It stood there below, one could call it and take it out by the hand. In its tangibility and extraordinariness it somehow resembled the dead man. So striking was the link between them both, they could have been twins. (4:239)

This excerpt is suggestive but not revealing. Pasternak's ambivalent attitude toward Mayakovsky is intensified by the words "impossible," "unprecedented," and "bursting in upon the centuries." Since for him the Soviet state and Mayakovsky resemble each other, the characteristics Pasternak uses for the state extend to the poet and acquire a judgmental tone. The adjectives quoted above resonate with the negative image of the bohemian actors from "Letters from Tula" and cast the shadow of a moral judgment on the portrait of Mayakovsky. But this is a conjecture while the ambiguity remains.

Pasternak wants the reader to pay attention to the uncertainties and ambiguities that accompany life experiences. Therefore, he emphasizes the impossibility of defining a life by a cause-and-effect relationship; neither can life be explained by documentary sources. Pasternak tells the reader that efforts to understand the causes of Mayakovsky's death are doomed if one trusts his suicide message, in which he asks the government to treat his love Veronika Polonskaia as a member of his family and take care of her (4:234). The causes of Mayakovsky's death were much too complex to be reduced to a love story and expressed on a scrap of paper. The suicide message, in the larger context of Mayakovsky's life, loses its strict referential quality and becomes an artistic potential. Pasternak says again that where one looks for the solidity of information there is only an illusion of it, memory and fiction.

The fictionality of Pasternak's autobiography is consistent with his aesthetic views, which are scattered throughout the text. His views on art in *Safe Conduct,* especially in part 2, constitute his artistic manifesto, his profoundly modern view of art and his rejection of verisimilitude and mimesis: "It [art] is concerned not with man, but with the image of man. The image of man, as it turns out, is greater than man" (4:179). For Pasternak art is only an illusion of truth, as there is nothing absolute about it: "What does the honest man do when he speaks only the truth? Time passes by as he speaks, and in this time life moves on. His truth lags behind and is deceptive. . . . In art man is silent and the image speaks. And it becomes apparent that only the image keeps pace with the successes of nature" (4:139). Artistic truths, in their turn, are also relative because they "are not depictive but are capable of endless development" (4:139). This view, consistent with general tenets of modernism, can serve as another explanation of the fictionality of Pasternak's autobiography.

Pasternak readily attributes the transformation of material facts into fiction to the narrator's subjectivity, or as he puts it, to his "feeling." He characterizes this feeling as "a beam of energy" that passes through life. "Focussed on reality dislocated by feeling," writes Pasternak, "art is a record of this dislocation" (4:187). If the reader accepts Pasternak's terms, any artistic creation, his autobiography included, is always a displacement, an alternative way of storytelling, a destruction of one's hope to see things as they really are.

When Pasternak turned historical data into perceptions, impressions, and memories in *Safe Conduct,* he did away, at least partially, with chronological narrative and replaced it by disjointed sketches of episodes from his life, instrumental in the formation of his autobiographical image: his reading of Rilke, his admiration of Scriabin and his music, his studies in Marburg, and his friendship with Mayakovsky, among other things. By choosing this selective approach of events in his autobiography, Pasternak emphasizes personal rather than historical time. For example, he skips the revolutionary time of 1917 almost completely even though it played an important role in the fate of Russian history and his own life. Pasternak's description of the revolution occupies about a dozen lines in *Safe Conduct* and is represented through metaphor and personal attitude:

> The winter twilight, the terror, and the roofs and trees of the Arbat gazed from Sivtsev Vrazhek Street into the dining-room which had not been cleaned for months. . . . When darkness fell, the sentries opened fire enthusiastically from their revolvers. Sometimes they fired salvoes, sometimes just an isolated, rare enquiry into the night, filled with pathetic unanswerable deadliness. And since they could never pick up any rhythm and there were many deaths from stray bullets, in order to establish safety in the alleys one felt that metronomes should be stationed out there instead of the militia. (4:228–29)

In this description history is turned into aspects of the narrator's being and is no longer an arena for his performance. The sounds of metronomes, the musical device for measuring meter, remind the reader of a disordered world of political-revolutionary events. With history an elusive frame of reference and chronology displaced, the narrator exists in a partially ahistorical world—the word *partially* used here because history is never actively eliminated and the narrator never completely withdraws into his inner states. Yet the narrator uses every opportunity to express his feelings and states of mind at the expense of the continuity and chronology of the story. His time becomes psychological, reminiscent of Bergson's *durée,* whereas historical time becomes marginalized.

The structure of Pasternak's own temporal consciousness in *Safe Conduct* is close to that of Sergei's in "The Tale" and is profoundly modern in its resistance to separating the present from the past. In consciousness everything exists in continuity, and images of the present and the past interact in one free movement of different interpenetrating dimensions:

> But who will ever understand or believe that the Pushkin of 1836 might

suddenly recognize himself as the Pushkin of any year? As the Pushkin, say of 1936? Who will believe that there comes a time when one expanded and regenerate heart suddenly unites with the responses that have long been coming from other hearts; that prime heart is still alive, pounding, still thinking and wanting to live. Who will believe that these irregular multiplying heartbeats become so fast that suddenly they even up and coincide with the main heart's tremors and begin to live one life with it? (4:232)

Here the emphasis is on the resonance of the epochs and its perception by the narrator. The figure of Pushkin suddenly appears in the Mayakovsky part, and the insistent sense of parallel between the tragic fates of the two poetic geniuses harassed by their respective regimes enters the picture. This parallel becomes more than words. In an oblique way, through Pushkin's death, it suggests a reason that might have led to Mayakovsky's death: the confrontations between the poet and the state, the poet and the crowd, the poet and time. Epochs intermingle with one another, and Pasternak shows what a fine line exists between them. The reader thinks Mayakovsky's death is unprecedented, but in fact it connects with another death in the past. This evocation of the past is through *durée,* which defines a new way of communication between the temporal dimensions as they are integrated in one individual consciousness.

This connectedness of things is perceptible throughout *Safe Conduct.* Not only are temporal dimensions in a dialogue with each other, but each event is in a dialogic relationship with Pasternak's entire life. In fact, he enriches the reader's understanding of an individual event with allusions to history and descriptions of new encounters and places. Curious in this respect are the Venetian episodes. They are saturated with connections between personal experience, history, and art. Pasternak's attempt to relate his life story takes readers once again beyond primary events to the intensity of his aesthetic-philosophical experience: "I discovered the syncretism that accompanies a flowering of craftsmanship, when once a complete identity between the artist and his medium is achieved, it becomes impossible to say which of the three and for whose benefit is more actively manifest on canvas—the executor, the thing executed, or the subject of that execution. It is owing to this confusion that misunderstandings are possible, in which time, posing for the artist, might imagine it is elevating him to its own greatness" (4:207). In this comment Pasternak's principle of connectedness reaches out to all aspects of creativity: the object of art, the artist, and the work of art itself. His idea of syncretism manifests itself in his autobiography, whose focus is precisely not on differentiating biographical data from "non-facts" but rather on integrating them into one narrative flow.

Safe Conduct thus creates the syncretism of the autobiographer, his life with all its nuances, and its fictional transfiguration. Pasternak offers a self in perpetual creation, a self that can be understood only through fiction because facts do not describe the "truth," certainly not the whole truth, or nothing but the truth, but always only aspects of it. His life exists not in commonplace reality but rather in his writing. His remarks about Chekhov apply to his own autobiography:

> the chief merit and value of his plays consisted in his having inscribed man in a landscape on equal terms with trees and clouds; that . . . he was against the over-rating of the social and the human; that the conversational texts of the plays are not written in obedience to any logic of interests, passion, characters, or plots, but that the cues and speeches are taken and snatched out of the space and the air they were spoken, like spots and strokes of a forest or a meadow only to render the true simultaneous resemblance by the subject of the play; to life in the far broader sense of a unique vast inhabited frame, to its symmetries and dissymmetries, proportions and disproportions—to life as a hidden mysterious principle on the whole. (Pasternak, "Three Letters," 4)

In *Safe Conduct* Pasternak is in search of these hidden mysterious principles of life and the self that usually escape the realist autobiographer.

There is in Pasternak's early fiction something like a summary of his modernism. In his fiction he succeeds in expanding the range of sensations and experiences by displacing external realities and moving toward inner states of being, such as memories, associations, and stream of consciousness. Although he retains a realistic frame of reference, the narrative itself reflects his move into inwardness, with chronology becoming convoluted, space stripped of its specificity, and time turning irreversibly subjective. Yet Pasternak does not turn the world into a complete abstraction, as Wassily Kandinsky does in his painting, but endows it with a stunningly new appearance. He suggests uncertainty and ambivalence where one hopes to find stable ground. Pasternak's language is only an approximation of a realistic representation. Although history is often internalized in the world of his characters, it does modify their circumstances and fates and prevents them from perceiving the world as nonexisting, as a dark place. And as historical beings, in a characteristically Russian manner, Pasternak's characters appear as moral beings, concerned with their self-perception and moral responsibility. The Tolstoyan heritage is thus ever present in Pasternak's fiction. Despite this, however, two points must be remembered:

Pasternak's maturation as a writer in the 1920s is above all defined by modernism; and his goal in art is aesthetic rather than ethical. In his short fiction, as in his poetry, Pasternak's aim is to extract the "original, extraordinary, and inexplicable" out of life and reveal "the unusualness of the usual" in it (Pasternak, "Three Letters," 5). By the time he completes his last modernist piece, *Safe Conduct,* he has become an accomplished writer whose contributions to Russian literature in narrative fiction are as significant as his contributions in poetry.

CHAPTER THREE

Epic Poems

The 1920s mark Pasternak's transition from "lyrical thinking to epic"[1] as he tries to capture and convey the magnitude of the revolutionary events he witnessed and the complexity of his feelings toward them in four epic poems. Pasternak's new image of the revolution is much more dramatic and political than its earlier impressionistic and lyrical portrayal in the collections *My Sister-Life* and *Above the Barriers*. Pasternak's correspondence of the 1920s demonstrates how his romantic perception of the October and February 1917 events was replaced by his deep disappointment about the social-political aftermath of the Bolshevik's accession to power. In his 1922 letter to Briusov he conveyed that it was "the revolution's morning and its outburst" that was really close to his heart (5:134). During "the revolution's morning" Pasternak does not dare nor is he willing to explore critically the nature of the grand political events that took place in Russia. As time went by, however, he began to look at the October revolution skeptically and unsympathetically, and in his 1926 letter to Rilke he compared it to "a fragment of gliding time, in the form of an immobile, fearful sight" that turned "personal fates" into "immobile temporal subjects of the somber and exalted historical portent, tragic in its smallest, even ludicrous detail" (5:179). Written two years after "Aerial Ways," this letter communicates both the oppressive external reality of the new Soviet state and Pasternak's own state of mind. The "immobile, fearful sight" of the revolution, so reminiscent of the image of the aerial ways in his short story, is no longer compatible with the bright future the revolution promised to bring.

By now Pasternak had been harboring the idea of writing a novel and had in fact been composing fiction throughout the 1920s to prepare himself for such a project. His interest, therefore, in the "big form," the poetic epic, is not altogether unexpected. His transition toward it, however, was not solely motivated by his internal need to break out of the fetters of lyricism. Like many other writers, Pasternak felt some external pressure from the party ideologues, who were in the process of establishing control over literature, to portray the "epic" revolutionary age in a corresponding epic form. His interest in the epic genre, therefore, was mixed with disappointment about the decline of lyrical poetry and contempt for the party enforcement of the epic. Answering the question-naire of the newspaper *Leningradskaia pravda* (*Leningrad Truth*) in 1926, he comments negatively on the forced rise of the epic form and calls it a "second-class genre."[2] Pasternak connects the revival of the epic with the pressures of the historical present and the change in the cultural atmosphere. On many occa-sions he laments the pitiful state of lyric poetry due to the destruction of the old bourgeois personality and the absence of a new socialist one. Like many lyrical poets of his generation, he feels forced from outside to make decisions about the future direction and shape of his art. In the same questionnaire he pledges his devotion to lyric poetry no longer as a poet but as a "person engaged in history" who hopes that socialism will gain its "ethical content" (4:620). But despite his pledge of devotion to lyric poetry, Pasternak had already completed his first experiments in the "second-class genre" by 1923. The epics *Vysokaia bolezn'* (*Sublime Malady*) and *Deviat' sot piatyi god* (*The Year Nineteen-Five*) appeared in 1923 and 1927 respectively, while he was working on a third epic poem, *Leitenant Shmidt* (*Lieutenant Schmidt,* 1926). To the puzzled reader who might have detected a discrepancy between Pasternak's public statements about the epic and his actual poetic production of the mid 1920s, Pasternak offers a pragmatic explanation: "I consider that the epic is what our time inspires, and accordingly, in the book '1905,' I move from lyrical thinking to epic, although this is very difficult" (4:621).

Yet despite this explanation—if an explanation it is—Pasternak's contra-dictory statements suggest his uncertainty about the state of literature, the party's determination to reform it, and his own place as a lyrical poet. His mood vacil-lates between outright criticism and appeasement throughout the 1920s. In re-sponse to the party resolution in the field of literature, "O politike partii v oblasti khudozhestvennoi literatury" ("About the Party Policy in Literature," 1925), which formulated the party's commitment to help proletarian writers establish their hegemony in Soviet culture, he criticizes the state of culture with resent-ment, pessimism, and sarcasm: "We do not experience any cultural revolution, it seems to me, we experience a cultural reaction. The presence of a proletarian dictatorship is not enough to produce an impact on culture."[3] Pasternak objects to the party's idea that the new proletarian culture could find a style appropriate for the historical epoch. The new style, says Pasternak, has already been found. It is the style of mediocrity and statistics, in other words, the style of bureau-cracy. But directly attacking the new party policies would have been nonpro-ductive and self-destructive for him. Pasternak was not a fighter interested in assuming a confrontational position in a political struggle. Since he did not want to be silenced as a writer, his goal was to preserve his freedom of writing, and the price for that was tolerance of and compromise with the new literary policies. But his pessimistic mood is clearly evident in his last bold public statement published in the newspaper *Vecherniaia Moskva* (*Evening Moscow*) in 1928: "Society has changed in a different and incomparably more complex degree than is commonly thought. It does not have a real structure. . . . I do not believe in the life of books in our time. . . . Recently art was blamed for its individualism. But now it is more than individualistic, it is physically lonely, and this is inhuman."[4]

In order to be able to exercise what was left of his freedom of writing, he had to listen to the age. He must try the epic form. His revolutionary poems of the 1920s thus reflect his attempt to survive as a lyrical poet and also to overcome his resentment of the epic form and adapt it to his poetic temperament. Lyricism had to be aligned with politics. The literary atmosphere was especially favorable to the portrayal of the heroic events of the revolution and the civil war, or anything, for that matter, that glorified the new ideals of the Soviet state. The ideological trend of the new art was toward collective experience and heroism, away from self-reflection and inwardness, and the emphasis was on "we" rather than on "I." In connection with these changes, Pasternak had to resolve important issues: how could he, a lyrical poet and short-fiction writer of modernist inclinations, adopt a social-historical orientation? How could he express his sensibilities in an epic form? He found an answer of sorts in creating his own epic form. In the words of Ronald Hingley, when Pasternak used the term *epic,* he meant "something elusively different from the stale conceptions that lurk in less original minds" (Hingley 1983, 81).

Pasternak's revolutionary poems are not traditional epics. They certainly defy the genre description in the *Princeton Encyclopedia of Poetry and Poetics,* which lists the following common characteristics of the epic genre based on its twentieth-century interpretations: a narrative of specified length which "deals with events which have a certain grandeur and importance and come from a life of action, especially of violent action such as war"; "seriousness of tone and excellence in expression"; "scope and inclusiveness"; "structural control throughout"; a "notable exercise of will in the conduct of the hero or in the poet's own accomplishment"; and, finally, "the poet speaks for his own time, sometimes for a people, sometimes for a whole age."[5] According to these genre parameters, Pasternak's epics are flawed in several areas. First of all, they hardly have a developed narrative; in fact, *Sublime Malady* has none at all. Second, the "seriousness of tone," at least at the beginning of *Sublime Malady,* where Pasternak questions the very idea of epic, is unreliable. Third, Pasternak's epics lack "structural control" and "consistency" in portraying the revolutionary events.

His poems, like his short fiction, are fragmented and impressionistic. Fourth, his "scope and inclusiveness" are limited, largely because the characters portrayed are undeveloped and hypothetical. In Sinyavsky's opinion, Pasternak "fails to allot much space to the delineation of human fates and characters." And finally, the distinct lyrical voice heard in Pasternak's epics was simply not suited to speak "for his own time," or "a people," or "a whole age." The lyrical tone in these long revolutionary poems prevails over the epic. In his historical endeavor he remains a lyric and, as Sinyavsky observes, is "more apt to tell us what the weather was like at some historical moment or other than to recount in consecutive order the course of what has happened" (Sinyavsky 1978, 95). In other words, despite his desire to represent the revolutionary epoch on a grandiose scale, Pasternak is unable to overcome his lyrical drive completely and give his long poems a strong and convincing historic-political ring.

Sublime Malady

Sublime Malady, the only Pasternak's poem that deals with the October revolution, was first published in the journal *Novyi LEF* (*New LEF*) in 1924 and four years later appeared in the journal *Novyi mir* (*New World*) with some revisions. The poem, although written with a view to an epic stance, hardly achieves its goal and reads as "a strange lyrical monologue on his [Pasternak's] own position" (Gifford 1977, 100). Sinyavsky describes *Sublime Malady* as "a kind of extended lyrical digression, which, taking certain contemporary facts as its point of departure, tries to encompass that age in a broad epic manner and to reveal its image, without recourse to a plot, by means of metaphoric imagery, syntactical constructions, and varying vocal intensity" (Sinyavsky 1978, 92).

The poem opens with Pasternak's ironic, if not mocking, attitude toward the classical epic. He describes the siege of a fortress in the Graeco-Trojan War as a boring hustle-bustle of everyday war routine, devoid of any glamour and heroism. The opening further emphasizes the repetitiveness and tedium of the events, as well as a slow progression of time, through the repetition of the phrase "day after day," which occurs three times in the sixteen lines of the first stanza. Yet, despite its unheroic and destructive nature, the poet-persona tells us, the war gives birth to an absurd epic that mythologizes the events and blatantly misinterprets them. The poet expresses his shame and dismay at this falsification of the truth by means of poetry: "I am ashamed, each day ashamed, / That in an age of shadows / Our sublime old malady of thought / Still calls itself a song. / Are alleys, shrill in their upheaval, / Our song of toil and soil— / Our song from books and ages hurled / Against steel bayonets? / But hell is paved with good intentions; / It is our modern view / That if verses too are paved with them / Our sins will be forgiven."[6] The "sublime old malady" thus turns out to be poetry, or "a song," as Pasternak ironically calls it. Throughout history epic poetry inappropriately and blasphemously aggrandized and beautified bloody events and endowed them with a heroic aura. It is, therefore, up to the poet's conscience how he or she uses poetry. However, the "sublime malady" symbolizes more than poetry. In Fleishman's opinion, "sublime malady" is also a metaphorical disguise for the revolution, a term not used a single time in the poem (Fleishman 1981, 30). Like epic poetry, the revolution conceals destruction and violence behind its rhetorical facade and evokes in the poet a feeling of shame.

But there is more to the opening of Pasternak's poem. In the context of the Soviet literary-political disputes about the function of literature in society, "sublime malady" acquires an additional meaning. Fleishman perceptively interprets the first stanzas of the poem as a hidden polemical challenge to LEF's literary agenda to produce political propaganda poetry (Fleishman 1984, 34). Like epics of the classical age, LEF's literary production vulgarizes history through praising the regime and ignoring true hardships inflicted on people by the ruthlessness of the revolution. Through reinventing history in its art according to the political demand of the regime, LEF abandons the ideals of honesty and social responsibility. A few stanzas into the poem Pasternak returns to the revolutionary propaganda created by the artists in support of the regime. This time, however, the focus is not so much on the content of the artistic production itself as on the fate of the artistic intelligentsia sympathetic to the revolution. Pasternak's tone is bitingly ironic: "Behind it all, in a glow of legends, / The wise, the hero, and the fool / Blazoned in print their happiness / About the sunset of their age" (92). These lines adumbrate the tragic fate of a large segment of the creative intelligentsia that through its own idealism and blindness wasted its talents on fulfilling the party's literary agenda. Above all, these lines seem to have targeted Mayakovsky, whose ardor to serve the revolutionary cause resulted in his profound disappointment and alienation. Misunderstood by the masses and unable to deal with the obscurantist campaign unleashed by the party and literary hacks against him, he shot himself at the age of thirty-seven.

But the revolution has not purged all the old cultural ideals. Vis-à-vis the revolutionary creative intelligentsia, there are still artists who feel that their old values are not easily replaceable by the new ones and therefore, while they do not go against the political current, choose the path of noninvolvement. Pasternak associates himself with these individuals who refuse to "play a role," or be performers, like Mayakovsky, in the building of socialism. His nostalgic description of this group of writers, however, changes to anger against the regime that trumps up unfounded accusations against these people: "We were that music in the ice: / I speak of my own society / With which I now intend to leave / The stage, as I for one must leave. / There is no room for shame: / I wasn't made to coax three times / And flatter men in sundry ways; / Yet more absurd than any song / Our word 'the enemy.' / I'm grieved to find in each far land / This malady of mind. / All my life I've longed to be like others, / But the world's great age / Is stronger than my private yearning / And wants to be—like me" (93). The reference to art as stage and the artist having to "flatter men" once again raises the question of the moral responsibility of the artist before his own self. Pasternak has made his choice, and the reader might feel in these lines that he, like Akhmatova, Tsvetaeva, and Mandelstam, considers the possibility of withdrawing into silence and accepting the official nonrecognition of his poetry. He tried to be "like others" but could not bear the burden of that role.

Pasternak's isolationist mood in *Sublime Malady* is only intensified by the devastation the revolution wreaks on the physical world around him. The images of the revolutionary transformations are uncanny in their explicit metaphors of deprivation and suffering: "The winter nights twitched unweariedly from lice," while days "gurgled, spewed their blood" (90); "the intolerable frightful typhus, clasping us quietly by the knees," the poet notices as well as the ubiquitous "weary strains of slow decay" (93). As Pasternak describes the horrors of the civil war, the future appears surrounded by dark shadows: "In sober mood, by sober roads / I came. Around me lay a city / In ruins, ravaged, and unreal, / Refusing flatly to recover, / To rise, get going, to rebuild" (94).

Deeply affected by the environment, the poet is unable to perceive the revolution as a cleansing force and a hope for a better future. He sees the state's new policies as based on lies, injustice, and disrespect for individual freedom and makes perceptible the contrast between the real human tragedy and the ridiculousness of the government's reaction to it. He is equally dismayed with the insensitivity and cynicism of the Soviet gesture in response to the Japanese earthquake of 1924 that killed about 250,000 people: "I long remember as by rote / That wicked telegram we sent / For victims of the tragedy,—/ That hackneyed workers' proclamation / To ease the terror of Fujiyama" (96).

The figure of Lenin, the mastermind behind the revolution, added to the poem's revision in 1928, creates an ambiguous feeling about the mission of the Bolshevik revolution. Lenin's name is not mentioned in the poem a single time, but his image is easily recognized from the features Pasternak briefly sketches:

"his thumb hooked in his vest; his foot swung slowly up and down" and "his burr" were familiar to many people from his public appearances (98). In Pasternak's portrayal Lenin appears as an embodiment of the fanatical revolutionary genius rather than a positive hero of epic stature. Pasternak's Lenin tries to establish a new social order at any cost—even if brutality and terror have to be used in the new Soviet society. In Pasternak's portrayal Lenin also appears as an enemy of individualism and prefers ideologically monolithic masses to individual thinkers. Only his will matters. He means happiness and yet inflicts grief. The portrait of the first head of the Soviet state at the Ninth Congress of the Soviets in 1921 is hardly favorable: "he struck out hard. . . . His words, which all men heard too well, / Were traced in the blood of great events. / He was their voice, their proclamation. . . . Alone, he ruled the tides of thought, / And through that mastery—the State" (98–9). This description of Lenin's speech resembles to a certain extent that of the Bolshevik Polivanov in "Aerial Ways" who, in a conversation with his former lover and alleged mother of his son, spoke as if he were writing a newspaper article, with all its punctuation marks and "whiches." As in Polivanov's words, it is hard to find any concern for human lives in Lenin's speech. And Lenin himself appears more as a metaphor of the omnipotent power of the revolution than a living human being. His performance on the congress stage is described by Pasternak as puppetry. Not only does the state leader's speech read as a prepared text, but his very entrance and reception by the public assume in Pasternak's text an atmosphere of theatricality: "We rose up with a shout, our eyes / Ransacking thoroughly the platform . . . / He entered, unobserved, through lanes / Of crowded doors and helping hands, / As a ball of lightning in a storm / Flames bright and blinding in a room. / The thunder of wild applause rang out . . ." (98). The last two lines of the poem sum up Lenin's meaning in Russian history: "Great men are heralds of new rights— / And burdens too as they leave the stage" (99).

At the end of the 1920s, when the poem was published in revised form, this image of Lenin not only failed to resonate with the growing body of literature eulogizing the revolution and Lenin's revolutionary stature, but the whole poem kept the reader off balance by its ambivalent message as to what revolution really meant. *Sublime Malady* does certainly nothing to give the reader a convincing and positive picture of the revolution. Where the reader wants to find hope and optimism, he finds a void and ambivalence. Needless to say, the poem's generic strangeness and contextual vagueness immediately excluded it from the official Soviet poetic mythology about the revolution. The meaning of *Sublime Malady* remained personal: it addressed the poet's decision to settle for the unadorned image of the revolution rather than for its official myth. Therefore, the poem resembles a peculiar "lyrical monologue" rather than a grandiose picture of a great historical time. Pasternak's first effort to present revolution in an epic manner ended in his confirmation of his strong lyrical voice that, above all, contemplates the fate of the Russian intelligentsia.

The Year Nineteen-Five

In the first issue of the journal *Na literaturnom postu* (*On Literary Guard*) in 1925 Pasternak announced to his readers that he had begun work on a project devoted to the revolution of 1905 (4:695). He further emphasized that he was not interested in composing a traditional poem but rather planned to create "a chronicle in verse form" (4:695). Since it was his first venture into the new area of factography, Pasternak spent several months studying a mass of documentary and historical materials about the first Russian revolution and was completely absorbed in this research (Barnes 1989, 356). A year later in the same journal he revealed that his new poem, *The Year Nineteen-Five,* would consist of "separate epic excerpts" (4:695). When it was published in 1927, the poem was praised by the critics. Gorky, who by that time was the patriarch of Soviet literature, praised Pasternak for his new poetic idiom. He responded to Pasternak's new artistic accomplishment in a laudatory letter: "This is an excellent book; it is among those books whose merit is not appreciated immediately, but which are destined to have a long life. . . . In *The Year Nineteen-Five,* you are more laconic and simpler. You are more of a classic in this book, which is saturated with pathos. As a reader, I am quickly, easily, and powerfully infected by this pathos. . . . this is a voice of a real poet, and also a social poet, social in the best and deepest meaning of this concept" (1:695).

The success of the poem was not surprising since it satisfied the demands of the new literary market. Almost anything about the revolution was certain to be published, and a revolutionary epic written by such a recognized and respected poet as Pasternak was predictably a major event. Also, unlike *Sublime Malady, The Year Nineteen-Five* was accessible even to an unsophisticated reader. More straightforward than the former, it was composed in a simpler poetic style and had a defined narrative structure. To Pasternak's old admirers, however, *The Year Nineteen-Five* appeared as a different poetic universe, for, to use Barnes's words, the new poem was not "organically bound up with Pasternak's personality" (Barnes 1989, 358). By choosing a political topic somewhat removed in history, Pasternak avoided the pressure to present his loyalties to the Soviet regime, which he would have had to do if he had chosen to chronicle the October revolution. But he was addressing a revolutionary topic. *The Year Nineteen-Five* was of great professional significance for Pasternak since it helped him secure his place among Soviet writers as well as improving his miserable financial situation. The choice of topic thus proved to be wise, at least from a utilitarian point of view, and the poem was subsequently published in many Soviet editions of Pasternak's poetry—in contrast to *My Sister-Life* and *Above the Barriers,* which, because of their subjective lyrical voice and stylistic complexities, appeared much less attractive to Soviet publishers during Pasternak's lifetime.

As Pasternak promises in his announcement in *On Literary Guard,* his poem is some sort of a chronicle. With the exception of one biographical digression, it is entirely devoted to the actual events of the 1905 revolution. But in spite of having a defined structure, an introduction, and six parts describing different episodes of the revolution, the poem does not form a coherent narrative. Its only binding principle, as Barnes rightly remarks, is its meter, anapestic pentameter (Barnes 1989, 359). Pasternak uses it so consistently that by the end of the poem the verse seems in fact monotonous. Yet the consistency of the meter does not interfere with the decisive rhythmical patterning of the poem, which adequately expresses the nervous energy of the revolution. The introduction is permeated with the revolutionary spirit symbolized by Joan of Arc, who is associated with Siberian convicts and a socialist maid. Each line builds up the romantic pathos and the energy of the revolution. As in Blok's poem *Dvenadtsat'* (*The Twelve*), which deals with the 1917 revolution, Pasternak's revolutionary winter of 1905 is shrouded in blizzards and miserable cold, both of which become permanent features of the poetic revolutionary landscape. The first episode is entitled "Ottsy" ("Fathers") and outlines the history of the Russian revolutionary movement. Pasternak refers to these first steps that culminated in the 1905 revolution as "our teachers' raw youth"[7] and recalls the fate of the most prominent revolutionaries. He makes references to serfdom and political oppression that gave birth to the young underground political opposition, the generation of "circles and heroes, / Dynamiters, / Daguerrotypes" (9). This generation helped to shake the foundation of czarism after the emancipation of the serfs in 1861 and spent its life in permanent conspiracy, defying the constant threat of searches, purges, imprisonment, and death. Although Pasternak mentions names of a few revolutionaries of the 1870s—for instance, the anarchist Sergei Nechaev (1847–1882), nicknamed "Jacobin" in memory of the Jacobins who seized power during the French Revolution, and the terrorists Sofia Perovskaia (1853–1881) and Stepan Khalturin (1856–1882)—as well

as alluding to Dostoevsky's political background, his image of the revolutionary hero is collective. It includes the members of the organization Narodnaia
volia (People's Will), the nihilists, and sympathetic students who wanted to
remake Russia in a social revolution. Pasternak's goal is not to introduce individual destinies but to pay homage to the radical intelligentsia that gave the
initial impulse to the revolutionary movement in Russia. Therefore, his poem
does not have real epic heroes: individual names are metaphors for the driving
forces behind the revolution. It is not the individual personality but the entire
cohort of the radical intelligentsia that Pasternak endows with a heroic halo.

In reality Russian political radicalism was born of nihilism, individualism,
and the uncontrollable desire for self-expression that translated into anarchy
and terrorism. Initially the main issue for the young revolutionaries of the 1860s
and 1870s was total personal emancipation. When a political agenda was adopted
by some of these radicals, one of its points was to merge with the masses, that
is, the peasants, and try to improve their conditions. This movement was called
"populist," and its major problems were political shortsightedness and naïveté.
Populism was ineffective and largely ignored by the masses. On occasion the
peasants even handed over the populist agitators to the police.[8] Another faction
among the political radicals were the terrorists, who believed that assassination
of top government figures and regicide were the ways to change Russia. The
point of both extremes, populism and terrorism, was sociopolitical expression
at any cost, and the end product of their political activism was, ironically, the
Bolshevik dictatorship. But in *The Year Nineteen-Five* Pasternak needed to
portray the revolutionary history in a heroic light and had no intention of revealing the failures and contradictions of its forefathers.

The second part, "Detstvo" ("Childhood"), is a glimpse into the author's
own biography: his recollection of Scriabin, music, expectations of Christmas,
games with his school friends. Childhood memories appear at the beginning
and the end of "Childhood," whereas the central part of the chapter describes
22 January 1905, the day known in Russian history as "Bloody Sunday." On
that day the priest Georgii Gapon led a large peaceful demonstration of workers
to the czar's winter residence, the Winter Palace. The workers' demands were
humble, and they essentially appealed to Czar Nicholas II to help his pious,
faithful subjects to improve their condition. The police met the demonstration
with gunfire and killed and wounded several hundred people. The brutality of
the massacre caused a wide wave of indignation and protests and ignited the
subsequent revolutionary explosion. As in the previous part, there are no individual heroes in "Childhood," as Pasternak's narrative centers on the fate of the
masses. The only historical figure mentioned in the chapter is Gapon, and the

whole action takes place between the two forces on the streets of Petersburg: the demonstrators and the police.

In the third part, "Muzhiki i fabrichnye" ("Peasants and Workmen"), the revolutionary tension results in the first outbursts of urban strikes and confrontations between the police and the people. The three-page sketch ends with a straightforward description of the first armed workers' uprising in the Polish city of Lodz, which belonged to the Russian Empire at the time: "All the offices shut at midday, / And from five traffic's halted. / Then across lifeless Lodz / Amid petrol / The twilight's aflow. / But this town without folk / Starts to writhe in the barricades' halter. / While the wrath of the workers / Takes aim at the mounted patrols. / The troops mustered by night" (37). The next part of the poem is entitled "Morskoi miatezh" ("Mutiny on the Sea") and deals with the sailors' rebellion on the battleship *Potemkin* in the Black Sea. The episode is animated through direct speech, the voices of the officers and the rebellious sailors. It should be mentioned in passing that at about the same time as *The Year Nineteen-Five* was being written, Sergei Eisenstein was working on his famous movie, *Battleship Potemkin*. Pasternak's technique in the poem is tangibly cinematographic: his eye, like Eisenstein's, moves from one face to the other, from one detail to the next, and, as Gifford comments, "there are countless individual moments, but very few individual men" (Gifford 1977, 104). In other words, Pasternak makes a serious attempt here to represent the epic forces of the revolution, but his inherently impressionistic manner thwarts this intention. Once again he fails to portray a collective revolutionary force in its unified revolutionary action.

From *Potemkin* Pasternak moves to the confrontation between a large student demonstration and the police in front of Moscow University on the occasion of the funeral of the Bolshevik student Nikolai Bauman, who had been killed by a member of the far-right group Black Hundreds. *The Year Nineteen-Five* closes with the episode "Moskva v dekabre" ("Moscow in December"), which recounts the last organized battle of the workers and the radicals against the police and the soldiers in Moscow at the end of December 1905. The resistance lasted for about ten days in Krasnaia Presnia, one of the centers of revolutionary activities, and ended with the defeat of the revolutionary forces. The final two stanzas describe the morning of the surrender of Presnia in a truncated, unemotional style. The images describing the final page of the revolution include the snowstorm, the cavalry, and revolutionary heroes escaping from the Cossack bullets (73). At this point the monotony of the anapestic meter reflects the exhaustion of the action.

In *The Year Nineteen-Five* Pasternak is a lens through which his readers must see the first Russian revolution. Yet the poem has neither the depth nor the complexity of his previous work, nor does it convey the epic magnitude of the revolution in the way Eisenstein's *Battleship Potemkin* does. *The Year Nineteen-Five* tends to ally itself with the brand of official literature that was rapidly accumulating around specific social coordinates. Readers see the distance of this poem from Pasternak's previous works not only in a manner of style but in his use of the material as well. *The Year Nineteen-Five* bridges the gap between the vast majority of revolutionary poetry of the 1920s and his own. In a way *The Year Nineteen-Five* symbolizes the slowing down of Pasternak's poetic metabolism, a kind of willful act to preserve himself and his creative energy for the future. Nevertheless, *The Year Nineteen-Five* does not imply that Pasternak rejected himself as the lyrical poet of *My Sister-Life;* it means that in the mid 1920s Pasternak was beginning to redefine himself. He was too well aware of the utilitarian necessity of *The Year Nineteen-Five,* and his conscience seemed somewhat disturbed by this awareness. In a 1928 letter to Tsvetaeva he wrote acidly, "The praises of the majority [of critics] concern the theme of 1905, that is, they are some kind of certificates of good behavior."[9] Despite his cynicism about the critics' attitude toward the revolutionary theme, Pasternak returned to it in his next poem, *Lieutenant Schmidt.*

Lieutenant Schmidt

Pasternak began work on *Lieutenant Schmidt* immediately after *The Year Nineteen-Five* and finished it in 1927. Initially the poem was serialized in the journal *New World,* and each chapter had a title. Although *The Year Nineteen-Five* and *Lieutenant Schmidt* deal with the events of the same year, the latter is more reflective and personal in character than the former. In *The Year Nineteen-Five* Pasternak's intention had been to design a chronicle in which revolutionary history occupies center stage. In *Lieutenant Schmidt* history forms the background against which an individual fate develops. *Lieutenant Schmidt* is more complex than *The Year Nineteen-Five* because it plays with nuances and uncertainties of the lieutenant's own heroic stature. Schmidt, in Pasternak's presentation, is not a clear-cut hero. Pasternak's interpretation of Schmidt is in fact a subtle assault on the authoritative textbook version of the lieutenant's personality and role in history. The Schmidt who evolved into a revolutionary figure in Soviet history books does not correspond to the Schmidt who is evolving as a personality in Pasternak's poem. As the poem develops, readers perceive the incongruity between the official heroic image of the lieutenant and his real nature. As many critics have observed, Pasternak's Schmidt resembles distantly such vacillating and introspective characters as Hamlet or some Chekhovian intellectuals.[10] Schmidt is more a passive revolutionary martyr inadvertently drawn into the turbulent events than a quintessential, iron-willed, unbending ideological fighter. His portrait thus stands outside routine heroic definitions and in its ambiguity anticipates two future intellectual characters in Pasternak's work, Sergei Spektorskii and Iurii Zhivago.

To prepare himself for writing the poem, Pasternak thoroughly studied documentary memoiristic material related to his hero, the lieutenant of the cruiser *Ochakov,* Petr Petrovich Schmidt (1867–1906), and the naval mutiny he led on the Black Sea in 1905. Pasternak tried to be faithful to the historical truth and used some factual sources directly in his poem. For example, he includes actual, only slightly paraphrased lines from Schmidt's letters to Z. N. Rizberg, the lieutenant's unnamed romantic correspondent.[11] Pasternak also quotes lines from the czarist October manifesto and attempts to reproduce verbatim Schmidt's actual speech at the trial. Pasternak was so careful in his effort to preserve the authenticity of the lieutenant's tone that he even adjusted his poetic meter to the rhythm and energy of Schmidt's speech. Pasternak's search for historic verisimilitude is so clear that at least on the surface his poem seems to comply with LEF's idea of "literature of fact." This is the reason why Tsvetaeva, one of Pasternak's most devoted critics and friends, disliked this new poetic approach and reproached him for his "tragic devotion to the original," which, in her opinion, overloaded the narrative with details. Tsvetaeva also felt that the abundance of factual information prevented the reader from seeing a hero in Schmidt: "You have presented a human Schmidt, in the weakness of his nature, touching but so hopeless" (Pasternak, *Izbrannoe,* 1:576). Tsvetaeva's reaction is, although justified from the point of view of the epic portrayal of the hero, pointing in a different direction: there is more of the human than the hero in Schmidt.

Rather than creating a strong man of action, Pasternak, by interiorizing Schmidt through his correspondence and private thoughts, builds the figure of a rather quixotic hero. The historical Schmidt, who sympathized with revolutionary ideals but never belonged to any political organization, agreed to lead a mutiny on the unarmed cruiser in the idealistic belief that his noble background would be taken into consideration by the authorities and thus help the peaceful resolution of the conflict. His lofty ideals and humanism were the major driving forces behind his decision. He must have known, however, that defeat was unavoidable and everyone participating in the mutiny doomed. In other words, Pasternak's Schmidt did not actively seek to be a hero; history and fate determined his plight, and he passively assumed the burden.

The poem consists of three parts divided into individual sections. The first part opens with Schmidt's romantic encounter with a woman at the hippodrome in Kiev, which is immediately followed by their accidental meeting again on a train. Then the narrative leaps into historical events: the publication of the so-called "October manifesto" on 17 October, political demonstrations, strikes, Schmidt's speech of 19 October at the funeral of the victims of a peaceful demonstration killed by the police during their march, and his pledge to stand up for the revolutionary ideas until the end. Other events include a description of the sailors' meeting and a confrontation between them and the military forces that were sent to suppress their rebellion. Among these historical events are intermingled Schmidt's personal letters to his romantic correspondent, in which he recalls his life, anticipates revolutionary events and his participation in them, and expresses his desire to meet with the woman. The narrative of the first part is far from chronological: it is fragmented and retains the impressionistic qualities of Pasternak's lyrical poems. There are no logical transitions between individual sections, and the characters and setting are generally sketchy. Nevertheless, in writing his poem for an audience presumably adequately familiar with the 1905 revolution, Pasternak effectively provided a general outline of the historical events. What mattered above all, however, was Schmidt himself, and Pasternak shows him in three central aspects of his personality: Schmidt the romantic, Schmidt the revolutionary hero, and Schmidt the human being. The reader sees the lieutenant both through his own self-characterization in the letters and through the eyes of the narrator. There is an alignment between the two visions as Schmidt, like the narrator, has no illusions about himself. The narrator presents him as a "mysterious sailor" who "writes silly things the whole night" (1:308), and Schmidt himself comments on his need to communicate with the romantic stranger and refers to his own letters as "babbling" (1:309). The narrator's words about Schmidt read like emanations from the lieutenant's own thoughts and feelings. When the narrator says that Schmidt's decision to lead the mutiny depended on his "joy to sacrifice himself" and on the "blind whim of chance" (1:311), readers think they hear the hero's own voice. The blurring of voices is sometimes achieved through the stylistic diversity of the text, the use of bits and pieces of real-life material, dialogue often without clearly identified voices, direct speech without quotation marks, and the narrative voice shifting between a conversational tone and impersonal descriptions of the events. This medley of styles makes the story line hard to follow, and only a perceptive and historically well-informed reader is able to reconstruct the flow of events with relative ease. Pasternak has maneuvered himself into a position between lyrical and epic modes and is still unable to find a comfortable balance between them throughout the poem. This imbalance is intensified by his intention to mythologize the revolution through Schmidt, a misfit revolutionary hero.

The second part is, in Pasternak's own words, "a transformation of man into the hero of the deed in which he does not believe" (Pasternak, *Izbrannoe*, 1:576). It consists of short sketches: Schmidt's participation in meetings and demonstrations, his speeches, his survey of the cruiser's readiness to meet the attack of the forces loyal to the government, and the debacle of the uprising. Even more blatantly than in the first part, Schmidt appears as the wrong choice for heading the uprising: he does not believe in bloodshed and violence in a political struggle. Pasternak highlights this aspect in a dialogue between Schmidt and an unnamed character, in which the lieutenant appears as a pacifist and idealist: "'I am an enemy of bloodshed.' / 'Then what kind of a sailor are you? / What kind of a politician? / Are you a revolutionary? / One does not start a fight wearing lady's gloves.' / 'I am going to Petersburg. / Don't persuade me. I will not give in" (1:318). Schmidt's background, education, and lifestyle create distance between him and his sailors. He is incapable of a full understanding of the group he has decided to represent. The class difference is seen through the eyes of a sailor who visits Schmidt and immediately notices his comfort, ample quarters, books, portiéres, china cabinet, and a table cloth, objects that belong to the refined world far removed from the sailor's. Like this simple man, the reader too sees Schmidt as an individual foreign to the dark, elemental revolutionary world.

The third part opens with Schmidt's letter to his woman correspondent written before his trial. This letter elaborates Schmidt's ethical and humanistic motivations in taking his role in the uprising: "I lived and / Gave my soul for my friends" (1:326). From the letter readers also learn that he foresaw the tragic end of the uprising all alone and made unsuccessful attempts to explain it to the revolutionary sailors. Next is his correspondent's trip to prison to see him, followed by the trial, Schmidt's speech at the trial, and his execution. The last sections of the poem portray Schmidt's sacrifice as senseless and pathetic in the context of the revolutionary history. His accomplishment is mainly before his own conscience, but his conviction of having fulfilled a historical mission appears unfounded. If not slightly ludicrous, Schmidt's speech at the trial demonstrates that he stands alone in history and his act could only be understood by men equal to him in their sensibilities and ethical standards: "I was singled out / By the elemental wave. / Not to rise with the whole motherland / Would have been more difficult to me, / I feel no regret / For the road I have gone down. / ... I know that the pillar against which / I will stand will be the boundary / Of two different epochs of history, / And I rejoice that I was chosen" (1:335). Until the end he is incapable of feeling anger and rage even against his judges and the power they represent. In fact he sympathizes with their position and sees in them "martyrs of the dogma" and "victims of the age" (1:334). In his utopian world of lofty ideals there is no place for antagonistic feelings. Although Schmidt senses that he stands on "the boundary of two different epochs of history," the old autocratic epoch losing its power and the new revolutionary epoch emerging to replace it, he fails to understand that, if anything, he represents the class doomed by the new epoch and the "elemental wave" that will eventually devour the likes of him. As Gifford put it, "Schmidt does not clearly understand the process of history" (Gifford 1977, 114).

Spektorskii

In a letter from January of 1925 Pasternak complains to Mandelstam about the constant disruptions in his work due to the psychological stress, his miserable financial situation, and the inability to cope with the hostility of his social and physical environments: "Everything is corroded, broken up, unscrewed, everything has ossified layers of insensitivity, dullness, oppressive routine" (5:168). Opposed to the new political atmosphere, Pasternak nevertheless felt compelled to pursue the epic revolutionary form but tried at least to define his own terms for it. As has been seen in *Sublime Malady, The Year Nineteen-Five,* and *Lieutenant Schmidt,* his invocation of the epic mood was an attempt to establish himself as an epic poet in order to catch up with the grandiose scale of the events. A "novel in verse" (5:283), as he called *Spektorskii* in a 1929 letter to the Marxist critic Pavel Medvedev, was one in the series of his endeavors to record the texture of his experience of this epic age. In the same letter to Mandelstam, Pasternak describes his new project as "a return to the old poetic rails of a train that derailed six years ago and all that time lay by the slope" (5:167). Again he was preoccupied with writing a novel but, still hesitant, decided to try his luck in a more familiar medium, poetry. *Spektorskii* took years to finish (Pasternak worked on it from 1924 to 1930): it was published in segments throughout the process of its development. The introduction was published in *New World* as late as 1930, whereas the last two parts appeared in 1929, the same year "The Tale" was published. "The Tale" is important for an understanding of *Spektorskii* because from its opening page readers learn about the close connection between the two works, as well as the links to an earlier prose piece, titled "Chapters from A Tale," that was published in 1918 and

1922. But Pasternak's original intention to develop the events of World War I in "The Tale" and then use this piece to fill in the temporal gap in *Spektorskii* was never carried out. The novel's narrative line, therefore, seems incomplete: it describes the hero's life in 1912 and 1913 and ends in 1919, thus leaving a gap of several years and thereby omitting the characters' experiences during World War I altogether.

The choice of genre, a "novel in verse," unusual not only for Soviet literature in the 1920s, was explained by Pasternak in his letter from November 1929 to Medvedev as his intended tribute to the Russian literary tradition. Most likely the allusion was made to Pushkin's famous nineteenth-century novel in verse, *Evgenii Onegin* (*Eugene Onegin*). Another reason for Pasternak's choice of form seemed dictated by his expectation of changes in society that would make this genre possible again. Such hopes soon vanished, however, and disappointment with the social transformation set in and hence his realization that the novel in verse was becoming an anachronistic genre:

When I began writing [*Spektorskii*] five years ago, I called it a novel in verse. I looked not only backward but also forward. I expected some transformations in life and society, as the result of which the possibility of the individual tale would be restored, that is, the story of individual characters forming a representative model and comprehensible to anyone in its personal confinement, and not in its applied breadth. About this I was wrong, I childishly exaggerated the pace of the possible differentiation of the new society and a part of the old one in new conditions. . . . I began in a state of some hope that the shattered homogeneity of life and its tangible manifestation would be restored in the course of years and not of decades, in my lifetime and not in some historical fortune-telling." (5:283–84)

This letter sheds light not only on the choice of the genre but also on the slow progress and fragmentariness of *Spektorskii*'s final version.

The generic aspects of *Spektorskii* are interesting in more than one way. First, *Spektorskii* symbolizes the link with classical Russian literature by recovering the genre of *Eugene Onegin*. Comparable elements in the two novels include the characters' similarity, their failed pursuits of a place in society, and poetic meter. Like Pushkin, Pasternak chose a regular iambic meter arranged in quatrains; the only difference is that his are pentameters, whereas Pushkin preferred tetrameters. Second, by choosing to write a novel in verse, Pasternak hoped to accommodate his own lyrical inclinations while at the same time reflecting his age through an individual character, thus avoiding or at least reducing the prescribed epic scale. It was a failed attempt. The main character, Sergei Spektorskii, as Pasternak conceived him from the beginning, had unmistakable family resemblances with a group of such nineteenth-century Russian literary characters as Pushkin's Onegin, Lermontov's Pechorin, and Goncharov's Oblomov, to name but a few, known as superfluous heroes. Obsessively introspective, socially passive, contemptuous of their society, and pursuing only their own interests, these characters could hardly have become role models for the new hero that Soviet literature tried to foster. Although Pasternak must have felt spiritually close to his character and would have been content focusing on his story line, he realized in the course of his work that for the sake of accommodating pressure from the literary-political front, an epic dimension had to be added. He therefore felt the need to introduce social-historical milieu sketches in the third and fourth chapters. Because of Pasternak's lingering uncertainty about the narrative development of the novel, the project dragged on for years. It was also slowed down by his parallel work on *The Year Nineteen-Five* and *Lieutenant Schmidt.* Moreover, the idea of writing a novel in prose was also part of his plans at that time. It seems that from the 1920s on Pasternak tended to work on several big projects simultaneously, and works that he cherished—in particular *Doctor Zhivago*—took much longer to finish than those in which he, sometimes rather hastily, reacted to a certain political climate. The work on *Spektorskii* could have taken much longer had Pasternak not realized by 1929, in the midst of the Pilnyak affair, that there was no time for another big project and instead hurried to finish his novel. He felt compelled by the political circumstances and by his own conscience to make a statement about the revolution. The verse form was a much more familiar idiom for this occasion than prose—because of his more extensive experience as a poet rather than a prose writer—and therefore, it was more convenient for Pasternak to complete *Spektorskii* rather than proceeding to work on a novel about the revolution in prose (Fleishman 1990, 156).

Although *Spektorskii* hardly appears as a revolutionary novel, Pasternak believed that it had to say more about the 1917 revolution than his "factual and chronological book" *The Year Nineteen-Five* said about the first Russian revolution of 1905.[12] Whereas *The Year Nineteen-Five* and *Lieutenant Schmidt* have an explicit revolutionary context, *Spektorskii* barely mentions the revolution. One could read Pasternak's novel in verse "without realizing that a major political crisis was the main object of study" (Hingley 1983, 89). The object of the author's interest is Spektorskii himself. By following the life of his protagonist, hardly the epitome of the revolutionary hero generally favored by literary-political hacks, Pasternak exposes the inhumanity of the age and its suppression of individuality. It is therefore not the revolutionary events per se that preoccupy Pasternak in the novel but rather their devastating impact on people's lives. The last pages of *Spektorskii,* according to Pasternak's letter to Medvedev from November 1929, were intended to portray how time "rises against man and gets ahead of him" (5:285).

Spektorskii consists of an introduction and nine chapters. Not only did Pasternak look to Pushkin for formal models, he also used the same narrative strategy to open his work: an author-figure introduces himself to the reader and explains to him the novel's origin. The biographical details of the author's life provided in this introduction lead to an easy identification of the author with Pasternak himself at the time: "I was poor. Our son was born. / Childish things had to be given up for a while" (1:337).[13] The author's job collecting materials about Lenin in the foreign press is also a direct reference to Pasternak's employment by the Commissariat for Foreign Affairs in 1924. Familiar also are the lines of the author's reading Conrad and Proust and his interest in the Russian expatriate poetess named Mariia Il'ina, whose poetry he comes across in foreign journals. Presumably it is his excessive attention to Il'ina's work, whose models, according to Pasternak himself, were Marina Tsvetaeva and a minor poetess Vera Il'ina, that caused the author's dismissal from his job. Now unemployed, he begins to write about his hero, the writer Sergei Spektorskii, "a person without merits," who turns out to be a friend of Il'ina's (1:338). In the first chapter the author further explains that his strange choice of a hero is triggered by the coincidental rediscovery of Il'ina's poetry. This incident throws him back in history while illuminating his present: "I would not give anything for my hero / And would not have started to talk about him for a long time, / But I wrote about the knot of rays / In which he appeared before me" (1:339). Through Spektorskii, Pasternak not only gains access to his own past but creates his own recognizable double. Spektorskii experiences a kind of social indifference and has no desire to participate in any political transformations. Like his creator, Spektorskii is caught between two worlds, the dying aestheticized world of the fin de siècle and the world of Soviet Russia, both of which doom him to oblivion. Like his creator, Spektorskii also faces a dilemma: either to let life carry him along or rebel against life despite the danger of being devoured in the process. In neither case will the author or Spektorskii be able to escape the internal and external drama of being displaced artists and social outsiders.

The first chapter is highly lyrical and describes the hustle-bustle of the city life surrounding the author in a vein reminiscent both of Pushkin's authorial digressions and the uplifting spirit of *My Sister-Life.* The second chapter focuses on the love affair between Spektorskii and Olga Bukhteeva, the wife of an acquaintance of his. This passionate affair takes place in a snowbound country house, where Olga and Spektorskii go with a group of other young people to celebrate Christmas of 1912 and the new year. This chapter in its original 1925 edition contains perhaps the most daring erotic lines in Pasternak's entire poetic career, but the explicit love scene between Spektorskii and Olga was cut out from later Soviet editions. Chapters 3 and 4, set in 1913, describe the unexpected arrival of Spektorskii's sister Natasha, the wife of a provincial factory doctor, at Spektorskii's Moscow apartment. It is at this point, in a conversation between the brother and the sister, that the revolutionary theme is introduced. The difference between the siblings' social sentiments is established in the first lines of Natasha's part, where she reproaches Sergei for his indifference to changing the social order in Russia: "Look, you are young and that's a plus. / But you are separated from your generation and that's a minus. / You have no sense of a quest in life, to my shame. / Which camp do you belong to?" (1:350). Spektorskii's political noninvolvement is contrasted with Natasha's conscientious attendance of political meetings. She is embarrassed that because of her visit to Moscow she has to miss one such meeting that she had planned to go to with her husband. Spektorskii, however, experiences nothing but irritation about his sister's accusations and political preaching. All he wants is to be left alone, and he cuts his sister off abruptly: "You are right-minded? Good for you. / I would be full on silence without your salad dressing" (1:350). Spektorskii's distance from the radicalized young intelligentsia is thus established. The closing of the chapter highlights his aloofness as the author paints a picture of the city saturated with social injustice and vibrating with the anticipation of political turbulence. As a counterbalance nature still preserves and offers its primordial comforts, and Sergei finds his peace in them. But perhaps, like the author, he feels that "nature is an unreliable element" (1:352).

After Natasha's departure in chapter 5 reality, "like a beast that had enough sleep" (1:353), rushes into Spektorskii's life in the form of urban violence and the poverty he senses while walking through a rundown part of town to give a private lesson (another detail probably derived from Pasternak's own experience as a tutor during his student years). Sergei experiences the destabilizing and alienating effect of this environment on his sensitivity and tries to rush through the depressing neighborhood. On the way he runs into Sasha Balts, "something like a friend" (1:353). Like other characters, Balts is only briefly outlined in the novel, but he is again mentioned in "The Tale" and characterized by Sergei as "a bastard." His function, like Natasha's, is to establish Spektorskii's distance from his generation, but this time the difference is of another variety. Fleishman hypothesizes that Pasternak introduced the figure of

Balts in the novel "to set him [Spektorskii] up against an unequivocally nega-tive character" (Fleishman 1990, 155). While working on the fifth chapter in 1927, Pasternak probably felt compelled to present his hero in a more favorable light and thought that Balts's love for luxury, his cynicism, and his devious nature would build a contrast to Spektorskii's modesty and sense of justice and honesty. Sergei finds the world of Balts's values revolting and is afraid of being devoured by it.

In the seventh chapter Spektorskii's life changes when he meets Mariia Il'ina at Balts's place. Il'ina is the only character in the novel with whom Spektorskii can establish spiritual closeness. The chapter supplies sufficient biographical references (the death of her father, a professor, in 1913; her emi-gration from Soviet Russia to the West; and her subsequent success as a poet) to associate Il'ina with Tsvetaeva and thus her relationship with Spektorskii with the friendship between Tsvetaeva and Pasternak. Just as Balts provided a negative foil for Spektorskii, whose stature is thereby elevated, so Pasternak adds, through Il'ina's perception of his main character, further positive traits: "this man is not some sort of Don Juan or a liar," she thinks, and he is no dandy either (1:362). To Il'ina, Spektorskii appears as a serious and considerate man, although she has to realize that she knows nothing of his whereabouts when he unexpectedly disappears from her life and leaves for Petersburg after receiving a telegram—unbeknownst to her, the telegram informs him of his mother's serious illness. Unable to find him, Il'ina feels betrayed and goes abroad, fol-lowing her original plan that she had only been postponing because of her meeting with and attachment to Spektorskii.

The narrative now skips ahead some six years and places its protagonist against the background of the revolutionary reality of 1919. The picture of Moscow sav-aged by the hardships of the civil war is grim and unwelcoming. The author de-scribes it as "a farewell souvenir of the war" (1:364): cold, hunger, devastation, and the new "military" lifestyle characterize the city (1:365). The middle part of chapter 8 is the author's contemplation about his time and perhaps one of Pasternak's most bitter indictments of the age. Gone is the old world, and the author does not have any illusions about the fate of characters like Spektorskii in the new revolu-tionary Russia. Amid the suffering of the masses, any attention paid to people like Spektorskii is as irrelevant as counting individual "kernels in a loaf of bread" (1:365). The old, refined, prerevolutionary bourgeois intellectual with his individuality is replaced by a new breed of people born by the revolution and nourished by the hatred of the old world, "people as hard as the cliffs," their "faces as dead as clichés" (1:369). Confronted with this environment the author no longer believes "in the reality of the individual person" (1:365).

The ninth, and final, chapter is full of coincidences and brings surprises into Spektorskii's life. While participating in the redistribution of confiscated furniture conducted by the Union of Writers, Spektorskii comes across Il'ina's photos. This discovery triggers his deep nostalgia and thoughts about the vicissitudes of life. Il'ina, the woman who was his sole treasure in the past, symbolizes for him the whole world of his true literary and cultural interests, now totally confined to his memory and thoughts. In the same chapter he also encounters his other former love, Olga Bukhteeva, now a representative of the new regime. Readers can hardly recognize Sergei's former passionate lover in her. She wears the standard belted leather jacket and obviously enjoys carrying a revolver. There is nothing but contempt in her attitude toward Spektorskii when she tells him, "My friend, you are such a miserable squirt!" (1:372). Olga no longer has any interest in Spektorskii and sees him only as a representative of the class enemy that she is determined to eliminate: "I am a patriot by nature. / What kind of weapon should I finish you off with?" (1:373). Olga's image in the last chapter is grotesque. Her political zeal places her among the people of the future who have declared war on those like Spektorskii. And Pasternak makes it clear to the reader that his sentiments are with the latter. As Pushkin's narrator meets with Eugene Onegin, the narrator of *Spektorskii* meets with his hero at the end of the novel. In contrast to Spektorskii's meeting with Olga, the meeting between the author and the hero is warm and open. Given the literary-political climate in Russia at that time, the unwavering friendship between these two individuals and the author's implicit identification with Spektorskii seem provocative: neither the author nor his hero is the least bit interested in participating in the erection of the new proletarian state and rather remain the unwanted shadows of the past.

Spektorskii thus becomes Pasternak's fourth epic work that starts with the intention to celebrate the revolution and ends up challenging it. But the challenge is put ambiguously, indirectly so that only a sensitive reader, experienced in reading between the lines, could detect the authorial notes of discontent. Because of its subtlety and obliqueness of style, the Soviet censors never noticed the antirevolutionary sentiment in the novel. In *Spektorskii* Pasternak's characteristically abstract poetic style serves as a perfect disguise for a political statement. His artistic method is thus effective because, to use Sinyavsky's words, "he [Pasternak] likes to talk about the 'center' in terms of the 'edges,' to define a thing through its boundaries with neighboring things . . ." (Sinyavsky 1978, 95). Of the four poems reflecting the revolutionary age, *Spektorskii* is Pasternak's most personal and at the same time most revealing of the dark sides of the revolution. Despite Pasternak's impressionistic method of portraying his characters in this work, *Spektorskii* contains his most coherent and inherently interesting hero up to this point. Through Spektorskii he insists on the value of individual experience and perceptions as well as the uniqueness of the creative expression. Outside the crosscurrents of the revolution and after choosing his path of quiet social existence and spiritual inner life, Spektorskii reflects the internal human drama of the displaced creative individual in a ruthless age. Although Pasternak will not return to the theme of the Russian intelligentsia for more than two decades, Spektorskii clearly is an ancestor of Iurii Zhivago.

CHAPTER FOUR

Second Birth and Translations

The years of the First Five-Year Plan (1928–1932) greatly affected all aspects of Soviet life. During the four years within which the plan was accomplished the Soviet Union became a strong industrial nation and its agriculture underwent a major reform, in which individual farms were replaced with a new system of collective farms. It was also during this time that the Soviet Union turned into an ideological monolith dominated by a Stalinist dictatorship. As the new Soviet consciousness was developing, Pasternak's literary profile gradually changed from that of a creative poet and writer to that of a translator who increasingly seemed to be shunning his own creative writing. Whereas the first half of the 1930s elevated him to the rank of a premier Soviet poet, the second half of the decade witnessed the eclipse of his popularity and official support, bringing on a severe personal and professional crisis.

The changing political climate in the Soviet Union at the time was well described by the American journalist Louis Fischer, who covered the Sixteenth Communist Party Congress, held in June–July 1930: "A good comrade should advise Stalin to stop the orgy of glorification of his person. . . . Every day hundreds and thousands of telegrams full of compliments in exalted, exaggerated Oriental style—'You are the very greatest Leader,' 'the most faithful disciple of Lenin,' etc.—are addressed to him. Three cities are named after him, along with countless villages, collective farms, schools, factories, and institutions. . . . Though Stalin may not be responsible for this state of affairs, he tolerates it. He could put an end to it just by pressing a button."[1] Upon hearing this account, Stalin allegedly responded with only one word: "Scum" (*Utopia*, 245). Although a full-fledged cult of Stalin's personality did not begin until the end of 1931 with an article in which the Soviet leader pronounced himself as the "only legitimate interpreter of Marx," by the time Fischer wrote his remarks, the Soviet leader had already concentrated practically all political power in his hands and was able to dictate to the party what it should do and how (*Utopia*, 245). The years of the First Five-Year Plan were years of unprecedented tightening of control over all spheres of Soviet life, putting incredible pressure on the people to adjust quickly to the new standards of social, political, economic, and spiritual behavior. A massive propaganda campaign was launched in all realms of the public sphere to portray a bright socialist future. But in reality Soviet people during the First Five-Year Plan once again had to face vast economic deprivations and the fear of political persecution if they did not conform to the new rules. The ideological attack on the population was accompanied by the growth of the bureaucratic superstructure that would ensure the proper course of the building of Soviet socialism. At the same time the developing Stalinist machine also cultivated a system of privileges for its favorites and stoked the fear of losing them in those who had them.

The most outrageous among new policies and legislative measures that the government introduced was Stalin's campaign to "liquidate the kulaks as a class," launched at the end of 1929. The campaign amounted to the forced collectivization of the kulaks (successful and well-to-do peasants), supervised by the police and the army. Since many farmers but especially the kulaks vehemently resisted the process, they were forced from their land and deported to Siberia or central Asia. Many ended up in prison camps favored by the new criminal legislation of 1928. The new criminal legislation also permitted the prisoners' re-education through work, which in reality meant slave labor under the harshest conditions imaginable. About five million people "vanished" in the process of collectivization. As a result the countryside was largely devastated and large areas of land went untended. The peasants sabotaged the collectivization process as much as possible, and droughts and famine further contributed to the bleak picture in Soviet agriculture. At the beginning of the 1930s the system of internal passports that, by and large, has existed into the present was introduced. Antireligious campaigns were unleashed; strict discipline and strong ideological education were established in schools; science was put under Marxist tutelage; and the intelligentsia began to be viewed more and more openly as the class enemy. Stalin was committed to clearing the road for a system of political nonresistance and unanimity, and he needed scapegoats to justify means to achieve his goals.

In 1930 the first wave of arrests of members of the technical and cultural intelligentsia occurred. In November and December the witch hunt assumed ever growing proportions and culminated in the arrest and trial of members of the so-called Industrial Party, who were accused of conducting subversive activities on orders from French president Raymond Poincar, T. E. Lawrence (Lawrence of Arabia), and the Dutch industrialist Henri Deterding. There were no witnesses to these alleged crimes and no material evidence, but the eight defendants put on trial confessed to all the preposterous charges against them. Political repression, especially against the "technical" intelligentsia, went into

high gear. There were massive arrests of members of the so-called Toiling Peasants' Party, followed by the trial of Mensheviks[2] held in Moscow in 1931; the
list of new political criminals kept growing from day to day. In this atmosphere
of political paranoia, the cultural intelligentsia found itself under enormous pressure to demonstrate its loyalty to the party and its policies. As the 1930s pro-
gressed and the political terror intensified, conformism became a form of survival
for many writers. The First Congress of Soviet Writers in 1934 became a large-
scale demonstration of the commitment of Soviet writers to the Stalinist regime, their critical reevaluation of the Russian literary tradition, and their
readiness to pursue a new way in literature supported by the party. For instance,
the prominent formalist critic Viktor Shklovskii denounced Dostoevsky and
proclaimed that from the point of view of the revolution the great writer was a
"traitor."[3] The whole congress turned into an opportunity for the writers to de-
nounce each other and pledge their loyalty to Stalin and the party. After the
congress there were only four major writers who did not support the decision of
the party to nationalize literature. These writers were Mikhail Bulgakov, Andrei
Platonov, Mandelstam, and Akhmatova. It is in this context of inhuman political constraints that Pasternak's work in the 1930s must be understood.

The beginning of 1930 was a difficult period for Pasternak. He was
still distressed after Mayakovsky's suicide, and a trip to the Urals with a
group of writers in June 1931 depressed him even more. The trip was part
of an official propaganda campaign aimed at familiarizing Soviet writers
with the industrial achievements of the First Five-Year Plan and helping
them project their positive impressions into their writing. But if anything,
the trip made Pasternak's psychological situation even more difficult: instead of being fascinated by the truly immense scale of the social and individual enterprise, he was horrified by the "merciless deindividualization of
the people" (Fleishman 1990, 165). This trip was never reflected in his poems.

Pasternak's personal life at that time was also undergoing a crisis as his
marriage was falling apart. Pasternak's wife Evgeniia, a creative artist herself,
found it difficult to cope with the hardships of everyday existence. The mutual
resentment grew as Evgeniia wanted to devote herself to art and Pasternak needed
a stable family and a lot of personal space to work. The tension grew over the
years, and by 1927 the couple became estranged from each other. After this
Pasternak's life underwent a sudden metamorphosis, and in spring 1931 he
undertook a trip to Georgia with his new love and future wife Zinaida Neigauz.
The two had met in the summer of 1930.

Second Birth

The atmosphere of Georgia and the love for Zinaida were behind Pasternak's outburst of creative energy and lyrical revival that now set in and resulted in a book of poetry entitled *Vtoroe rozhdenie* (*Second Birth*). The twenty-six poems of the volume were written in 1930–1931 and published in 1932. Not since *My Sister-Life* had Pasternak written so many poems in so short a time. The volume is deeply personal and relates the poet's love, tenderness, and excitement for his lover, who is also his new muse, and at the same time his compassion for and pangs of conscience about Evgeniia. To this must be added his fascination with the landscape and people of the Caucasus and, lastly, his acceptance of socialism.

Pasternak's romance with Zinaida had begun in Irpen' (a small place near Kiev), where he stayed in the summer of 1930. The atmosphere there proved to be conducive to creativity and was made all the more so by the presence of Pasternak's brother Aleksandr and his friends Genrikh Neigauz, one of the leading Soviet pianists, and the philosopher Valentin Asmus and their wives. In Irpen', Pasternak seemed to gain the temporary emotional stability that he needed so badly to resume the work he had abandoned temporarily as a reaction to the increased ideological pressure on literature. His romance with Zinaida, Neigauz's wife, continued after Irpen', and in the following spring they undertook their joint trip to Georgia at the invitation of the Georgian poet Paolo Iashvili, whom Pasternak had met earlier in Moscow.

Georgia so completely overwhelmed the poet by its beauty and the warmth of its people that more than two decades later in his 1957 autobiography, "People and Situations: An Autobiographical Sketch," he remarked that if he were to revise *Safe Conduct* for a new edition he would add a chapter about Georgia and the Georgian poets. He wrote:

> Then the Caucasus, Georgia, individual people there, the people's life came as a revelation to me. Everything was new, everything surprising. . . . Spilling out from the court yards into the street, life of the poorest people was bolder, less secretive than in the north, it was vivid and sincere. The symbolism of folk legends was full of mysticism and Messianic feeling, that disposed one toward the life of imagination and as in Catholic Poland made everyone a poet. The high culture of the progressive part of society meant an intellectual life on a level already rare in those days." (4:342–43)

A year later, in a letter to Iashvili, Pasternak described the impact that Tiflis, the capital of Georgia, had had on him, comparable only to that of the cities of Marburg and Venice, or of artists such as Chopin, Scriabin, and Rilke. The Georgian poet Simon Chikovani talked of Pasternak's Georgian experience as "a new opening of the world, the beginning of a new life" and claimed that according to Pasternak himself, Georgia had as strong an effect on him as the revolution itself.[4]

The theme of the "second birth" was earlier encountered in Pasternak's poem "Marburg" (1928), where it was related to the birth of a poet. The 1932 collection was full of autobiographical moments and clearly alluded to the poet's spiritual rebirth. But in addition to the more intimate personal meaning of the "second birth," Pasternak was trying to reestablish a rapport with his lyrical audience by implying that the period of his epic poems was over and he was reborn as a lyricist. Pasternak confessed to a friend, the poet Sergei Spasskii, that "the common tone of expression does not come from the *perceptions* of a lyricist, not from the preponderance of one kind of *real* impressions over another, but is approached by him almost as a moral question. That is, when in the healthy time we considered it *natural* to talk in this way or that way, now . . . we consider it to be our *duty*" (5:310). As the letter shows, a return to lyrical poetry was a matter of great concern for Pasternak. He never stopped pondering the meaning of his poetry in a new society and reassessing his own role as a poet. The "duty" to speak in a certain way, as follows from the letter, is thus no longer a matter of feelings but rather of historical necessity and moral choice.

Second Birth opens with the long poem "Volny" ("Waves"), which introduces the reader to the themes of the book: "Here all things will come together: my past / And what I live by now, / My aspirations, my values, / The whole of life that I have seen" (1:374). These first lines set the reflective, contemplating tone of the poem as the poet-persona ponders the transitoriness of time and the connection between his present, past, and future experiences. It is his memory and his spiritual state that preoccupy him at the moment. He still cannot grasp the full meaning of his experiences and compares them to the waves that roll onto the shore one after the other: "My deeds and experiences return to me / Like crests of waves. / The waves are boundless, endless, / Their essence is still unknown, / But everything is touched by their change, / Like the foam of the waves changes the sounds of the sea" (1:374). The poet's use of this wave metaphor dissociates him from the immediate surroundings and brings him to the domain of his inner world. But it is not a world of lyrical narcissism. Rather than withdrawing into the past, he is alert to the present and sees it in unity with his former experience. What clearly remains from the past is the poet's union with nature and his work.

The sweeps of time in the poet's memory and his thoughts about his present life and work in *Second Birth* are set against the majestic Caucasian landscape, to which he returns throughout the poem. Exotic and strikingly romantic, the Caucasus provides the perfect refuge for the poet in search of peace and revives his desire to write. The inspiration comes from the surroundings themselves. The long spacious beach of Kobuleti on the Black Sea coast evokes in the poet's mind images of his own work in which he has to include twice as much as a normal person could (1:375). Pasternak celebrates the liberating romantic nature of the Caucasus: "The Caucasus was spread out as on a palm, / And like a rumpled bed, / And the ice of the mountain heads was bottomless-blue / From the warmth of the heated precipices. / Misty and out of sorts, / But accurate like a machine gun, / It raised the hatred of its icy peaks / Like salvos in an exchange of fire" (1:380). With skilled dramatic metaphors Pasternak re-creates the atmosphere of the grandeur and splendor of nature and sets his thoughts moving steadily toward poetry. Both in nature and poetry he finds peace and harmony as well as excitement and fulfillment. In fact he feels himself so bound up with his work that he seems willing to exchange his very existence for the life of his poems: "Instead of leading the life of a versifier, / I would lead the life of the poems themselves" (1:380). But as in reality happiness is not made to last in the poet's soul either, and soon that which gives him pleasure also becomes the source of his nostalgia. Looking at the marvels of Caucasian nature, he suddenly feels a gnawing desire to return to his empty Moscow apartment, to the cityscape, and to his writing. His Caucasian experience will always remain with him, but he must accept his fate in Russia "as his harness" and regardless of the "future insanities" he anticipates there (1:376). The chilly political subtext in these expressions is transparent enough, as is the poet's uneasy feeling about his plight, but Pasternak lets his readers know that he understands his return as a moral quest he must undertake.

There clearly is a confusing duality in Pasternak's perception of the changes in Soviet Russia. On the one hand he describes his life there as a "harness"; on the other hand, in "Waves," he appears as a supporter of Soviet socialism. Perhaps this double perspective, with the positive view prevailing, was caused by his sudden enchantment by the Georgian land and the cultural surroundings his friends provided. Sheltered from the material deprivations and poverty of Russia and temporarily liberated from political constraints, Pasternak finally felt like a truly free artist. This happy illusion colored his view of Soviet socialism—for a short time and from the distance. In Fleishman's interpretation of this period of Pasternak's life, the poet developed a "genuine faith in socialism . . . and personal independence" that existed in Georgia (Fleishman 1990, 166) and mistook it for a model of an ideal society. It is only in the light of this experience that sense can be made of Pasternak's short-lived enthusiastic alliance with Soviet socialism. In one lyric of "Waves" devoted to the happy life under socialism the allusion to Georgia becomes an example of Pasternak's romanticized view of the future: "You are near, the far-away land of socialism. / Or would you say you are close? / In the name of life / We came together in the thick of life. / Take us to the future. / You appear through the mist of theories, / Like a land beyond gossip and slander, / Like a passage to light and to the sea, / Like the passage to Georgia from Mlety" (1:380). These lines, written only a year after the publication of *Spektorskii,* stand in sharp contrast to Pasternak's earlier skepticism about the future of Russia and can be understood only in the context of his Georgian experience.

The moment the poet returns from his far-flung spiritual journey into the future, he wants to change his artistic expression. His journey revealed new sensations to him, as well as leading him to believe that the socialist future was close. Pasternak felt that his old poetic idiom was no longer adequate to describe the new epoch he was willing to embrace. The historic moment itself rejected ambiguity and demanded directness and clarity. Toward the end of "Waves" Pasternak declares his intention to search for a different stylistic path of linguistic simplicity: "There are in the experience of the great poets / Features of such naturalness / That it is impossible, having known them, / Not to end up in utter dumbfoundedness. / In kinship with everything, and in assurance / And knowledge of the future in real life, / It is unavoidable not to fall at last into heresy, / Into a never heard-of simplicity. / But we will not be spared / If we do not conceal it. / That is what people need most of all, / But complicated things they understand better" (1:381–82). Written with dispassionate equanimity and self-awareness, these three widely quoted quatrains outlined Pasternak's style for the rest of his life. Thus in "Waves," as in the rest of the volume, stylistic simplicity becomes the poet's quintessential artistic method. Although not completely stripped of metaphoric ornamentation, Pasternak's language in "Waves" lacks its earlier baroque quality and harks back to the clarity of classical models. Gifford sees Pasternak's choice of iambic meter in the book as a tribute to such classics as Pushkin and another nineteenth-century distinguished Russian poet, Fedor Tiutchev (1803–1873), who both favored iambic quatrains. In Gifford's opinion, Pasternak, by choosing this poetic form, "committed himself to a different relationship with the reader," a relationship that points to "a moral tradition which also supported the Russian novel" (Gifford

1977, 136, 138). In the final analysis, "Waves," as Sinyavsky observed, becomes more than the simple introduction to a new theme; it stands on its own, like a story about "a life incompletely realized, hiding within itself new possibilities and intentions resembling those schemes which inspire the poet and which are also only half-expressed and roll into the future" (Sinyavsky 1978, 96).

Some helpful narrative links among the poems in *Second Birth* can be found in Pasternak's biography. "Waves" is followed by two poems with biographical roots, both entitled "Ballada" ("Ballad"). The first is devoted to the musical talent of Genrikh Neigauz and the second to Neigauz's wife Zinaida, Pasternak's lover at the time. The first "Ballad" describes Neigauz's concert in Kiev in 1930 and celebrates the pianist's mastery; but it also alludes to the theme of a second birth in Pasternak's own life. It is his closeness to Neigauz and fascination by his talent that inspires the passionate intensity of the poem, as it describes the pianist's performance of Chopin. Pasternak sensuously describes Chopin's music as gliding above Kiev, intensifying, expanding, and filling with its sounds the still Dneper River and Podol, the part of Kiev where the concert took place. In the second "Ballad" the ecstatic energy of the prior poem is replaced by a more subtle expression of the poet's tender feelings for his beloved and his recaptured peace of mind. In a slightly restrained mood the poem expresses the poet's emotions in tones already familiar to readers: a breeze, the rustling of foliage, the rain—in other words, nature creating an accompaniment to the poet's dreams. Once again readers recognize the full manifestation of Pasternak's personality in the romantic touch of his nature description. What is new in his manner, however, as Dale Plank has noted, is the absence of any "illusion of spontaneity that distinguished his earlier works; . . . in its place we have, not a new poetics, but an application of the old poetics, perfected and enriched." What marks this poetics is the poet's more contemplative mood— Plank calls it "elegiacal" (Plank 1966, 112). This is certainly true for another poem in the collection, "Leto" ("Summer"), a biographical reflection on the summer of 1930 spent with friends in Irpen'. Through memory Pasternak revives the lost paradise of those moments, and at the end of the poem he laments with sadness that they are irretrievable.

The elegiac tone also carries through the following poem, "Smert' poeta" ("Death of the Poet"), composed on Mayakovsky's death. The poem resonates with the parts on Mayakovsky in *Safe Conduct,* especially the theme of the "poet and the crowd," the poet's helplessness and fear in the face of the pettiness and vulgarity of the slanderous crowd. Yet Pasternak treats Mayakovsky's suicide as an act of courage and a challenge to the crowd: "Your gunshot was like an eruption of Etna / In the foothills of the cowards" (1:391).

There is another poem on music and its capacity to trigger memories. This time it is the music of Brahms that evokes the past and makes the poet cry. The theme of music fades in and out of *Second Birth,* but, like the waves, it always returns. In the poem "Opiat' Shopen ne ishchet vygod" ("Again Chopin Does Not Seek Advantages") music makes all experience timeless, linking centuries and lives, resonating in every moment of existence. These two musical poems about Brahms and Chopin frame a series of love poems for Zinaida and the poet's tormenting estrangement from his wife. One of these poems, "Liubit' inykh tiazhelyi krest" ("To Love Some Is a Heavy Cross"), perhaps the most revelatory about Pasternak's own needs in love, celebrates the lightness and naturalness of Pasternak's relationship with his new lover. As in his language, there is a similar yearning for simplicity in the poet's love life. Zinaida's love and her uncomplicated and sincere nature appear as a near ideal for Pasternak, who is tired of the complexities of his psychologically demanding marriage. Zinaida becomes the personification of happiness for Pasternak in need of a spiritual revival: "To love some is a heavy cross / Yet, without subtlety, you are lovely; / And the secret of your charms / Rivals the enigma of life" (1:396). Zinaida is crucial in his artistic revival and brings him joy and inspiration, as clearly can be felt in another poem dedicated to her and expressing the poet's blissful state: "And fate dies in rhymes, / And the polyphony of the worlds / Enters our little world like truth. . . . / My beauty, all your essence, / Your whole stature, my beauty, . . . draws me to sing, and I like it" (1:401).

In comparison with the love lyrics of *My Sister-Life,* the love poems in *Second Birth* are not only more subdued in their style and tone, they also express a different scope of concerns. Love is no longer as easy and romantic as it used to be more than a decade earlier. In the background now lurk trivial family problems and material concerns. Perhaps inadvertently the poet casts a shadow on the future of his new love by introducing real life problems he senses he will have to deal with in the near future. In one poem Pasternak openly addresses his wife, "You look at everything in a different way" (1:394); in another he complains about his sense of guilt and his tormented conscience for leaving Evgeniia; and in a third he makes plans for the winter and says that he "will move into my brother's room" (1:403). Pasternak's mood throughout the whole book is unstable. He is anxious about the future and arduously thinks about what to do next. Confused and depressed about his relationship with his wife, the poet turns his imagination toward the Caucasus again and hopes for an answer to his personal crisis. The poem "Kogda my po Kavkazu lazaem" ("While We Are Climbing in the Caucasus") reflects the poet's heavy feelings about his broken marriage and his uncertainty about his personal life.

In addition to personal problems, however, there is growing pressure to deal with his own public role as a poet. Playing a role, then, is the theme of a poem titled "O, znal by ia, chto tak byvaet" ("Oh, Had I Known That It Happens This Way"). For him life shapes itself like theater in which the poet must become a performer. He must find a manner of performing that satisfies both himself and the audience. He is aware that he lives in tough times and that a poet's public image is being judged more harshly than ever and may even cost him his life. The image of blood in the opening quatrain of the poem captures the poet's perception of the current literary-political situation: "Oh, had I known that it happens this way / When I decided to make my debut, / That lines written with blood can kill, / They choke you and kill" (1:412). If "lines written with blood" refer to the poems that come from the soul of the poet or are inspired by passion, then it is dangerous to open up to the reader. It was this kind of danger that led Sergei Esenin (1895–1925) and Mayakovsky, once they became aware of it, to take their own lives. According to Pasternak, the mature poet must take intellectual control of his feelings and overcome the unmediated identification of art and emotion. Only a rational approach to his own image as well as to his writing can save the poet from being a public slave and unnecessarily jeopardizing his soul: "But old age is Rome, which / Instead of twaddle / Demands from the actor not a recitation / But a real death. / A line is dictated by emotions, / Sends a slave onto the stage, / And art ends here, / Whereas earth and destiny breathe " (1:412). Finding the balance that he needed so badly between his public image and his real self in order to be able to walk the political tightrope preoccupied Pasternak at the time and is revealed in this poem as well as in his letter from 11 February 1932 to his parents: "how it changes one, how this fate makes one a prisoner of time, this realization of being public property. . . . And this is the eternal cruelty of unhappy Russia, when she endows someone with her love, the chosen one will no longer find a refuge from her eyes. He somehow appears in the arena before her and owes her a performance for her love" (1:724).

The remaining lyrics of the book confirm Pasternak's contradictory attitudes toward socialism. The poem "Kogda ia ustaiu ot pustozvonstva" ("When I Get Tired of Empty Words") is indicative of his vacillation. Three thematic lines: the poet's retrospective evaluation of his life; thoughts of the two women in his life, Zinaida and Evgeniia; and his optimism about the last year of the First Five-Year Plan, come together in a confusing confessional context. On the one hand, he alludes to the hardships of the last year of the First Five-Year Plan—possibly the tightening political control of the party—from which he escaped into his personal world dominated by Evgeniia and Zinaida. On the other hand, as a counterbalance to his personal situation, he cherishes hopes about the idealistic future that will move his country up toward the light, toward "that faraway land into which the Second Five-Year Plan / Is extending the theses of the soul" (1:413). But already the following quatrain voices dissonance: "We are living our future, I tell them, like everyone, who / Is alive now. But if crippled, it does not matter: We are run over / By the wagon of the plan, driven by the new man" (1:413). There is more submissiveness and fatalism in these lines than a hearty welcome of the new society. The graphic and violent image of the wagon of socialism overrunning everything in its way harks back to Pasternak's earlier representation of communism in the oppressive imagery of the revolutionary ideas in "Aerial Ways" in 1924. Olga Hughes, for one, is clearly doubtful about Pasternak's poetic celebration of the socialist state when she says that "his consistent emphasis on the future relegates socialism to the realm of the unattainable" (Hughes 1974, 93).

The last three poems of *Second Birth* also reflect Pasternak's contradictory attitudes. The first of them, "Vesennii den' tridtsatogo aprelia" ("A Spring Day on the Thirtieth of April"), sounds disappointingly programmatic and trivial if placed in the context of official Soviet poetry: "But with every anniversary richer and richer / Will bloom the bud of the rose, / More noticeably will it gain health, / More obvious will be sincerity and honor" (1:419). Pasternak tries to find support for his optimism in Russian history, and in the following poem, "Stolet'e s lishnim—ne vchera" ("More than a Century Ago—Not Yesterday"), he draws a parallel between the Soviet epoch and that of Peter the Great that pushed Russia from medieval backwardness to a kind of Western enlightenment and relative economic and military strength. In a hopeful tone, Pasternak opens the poem by paraphrasing the lines of Pushkin's poem "Stansy" ("Stanzas," 1828): "More than a century ago—not yesterday, / But there is the same power in the temptation, / In hope of glory and the good / To look at things without fear" (1:421). But Pasternak's allusion to history creates ambiguity of meaning. Although in his poem Pushkin appeals to Nicholas I to show mercy to his political opponents, as Peter the Great had done nearly a century earlier, Pushkin's hope that the czar would liberalize his policies proved to be unfounded. Pasternak knew that well, and therefore his "implicit misgivings about the regime [appeared] only too evident" in this poem (Hughes 1974, 92).

Pasternak obviously wanted to believe that life under socialism would bring positive changes and tried to find every shred of supporting evidence for that. One case in point is the subordinate position of women in society that socialism set out to change. Pasternak supported such change; he had already voiced his concern about improving women's social and economic condition in "The Tale" and addressed it again in *Second Birth*. He wrote: "And because from my child-hood / I have been touched by women's lot, / And the poet's trace is only a trace / Of her path, no more, / And because I am touched only by her, / And she is free in our country, / I am ready to sacrifice myself / For the revolutionary will" (1:90).

Pasternak's praise of socialism is not startling in itself, given that it re-flected a temporary concession to protect himself against the regime that had crushed Mayakovsky and many others among Pasternak's friends in the 1930s. Another reason for Pasternak's acceptance of socialism, as has been mentioned earlier, was his warm Georgian impressions. What is more striking is that to-gether with accepting socialism, the poet abandons his unique poetic idiom almost completely in *Second Birth* for some traditional realist verses and makes a break with his modernist past. He turns to the qualities of Russian classical verse; his emphasis is on simplicity, subtlety and clarity. And although ambi-guity does not completely disappear from his poems, it is hard to find it. Fleishman explains Pasternak's quest for a different literary style by his fear of "belonging to a superfluous generation" (Fleishman 1990, 225). If earlier he believed that the poet was his own supreme judge, in 1937–1939 he developed a need to get closer to the reading public. Fleishman writes: "The new idea of the poet's unity with the people crowded the sensation of being a 'superfluous' hero out of Pasternak's consciousness" (Fleishman 1990, 225). But besides his longing to establish a closer rapport with readers, *Second Birth* demonstrates Pasternak's willingness for political compromise, which manifests itself not only thematically but inevitably in an inferior style.

Despite its relative simplicity, the book did not satisfy the RAPP critics traditionally critical of Pasternak and was subject to a harsh attack. Pasternak himself was displeased with the book. The truth of the matter was that the life-affirming title of the book was a far cry from the actual state of things in the poet's life. Personally he still felt torn between the guilt about his abandoned family and his commitment to Zinaida. Soviet life had not become any happier either and hardly corresponded to its bright portrayal in *Second Birth*. Indeed, this collection marked the beginning of "an interval of silence," as he and his biographers have called the years without publication of new poetry or prose that followed (Fleishman 1990, 172). Only in 1940 did Pasternak return to origi-nal writing.

This personal and creative crisis was aggravated by the events taking place in Soviet Russia at the time. In 1932 the Central Committee of the Communist Party abolished all literary schools and associations and moved decisively toward consolidating its control over all writers' activities and their artistic production. In 1934 the nationalization of literature was completed with the establishment of the Union of Soviet Writers, approved by the First Congress of Soviet Writers in 1934. Unions were also established in other fields of art. These unions transmitted the guidelines of the party and implemented the official new artistic style called "socialist realism" that was introduced by Gorky at that First Congress of Soviet writers. As defined in the newspaper *Pravda* of 6 May 1934, socialist realism demanded from the artist "truthfulness" and "an historically concrete portrayal of reality in its revolutionary development." Writers were now treated as builders of a new life and "engineers of human souls." But even before the formation of the Union of Soviet Writers the party had tightened its grip on literature, and censorship had become more brutal. Pasternak's *Safe Conduct* was banned in 1933 and was not published again until the 1980s. The ban distressed Pasternak immensely and contributed to his creative hiatus. But he was not altogether inactive on the literary scene, for his 1933 trip to Georgia with a group of Soviet writers helped him to become creative in an unexpected way: it refocused Pasternak's attention on translation.

Translations

By 1934 Stalin had acquired unlimited power in the Soviet Union, and he maintained it until his death in 1953. That this regime was one of terror and suffering for vast numbers of Soviet citizens is well known today and becoming increasingly better documented with the opening of former Soviet archives.[5] Fear was not the only means of control of the population. A powerful ideology and cult of Stalin's personality became another tool in the manipulation of the masses. Stalin and other "spiritual teachers" had to create "a mirage that they tried to make people believe by claiming that the mirage was more real than reality, that it was reality" (*Utopia,* 276). In the process of creating this "virtual reality" writers had to play an important role.

Pasternak's role in Soviet literature in those days was ambiguous. He was the only one among the remaining great poets of his generation who had not been disgraced by the regime; and he maintained, despite being criticized for formalism in the past, the reputation of a major Soviet poet. With Esenin and Mayakovsky dead, Mandelstam exiled to Voronezh (a town in the southern part of Russia) after his arrest for writing a satirical poem about Stalin, Tsvetaeva having immigrated to the West, and Akhmatova in obscurity and proud isolation, it was perhaps not surprising that Pasternak would be distinguished by the regime. After all, a first-rate poet could be a valuable cultural asset—particularly one like Pasternak, who seemed to have had a change of heart and made efforts to conform to the new Soviet literary requirements. This became clear when at the First Congress of Soviet Writers Nikolai Bukharin, a prominent and still influential although already doomed politician (he was sentenced to death on charges of treason and conspiracy and executed in 1938), delivered a speech supportive of Pasternak's work. Gorky was Pasternak's other ardent and influential supporter.

As Pasternak was thus lifted into the front rank of Soviet writers, he inevitably became involved with the politics of literary activities. In 1935 he was ordered, against his will, to go to Paris on short notice to attend the international Congress of Writers for the Defense of Culture organized by a group of prominent French writers—André Malraux and André Gide, among others—concerned about and working to counteract the spread of fascism. Pasternak's speech at the congress was short and reflected his resistance to the bureaucratization of literature and his strong belief in creative freedom—a viewpoint that could be interpreted against fascist as well as socialist totalitarianism: "Poetry will always remain that celebrated height, higher than any Alps, which lies in the grass underfoot, so that one needs only to bend down in order to see it and pick it up from the ground. It will always be simpler than the things one can discuss at meetings; it will always remain an organic function of the happiness of the human being, who is overfilled with the blessed gift of rational speech, and therefore the more happiness there is on earth the easier it will be to be an artist" (4:632–33). Pasternak told Isaiah Berlin in 1945 that his speech at the Congress of Writers for the Defense of Culture had a much stronger message against the unionization of writers than it appeared in the minutes of the congress: "Do not organize! Organization means the death of art. Only personal independence is important" (4:883). The trip to Paris was a depressing experience for Pasternak. The exposure to the free world only intensified his disillusionment with Soviet life. It was clear to him that upon return he would have to come to terms with reality in order to maintain "his personal independence in light of the profound falseness of the official status he had been accorded" (Fleishman 1990, 193). For better or worse—but probably for the better—his high official status in Soviet literature was considerably reduced after Stalin pronounced Mayakovsky "the best Soviet poet" in a 5 December 1935 issue of *Pravda*. Pasternak was relieved that he did not have to play the role of the premier Soviet poet any longer, but he also had to accept that from that time on his position among Soviet writers became increasingly marginalized.

By the end of the Second Five-Year Plan (1933–1937) Pasternak had fallen from grace. In 1936 the most oppressive period in Soviet history began with the Kamenev-Zinov'ev trial, and a reign of terror was unleashed for the next few years in Russia. No one was spared as whole segments of the population were accused of and prosecuted for Trotskyism, espionage, treason, and other fabricated crimes in Stalin's final drive to gain the nation's complete submission— if not loyalty. The punishment for political crimes consisted of the death penalty or long sentences in forced labor camps. The "Great Terror" claimed the lives of many of Pasternak's friends, among them Paolo Iashvili, who committed suicide; Titsian Tabidze; Boris Pilnyak; and Osip Mandelstam. It is truly miraculous that Pasternak himself was not arrested during those grim days of Stalinism, and it is pointless to speculate why that did not happen. Stalin's terror operated on the premise that if a certain proportion of the group is liquidated, "the remainder will be cowed into uncomplaining obedience" (Conquest 1966, 67). However, anyone whom Stalin personally disliked was doomed to vanish in the purges. Pasternak apparently was not on the dictator's list of personal enemies and survived by mere chance, although it was rumored that the attacks in the press against him were engineered by Stalin himself, who had supposedly read his 1936 collection of poems and been disgusted by it (Fleishman 1990, 208). It was during that horrifying period of Russian history that Pasternak ceased to be a "premier" Soviet poet. A 1937 article in the journal *Oktiabr'* (*October*) criticized the earlier attempt of the literary authorities to honor Pasternak as a "premier Soviet poet" in 1934 and proclaimed "the fading of his talent." He was assigned only a secondary role in Soviet literature as a translator of national minority writers, primarily on the basis of his translations of Georgian poetry (Fleishman 1990, 209–10). But this peripheral position provided a sort of shelter for Pasternak and relieved him from the pressure of writing pro-Stalinist poetry during the worst years of the Great Terror. It also allowed him to devote himself almost completely to the art of translation, at which he began to excel. This newly discovered vocation saved him from Akhmatova's fate: relegation to complete silence, isolation, and poverty.

In addition to translating a number of Soviet minority poets into Russian, Pasternak made an outstanding contribution to the translation of major works of European literature into Russian. Sinyavsky points out that Pasternak's translations created their own chapter in the poet's literary biography (Sinyavsky 1978, 97). He translated mostly from the languages he knew best: German, English, and French. But he also worked from Georgian, Armenian, Ukrainian, Polish, and Hungarian using interlinear translations done by others for him. Rilke was the first poet Pasternak had attempted to translate while still a student in 1910–1913. In 1917 he made a translation of Heinrich von Kleist's play

The Broken Jug, published in Gorky's journal, *The Contemporary.* Among the Western European authors he translated were Goethe, Schiller, and Hans Sachs from German; William Shakespeare, Lord Byron, Percy Bysshe Shelley, Sir Walter Raleigh, and Ben Jonson from English (his translations of Shakespeare were particularly well known and respected); and Paul Verlaine, André Gide, Emil Verhaeren, among others, from French.

Pasternak's first success as a translator came in the 1930s when he rendered a few lyrics of Georgian poets. Among them were two blatantly programmatic odes to Stalin, written in a standard eulogistic manner and published in a 1934 issue of *Pravda.* These two pieces were "a political compromise" (Fleishman 1990, 176), but apart from them Pasternak had a genuine interest in popularizing the work of his Georgian friends in Russia. For the remainder of his life he continued translating Georgian poets, among them Paolo Iashvili, Titsian Tabidze, Vazha Pshavela, Akakii Tsereteli, Georgii Leonidze, and Simon Chikovani, to name but a few. Characteristically, Pasternak was dissatisfied with his translations since he felt uncomfortable working from a language he did not know at all, and in a 1933 letter to Tabidze he apologized for the "crude" rendition of his poetry: "all translations contain some violence against the original, regardless of whether they are bad or good, mine are more of the former variety. I probably vulgarize you because every artist in the course of his work forms his own idea of the permanence of his word, and mine is crude: in it dilettantism is badly mixed with life" (5:341). Tabidze, on the contrary, was impressed by Pasternak's accurate rendition of the intonational patterns and the "inner melody" of his lyrics (Gifford 1977, 149).

In the case of the Georgian poets, Pasternak seemed not to have had any problems with the "inner melody" of the verse since he knew many of the poets personally and was enchanted by all things Georgian. He counted Tabidze and Iashvili among his closest friends and described them as a "constitutive part" of his personal world ("Autobiographical Sketch," 4:344). He considered their fate, together with that of Tsvetaeva, who committed suicide in 1941 after her return to the Soviet Union from the West in 1938, his greatest tragedy ("Autobiographical Sketch," 4:344). Pasternak's words about the poetry of Iashvili and Tabidze are saturated with a deep understanding of their emotional potential and their relation to the surrounding world. He wrote in 1946: "Memories about the legends and impulses that inspired these translations, as well as the details of the environment in which they were done, came together as a whole world, far-away and precious. . . ."[6] What made Pasternak's translations successful was his own conception of art, which applied also to the art of translation itself, as an expression of displacement and emotional force rather than the slavish reproduction of a model (*Safe Conduct,* 4:187).

But despite his rewarding experience as a translator of Georgian poets, it was his translating from German and English that offered particularly gratifying, although challenging, experiences for him. Since the Russian tradition in translation from these two languages was rich and had produced a great number of superb works, Pasternak had to compete with such famous and well-established masters as Mikhail Lozinskii and Samuil Marshak, both of whom were excellent translators of Shakespeare. Yet his own renditions of Shakespeare and Goethe remain respectable achievements among the translations of foreign classics into Russian in the modern era. Pasternak's success is not ultimately owing to his ability to make the words of the classics accessible to the contemporary audience without losing the authentic power of their work. In "Zapiski perevodchika" ("Notes of a Translator," 1943) he explains his views on translation. In his opinion, a direct textual correspondence between an original and its translation is senseless because it produces "pale retellings," whereas the essence of a translation lies in the power of its artistic expression (4:393). Pasternak writes: "The relation between an original and its translation must be that between a base and its derivative, between a tree trunk and its branch. The translation must come from an author who has experienced the effect of the original long before he starts work. It must be born from the original and its historical consequence" (4:393). In his "Zamechaniia k perevodam iz Shekspira" ("Notes on Translations from Shakespeare," 1946–1956), Pasternak reinforces the same idea in a more laconic and precise form: "Like the original, the translation must produce an impression of life, not literariness" (4:413).

Shakespeare was among Pasternak's favorites, and he translated a great number of his works, including *Hamlet, Romeo and Juliet, Antony and Cleopatra, Othello, Henry IV* (first and second parts), *Macbeth,* and *King Lear. Hamlet* was of particular significance for Pasternak, and a close reading of the translation helps readers' understanding of Pasternak, since this play clearly conveys "lyrical reflections and moods of the poet at this time" (Fleishman 1990, 218) and because of its unmistakable connections with *Doctor Zhivago.* Pasternak had first attempted *Hamlet* in 1924, but only in 1939 did he seriously undertake this project at the request of Vsevolod Meyerkhold (1874–1940), the great and justly renowned avant-garde stage director. Meyerkhold was among the generation of artists whom Pasternak admired in his youth and felt honored to work for later. However, Meyerkhold's long-cherished project to stage *Hamlet* was never realized. In 1939 he was arrested as an "enemy of the people" and brutally tortured in prison. He completely vanished in 1940, and the circumstances of his death remain unknown to this day. Any association with

Meyerkhold's name became dangerous. Yet instead of abandoning the project, Pasternak, who anticipated his own arrest any day, rushed to finish it.[7] Pasternak described his work on *Hamlet* as "happiness and salvation."[8] Translating *Hamlet* turned for him into a lifetime preoccupation, as he produced at least twelve different versions of the play. He put all considerable talent as a translator into this work because he saw the parallels between Hamlet's and his own situations.

Pasternak's notes on his *Hamlet* translations shed light both on his approach to Shakespeare's language and his attitude toward the character of Hamlet. Pasternak finds Shakespeare's language rich yet sometimes excessively rhetorical and metaphorical, which "hurts naturalness" and "verisimilitude" ("Translations from Shakespeare," 413). On the other hand he fully appreciates Shakespeare's use of "widely different stylistic extremes" and his ability to make the verse episodes sound like "rough drafts for prose" (414). For Pasternak the power of Shakespeare's poetry is manifested above all in its "being a free sketch that knows no restraint" (414). It is Shakespeare's linguistic "sketchiness" that permitted Pasternak his own expressive freedom in the translation. He gives up much of Shakespeare's metaphoric language, difficult for the contemporary reader, and paraphrases it without simplifying. Pasternak's *Hamlet* is also original because it responds to the political atmosphere in Stalinist Russia through subtle linguistic manipulations in Shakespeare's play (Gifford 1977, 153–56).

Taken in Pasternak's historical context, the figure of Hamlet becomes the poet's "alter ego, assimilating features of Pasternak himself, of Meyerkhold, and of their entire generation" (Fleishman 1990, 220). In Pasternak's view *Hamlet* is not "a tragedy of will" or "a drama of a weak character," as the critics claim, but rather a drama of duty, self-denial, and self-sacrifice ("Shakespeare," 416). Pasternak's Hamlet is an honest and courageous hero who upon the discovery that "appearance and reality do not coincide," faces the world of lies alone (416). And it is only by chance that Hamlet, like Pasternak, becomes a "judge of his time and a servant of the future" ("Shakespeare," 416).

In the "Notes on Translations from Shakespeare," Pasternak also offers his insights into other works by Shakespeare. Thus, *Romeo and Juliet* is a tragedy of the power of first innocent love and of its juxtaposition to the world of lies and hatred (417–18). Pasternak observes that the play is written for the most part in blank verse, especially in conversations between Romeo and Juliet, a form chosen by Shakespeare in order to avoid the effect of declamation. For Pasternak the dialogues between Romeo and Juliet become, despite their "prosaic form," examples of the highest poetry, through which one can sense the "simplicity and freshness of prose" (418). This echoes Pasternak's earlier state-ment at the First Writer's Congress that "pure prose in its primordial intensity is poetry" (4:632). In the "Notes" Pasternak once again affirms originality as the highest principle of art: "The highest thing that art can dream about is to listen to its own voice, its always new and unusual voice. It does not need sweet sounds. It is not sounds but truths that are alive in its soul" (418). Phrased in this way, Pasternak's comment not only confirms his old aesthetic principles and his understanding of the artistic truth but implicitly also takes issue with the prescribed formulaic principles of socialist realism.

Closest to *Romeo and Juliet* for Pasternak was *King Lear,* and he called both of them "quiet tragedies" because positive characters in these works are irrational, contradictory, and quiet whereas the villains are rational, eloquent, and do not hesitate to cover up their vile deeds with the concepts of responsibil-ity and honor ("Translations from Shakespeare," 4:429). Pasternak also ob-served a similarity between the tragedies in their representation of love as an object of persecution. But whereas in *Romeo and Juliet* it is a love between the two young people, in *King Lear* it is love and devotion of the daughter for her old father, which translates for Pasternak into love and devotion for truth, a quality important for Pasternak's own moral persona.

In his discussion of *Othello,* Pasternak displays a much broader interpreta-tion of the play's meaning than its racial juxtaposition might suggest. Accord-ing to Pasternak, Shakespeare was concerned in this tragedy with aspects of Christian ethics; he was not interested in the racial origin of human beings but rather in what they became in life. Othello therefore appears in Shakespeare as a historical man and a true Christian, whereas Iago, for Pasternak, is a "prehis-toric animal" ("Translations from Shakespeare," 4:421).

In general, Shakespeare was for Pasternak a kind of father and master of realism, and his works allowed the poet to take a closer look at the nature of great art and the power of language. Shakespeare's most prominent achieve-ment, for Pasternak, is in the originality of his realism that makes us see the vulgar and narrow-minded side of life ("Translations from Shakespeare," 4:430). What Pasternak found especially familiar in Shakespeare was the element of vagueness and open-endedness, the characteristics so typical for Pasternak's own conception of realism. It is these characteristics that underlie truth in art. Pasternak claims that art, like life, cannot be understood completely and does not survive "without a share of darkness and insufficiency" ("Notes," 4:423). In other words, the realism that Shakespeare taught Pasternak and other writers was based on creativity and imagination and thus allowed for freedom in any political situation. It is no wonder that Hamlet's famous soliloquy "To be or not to be" published in 1947 in Pasternak's rendering has only a slight resemblance to the original as well as to previous Russian versions, as Vladimir Markov has demonstrated.[9] The five lines that Pasternak inserted into the text read like "a lyrical confession camouflaged as a translation" and make a strong statement against the oppressive forces of his time.

The voluminous translations alone would assure Pasternak a notable place in the history of Russian literature. They remain among the most accomplished achievements in translation into Russian. Although translating could never suppress Pasternak's yearning for his own writing, it provided an outlet for his creative energies and turned into a source of material survival for him during the darkest years of Soviet history.

CHAPTER FIVE

On Early Trains

When after the First Congress of Soviet Writers in 1934 the literary-political situation had gradually become more and more constricting, Pasternak devoted himself primarily to translations, a vocation he followed for the rest of his life. The number of his own original works published during the last two and a half decades of his life, therefore, diminished considerably and consisted only of two thin collections of wartime poetry and the novel *Doctor Zhivago,* published in the West in 1957. Moreover, the second of these two collections, *Earth's Vastness,* 1945, contains a large number of revised poems from the first, *On Early Trains,* 1943. With socialist realism as a cultural model, Pasternak found it difficult to pursue his old path in literature. He needed to find another kind of language with new images, fewer tropes, and simplified syntax in order to meet at least in some way the acceptable cultural standards. In order to achieve "simplicity" he had to forsake his personal idiom, and he attempted a more restrained and sometimes, as in some of his war poems, impersonal style.

Pasternak's quest for the "purification" of his style should be linked to both external and internal factors. With the pressure of the literary authorities on Soviet writers to comply with the rules of socialist realism, Pasternak could no longer preserve the strikingly individualist and self-reflexive style of his early poetry and prose. Whereas in his earlier writings his sole responsibility was to himself and his art, now he was responsible before the readers and the Soviet literary institutions. In a letter to his cousin Olga Freidenberg of 30 July 1944 Pasternak wrote: "My tragedy is not in the exterior difficulties of life, my tragedy is in the fact that I am a man of letters and have things to say; I have my thoughts, but we do not have literature and under the present circumstances, it cannot and will not exist."[1]

Pasternak's internal desire to be accessible to his readers also appears considerable. He sincerely wanted to find a stylistic level at which he could reach a larger part of the reading public. The adjustment to the tastes of the new Soviet reader was possible for Pasternak only by cutting the ties to his avant-garde modernist past. It is therefore not surprising, perhaps, that in his "Autobiographical Sketch" from 1957 he renounces his literary style before 1940 and criticizes it for "the general disintegration of form" and "the impoverishment of thought" (4:328). This statement must be read at least partially as Pasternak's genuine indictment of his modernist period and his commitment to reach the verbal simplicity and lucidity of Russian classical poetry exemplified by Pushkin. But his seeming embarrassment and irritation about the modernist works that brought him recognition in the West are less an open and voluntary embracing of Soviet socialist realist doctrine than a major Russian writer reflecting on his honest determination to change his literary course.[2]

Pasternak's speech at the third plenary meeting of the Board of the Union of Soviet Writers in Minsk in 1936, published in the newspaper *Pravda* under the title "O skromnosti i smelosti" ("About Modesty and Boldness")[3], reflects the complexity of his situation and his motivation to change the poetic route. In this speech he tries to accept historical necessity yet at the same time attempts to remain loyal to his moral principles. In this speech Pasternak defines his attitude toward socialist realism and the growing bureaucratization of literature and comments on his own role as a Soviet writer. Taking into account the harsh political reality at the time, Pasternak's speech appears as a courageous statement about his difficulties in following the official literary procedures approved by the party and his fundamental belief in the freedom of creativity and originality of writing.

At first glance there seems to be a profound contradiction in his speech: while stressing freedom of literary expression Pasternak accepts socialist realism, the style that unquestionably modifies and limits creative potential. At a closer look, however, Pasternak's understanding of socialist realism is characteristically idiosyncratic. For him socialist realism can be traced back to Tolstoy's realism that exposes "noisily exaggerated and rhetorical" aspects of literature through "unmaskings" and "bluntness" (4:634). It is therefore shameful that sometimes socialist realism becomes "noisy" and "rhetorical" in its depiction of life and appears vulgar and false. Through juxtaposing the sincerity and ethical principles of Tolstoyan writing to the morally corrupt principles of the majority of socialist realist works, Pasternak emphasizes the moral superiority of Tolstoy's heritage in Russian literature and suggests that the growing political profiteerism and the vulgar, self-serving practices of contemporary Soviet literature are incompatible with it.

The juxtaposition of the old classical and the new Soviet literary traditions acquires especially strong moral overtones when Pasternak compares the professional behavior of prerevolutionary and Soviet writers. Whereas in the nineteenth century Pushkin and Tiutchev reached prominence because of their books' merits, Pasternak accuses many Soviet writers of seeking fame through advertising themselves in officially organized meetings with the public (4:635). For Pasternak, self-advertising represents a betrayal of the moral stature of literature and a step toward establishing a new model of literary life, "repulsive in its cheap brilliance, false and artificial" (4:635). Pasternak declares his solid devotion to the moral tradition of classical Russian literature and expresses his concern with the more and more common attitude among critics and writers toward the writing of poetry as some kind of a mechanism whose "output is directly proportional to the labor applied" (4:636). To Pasternak, such a mechanistic understanding of the writing process, fostered by official literary politics, presents a serious threat to the very nature of creativity.

But Pasternak does not mean to battle socialist realism. His tone toward the end of the speech is reconciliatory: he is willing to make changes and announces his transition to a new creative path. Although he is not ready to erase his past completely, the pressing circumstances ("I have no choice," 4:637) dictate his decision. Without going into detail about what the future expects from him, Pasternak declares his own program:

> For a while I am going to write badly—from my previous point of view—until I get used to the novelty of the themes and propositions that I want to touch on. My writing will be bad in several respects, starting with the artistic, for this leap from one position to another will have to be accomplished in a space that has become rarefied by journalism and abstractions and is poor and vague in imagery. My writing will also be bad in regard to the aims for the sake of which it is being accomplished, because on these themes that are common to us all I will not be able to speak in the common language. . . . (4:637)

In reference to his new "bad" style, which should potentially lead to full-fledged "good" socialist realism, he says that for a while he will write like a shoemaker and has already published two such "shoemaker's" poems in a January 1936 issue of the newspaper *Izvestiia* (*News*).[4] But whereas the poet recognizes his temporary reconciliation with the shoemaker's style, he also expresses his strong belief that art must be innovative, courageous, and unexpected: "Art without risk and spiritual self-sacrifice is unthinkable; freedom and boldness of imagination have to be gained in practice, and it is here that the unexpected that we spoke about earlier is appropriate; do not expect any directives in this respect" (4:637–38).

Despite his courageous words about the freedom of expression as the basis of art, Pasternak saw himself caught more and more in tradition and authority and the dictates of the reading public. Thus his next collection of poems, *Na rannikh poezdakh* (*On Early Trains*), was in line with his commitment to appease the public. Not surprising, some poems of the collection are virtually indistinguishable from the flood of mediocre poetry printed in the Soviet Union at that time and appear bland, clichéd, and unimaginative. *On Early Trains* also projects to the reader the image of the politically obliging Soviet writer that Pasternak has now become, his avant-garde modernism completely purged by socialist realism. In *On Early Trains* Pasternak makes a stylistic leap that negates almost everything of what preceded it and emphasizes the author's sharper and realistic perception of the present, his Hamletian self-sacrifice, and the artist's duty to serve his people and his country. It is fair to say that in *On Early Trains* matter and reality return to Pasternak's poetry as his language becomes more representational in comparison with his earlier writing.[5]

On Early Trains originally consisted of four cycles: "Voennye mesiatsy" ("War Months," 1941), "Khudozhnik" ("The Artist," 1936), "Putevye zapiski" ("Travel Notes," 1936), and "Peredelkino" (1941). The twenty-five poems included in the collection were written between 1935 and 1941. In its selection of poems *On Early Trains* is close to Pasternak's following collection, *Zemnoi prostor* (*Earth's Vastness*). *Earth's Vastness* included, with the exception of one, all poems from the cycle "Peredelkino": "Prisiaga" ("Oath") was replaced by the poem "Val's s chertovshinoi" ("A Waltz with Devilry"). This collection also contained all poems from the cycle "War Months" with the exception of "Strashnaia skazka" ("A Frightening Tale") and "Zastava" ("A Frontier Post"). In his 1945 book, *Izbrannoe* (*Selected Works*), Pasternak combined the poems from *On Early Trains* and *Earth's Vastness* into one cycle, and the 1989–1992 collection of his works follows by and large the 1945 edition of his *Selected Works* but unites both *On Early Trains* and *Earth's Vastness* under the title *On Early Trains*.

The quality of the poems included in *On Early Trains* varies dramatically, from contemplative and serene pictures of nature in "Peredelkino" to trivial and ideologically programmatic war lyrics. The publication of this collection was initiated by the literary authorities in order to demonstrate their rehabilitation of an author who in the mid 1930s had been considered too aesthetic and bourgeois (Fleishman 1990, 232). In exchange for an opportunity to publish his original works again, Pasternak had to prove to both the authorities and the public that their trust in him as a true Soviet poet was justified, so he composed what was expected of him. The official critical reception of *On Early Trains* was warm, but Pasternak himself found the collection embarrassing and consistently apologized for the small number and eclectic selection of poems. In a letter to Freidenberg he characterized the book as "too skinny, very belated, and too dismal to be talked about."[6] He added that it contained only a few "healthy" pages in the cycle "Peredelkino" and described them as his ideal of writing from now on (5:423). Pasternak was even harsher in his critical evaluation of the book in a letter to the writer Daniil Danin, calling *On Early Trains* "a useless book."[7]

Pasternak's wish to shift stylistic gears in *On Early Trains* is expressed in his poem "Staryi park" ("Old Park") (Sinyavsky 1978, 106). The hero of the poem has been a soldier in World War II and now reflects on a play he would like to write after the war ends. He says that "There, in a provincial's language" he would like to "clarify and set in order / The unimaginable course / Of a fantastic life" (2:46). "A provincial's language" was to provide linguistic purity, if not naïveté, free from Pasternak's early metaphorization and hermetic symbolism. The use of a provincial's language thus signifies Pasternak's rejection of the elite literature to which his early poetry unquestionably belongs and a turn toward the route charted by the official literary politics aimed at the mass of ordinary Soviet readers.

The first cycle of the collection *On Early Trains* consists of five lyrics written in 1936. Four of these are united under the title "Khudozhnik" ("The Artist") and cited by Pasternak as an example of "shoemaker's work" at the Minsk plenum. "The Artist" is inspired by Pasternak's visit to the Caucasus and his friendship with the Georgian poet Georgii Leonidze, who embodies the qualities of a true artist. "The Artist" has an autobiographical touch: like Pasternak himself, the hero is a writer in the prime of his life. He looks back on his work and feels shame and dissatisfaction with it. He begins to shun his fame and feels an urgent need for change. This forces him to confront the questions that Pasternak himself faced at that time: his role in art, his relationship with time, and whose side to choose. Whereas in the past he was concerned primarily with himself, disregarding history, now he feels it is his duty to respond actively to the historical time. Through his hero Pasternak reiterates his discomfort with fame and honor, which mean nothing to him in comparison with poetry itself. And for the sake of poetry the artist is ready to sacrifice "friendship, reason, conscience, daily life" (2:9). Accordingly the artist declares his unbending allegiance to poetry, for which he is ready to forsake his friends and daily life. Not quite amounting to "a provincial's language," this poem is hardly a "shoemaker's" creation, but on par with the lightest lyrics of *Second Birth,* it is unburdened by linguistic and syntactical complexities.

"Bezvremenno umershemu" ("To the Untimely Deceased," 1936), the second poem of the cycle, was written on the death of the young poet Nikolai

Dement'ev. Dement'ev's suicide in 1935 triggers Pasternak's memories of Mayakovsky's and Esenin's deaths. Suicides were symptomatic of many artists' extremely difficult personal conditions of adjusting to their social and political environments. Moreover, many of them felt depressed because of the press's attacks against them. Pasternak himself felt despondent about his situation in literature and tried to take his life in 1932.[8] But what this poem says is that the artist should not capitulate before the critical reactions of his contemporaries against him, for history itself will judge right and wrong deeds. The poet's heritage does not die but will be rediscovered and appreciated by the next generation (2:12). In "To the Untimely Deceased" Pasternak thus expresses the idea of the poet becoming a part of life or nature after his death. This idea of the artist's immortality will resurface more prominently later in *Doctor Zhivago.*

"The Artist" is followed by the short cycle "Iz letnikh zapisok" ("From Summer Notes"), composed and published in 1936 and devoted to his Tiflis friends. As in *Second Birth,* in this cycle Georgia personifies the land of eternal beauty and bliss. Pasternak praises nature and the sky, colors and smells, as well as the prosperity and happiness of the people. He compares Georgia to a rose: as a rose is full of petals, Georgia's rich layers of experience are countless (2:21). Pasternak's idealization of Georgia seems to be even more overstated in this cycle than it had been in *Second Birth,* for he appears blatantly to adore this "land of those born with a silver spoon" (2:18). The difference lies in the degree of metaphorization: whereas in *Second Birth* Georgia still appeared in its metaphorical majesty and magnificence, now the image of Pasternak's beloved land is more representational, more material and concrete, with a focus on the details of daily life. And among the poet's heroes, on par with the poets Iashvili and Tabidze, readers find a simple shepherd in the mountains. The contact with ordinary people emerges as a new theme ("You are nothing without them [people]," 2:15). It is a new kind of experience that Pasternak seeks, defined by real time and space and different from his early quest for the timeless aesthetic moment. Pasternak's vision of Georgia, this time conveyed with more linguistic economy than before, projects a sense of a deepening spiritual bond between the poet and the country, and his love for this land appears more tangible and earthly than it was in *Second Birth.*

The third cycle of the book, "Peredelkino," includes poems written mostly between 1940 and 1942, with only one of them, "Zazimki" ("First Frost"), appearing later, in 1944. Peredelkino is a village some twelve miles southwest of Moscow, where a number of houses were built by the Soviet authorities as a privilege for the prominent men of letters. The implication of this official gesture was clear: the writer had to be cooperative with the party policy in literature in order to receive a house in Peredelkino. Pasternak acquired a house there in 1936, and together with his Moscow apartment Peredelkino became his permanent residence for the rest of his life. The cycle "Peredelkino" consists of eleven poems focusing on nature, the changing of the seasons, and the poet's reflections. In "Peredelkino" readers see the poet at rest, far from the stress and pressures of city life, finding peace in the small wonders of nature and satisfaction in garden work. In the poem "Letnii den'" ("Summer Day," 1940) the poet is shown as a hardworking gardener who enjoys a hot summer day and his closeness to the earth and nature. If earlier Pasternak's impulse was to defamiliarize nature in language, now his descriptions are more mimetic. With his reader in mind, he writes like a guide to some small familiar joys of life: a bonfire in his vegetable garden, the warmth of the earth, the heat of the sun, and the night filled with the smell of lilac. In comparison with his early style the imagery now is tighter and can be traced to his more concrete interests in the simple pleasures of life. If "Summer Day" appeals more to the senses, the next poem, "Sosny" ("Pines," 1941), shows the poet in a more pensive mood, contemplating his unity with nature. As the poet thinks of the life of the pines, he temporarily loses his fear of the ineluctable in life: pain, suffering, and death—because the unity with nature makes him feel immortal.

The imagery of nature in *Second Birth* contains both styles: Pasternak's early dazzling technique is not altogether erased; but the trend toward simplicity and more conventional realism in representation is clearly present. The poems of "Peredelkino" are very intelligible. As his imagery becomes sparser, his mood becomes more pensive. Now in his fifties, Pasternak strikes a more somber note and undertakes to express his feelings of aging and the coming end in a tone and voice more defined, controlled, and philosophical than before. In the poem "Lozhnaia trevoga" ("False Alarm," 1941) Pasternak's thoughts about death take shape against the background of the dying nature of fall and the approaching cold of winter, dark nights, and howling winds: "From my hall window, / I see the postponed approach / Of my final days drawing near. / Having cleared its paths, from the hill, / winter stares at my life, / Through the horror of yellow leaves" (2:25).

"False Alarm" is close in its mood to another lyric in the cycle entitled "Gorod" ("The City," 1940), in which the aging poet complains about the discomforts of country living in wintertime. The snowbound house, the cold of the rooms, an ice-covered well, and slippery stairs are part of his rather monotonous and isolated daily existence in Peredelkino. The specter of death almost predictably rises in this winter landscape. But much more pronounced than death in this poem, as well as in others, is the theme of alienation and loneliness. In his retrospective mental journey the poet travels to the city in an attempt to find comfort in its urban conveniences but unexpectedly experiences nothing but disdain for it. The city appears hostile, indifferent, even condescending toward the harsh conditions of life in the country. The city, quite simply, snobbishly ignores the countryside. And whereas in his youth the poet created an idol out of the city and felt flattered by its arrogance, now, as an older man, he finds unappealing what once seduced him. Pasternak's unfolding critical attitude toward the city is only part of the general shift of his perceptions. With the declining role of linguistic virtuosity, basic human issues and concerns become the focus of his attention, and form and content now acquire an almost tangibly direct correlation. There is an analogy between his altered perception of the city and his critical assessment of his earlier writing: he dislikes both for their elitism and detachment from ordinary human concerns. Although he cannot tolerate the physical discomforts of country living, he finds the city emotionally uncomfortable: "There is no life in the country in the winter, / But the city is full of indifference / Toward imperfections of life" (2:29). By analogy, it can be said that whereas he feels—still—uncomfortable with his new style, his old style feels foreign to him.

The poem "On Early Trains" (1941), from which the cycle takes its name, refers to the poet's commuting between his Peredelkino and Moscow residences and magnifies Pasternak's growing need to be close to human issues, to his land and his people. His trips to Moscow bring him into contact with ordinary people on commuter trains and make him take a closer look at them. The poem expresses his profound compassion and tenderness toward his countrymen: "Through the hardships of the past / And the years of wars and poverty / I silently recognized Russia's / Unrepeatable features. / Beyond admiration / I watched—worshipping. / Here were peasant women, people from working class suburbs, / Students, locksmiths. / There were no traces of servility in them / imposed by poverty, / Bad news and discomforts / They carried like masters" (2:35–36).

One other poem of the cycle that should be mentioned here is "Zazimki" ("First Frost," 1944). In six quatrains it describes a November landscape touched by the first signs of winter. It has been called by Vladimir Weidlé "one of the finest instances of [Pasternak's] new and truly unheard-of simplicity."[9] Analyzing Pasternak's new style, Weidlé argues that one of the main features distinguishing it from earlier work is not the use of a simplified vocabulary but rather the approach to identical words from a different angle of vision. If in his early poetry Pasternak's words acted as images or metaphors, now "the lyrical merger of the inner with the outer was brought under control. Imagery was supplanted by representation and the lyrical 'I' by 'feeling near to all things,' by the poet's broadened 'experience'" (178). This comment is certainly true for "First Frost": "The river is ice-bound and the osier frozen, / And the black sky is set / Above the bare ice / Like a mirror on the mirror table. / Before it stands, at the crossroads, / Half-covered by the snow, / A birch with a star in her hairdo / And gazes at herself in its glass. / She secretly suspects / That at the last cottage / Winter is full of unbelievable wonders / Like the sky at her height" (2:26). These images, presented with directness and verbal economy, together with the meter—iambic pentameter—remind readers of Pushkin's best nature lyrics. Yet the poem pulls in two directions: toward the classical clarity and concreteness of representation and simultaneously toward rapid impressionistic transitions in the poet's perception of the winter scene. Without the perfected continuity and directness of Pushkinian lyrics, Pasternak's vision contains an impressionist touch, as he is unwilling to strip his language completely of the metaphoric dimension. Pasternak's poetry meant, for the rest of his life, "the disclosure of hidden relations between things: hypothesis made actual in the concurrence of word and image" (Gifford 1977, 169). In "First Frost," as in the best lines of the "i eredelkino" cycle, Pasternak now manages to tame his former penchant for incessant verbal and syntactical manipulations and to paint his images with more linguistic restraint.

If "Peredelkino" contains some of the best examples of Pasternak's new style, the last cycle, "Stikhi o voine" ("Poems about the War"), written between 1941 and 1944, contains some of the weakest. The "Poems about the War" deal precisely with what the title says, World War II, which began for the Soviet Union on 22 June 1941, when Hitler's army unexpectedly attacked the Soviet borders in flagrant violation of the nonaggression pact signed by both countries in 1939. In order to discuss Pasternak's penultimate collection of poetry more meaningfully, a brief contextual-biographical sketch may be in order here. Hitler hoped for a quick victory over the Soviet Union and sent some 175 divisions against it. The German troops were simultaneously advancing toward Leningrad in the north, toward Moscow in the center, and toward Kiev and Rostov-on-Don in the south. Entire Soviet armies were rapidly defeated in the south, and Kiev and Minsk, the Belorussian capital, fell to the Germans within three months. In the north the Germans tried to capture Leningrad, but although during a nine-hundred-day siege the city was virtually isolated from the rest of the country and the population suffered indescribable hardships, they did not succeed in their effort. Eight hundred thousand people died of starvation, cold, and diseases, but the city remarkably held out. Hitler also hoped to take Moscow, but unlike in 1812 when Muscovites deserted their city for Napoleon's invasion, in

1941 the Russians decided to counterattack and threw all their strength into the defense of their capital. Hitler's armies stood only twenty miles from Moscow but were unable to take the city. As the war continued, the Red Army, although technologically inferior to the German army, began to regain lost positions. The unmatched patriotism of the Soviet people added immensely to the army's determination to drive the Germans out of occupied Russian territories. As early as the winter of 1942 it was clear that Hitler's blitzkrieg against Russia was a failure. His Russian front was overextended; his armies were unprepared for the harshness of the Russian winter and suffered severe losses. As the war dragged on, German chances of winning the Russian front faded rapidly. Despite the renewed offensive on the southern front the following summer, with some one million troops involved, the Germans enjoyed only a brief success and suffered a major defeat in the battle of Stalingrad. Thereafter the Russians began gaining the upper hand in the war and played a decisive role in bringing about Germany's unconditional surrender to the Allied British, American, and Soviet forces on 9 May 1945.

When the German forces approached Moscow and the evacuation eastward of the civilian population began, Pasternak's wife Zinaida and her children were sent to Chistopol', a town in the Tatar Republic 430 miles east of Moscow. Pasternak himself, together with other writers, was assigned to a civilian anti-aircraft brigade. According to numerous accounts, the poet demonstrated great courage during the German bombardment of Moscow, cleaning incendiary bombs from the roof of his apartment building. He also excelled in the two-week military training for which he was called up, and the newspaper *Literaturnaia gazeta* (*Literary Gazette*) of 10 September 1941 announced that Pasternak was among the best of Moscow writers in target-shooting practice.[10]

In October 1941 Pasternak was allowed to join his family in Chistopol', where he remained until the fall of 1942. In 1943 the fifty-three-year-old poet visited the front at Orel with a group of prominent Soviet writers. This two-week trip, in his own words, was important for him because it "liberated" him "internally": "Suddenly everything appeared very close, natural, and accessible, resembling what I usually thought [about the war] rather than what was portrayed [in the official press]."[11] It was also Pasternak's chance to get close to ordinary people fighting for Russia, and it reinforced his wish for closeness with them. Recollecting his encounters with Pasternak during those days, when the poet stayed with the ordinary soldiers, the Soviet army general Gorbatov wrote: "We liked him for his open character and his lively and sympathetic attitude toward people" (*Collected Works,* 4:890). Pasternak published his impressions of the trip in a series of sketches, "V armii" ("In the Army"), published in abridged form in the newspaper *Trud* (*Labor*) on 20 November 1943.

The cycle "Poems about the War" opens with the poem "Strashnaia skazka" ("A Frightening Tale," 1941), which conveys the poet's hope for the eventual victory of the Soviet Union over the German enemy, whom Pasternak labels "Herod in Bethlehem" (2:40). The poem is straightforward and stripped of all metaphor. It focuses on human suffering and especially on the fear of children who will remember the war as a frightening tale. The poet's pain for children mutilated by the war is conveyed in simple direct lines: "A new, better age will come. / The witnesses will disappear. / But the sufferings of children maimed by war / Will not be forgotten" (2:40). Despite its lofty concerns, "A Frightening Tale" is an example of mediocre programmatic Soviet war poetry.

Into that category also fall a large number of his writings from 1941. They are practically indistinguishable from the countless war verses that flooded Soviet newspapers and magazines at the time. They are flatly clichéd and unimaginative. The poem "A Frontier Post" provides a typical example: "And suddenly the skyline explodes; / And burning over the village, / The attacker, hit by a shell, / Falls down like a smoking piece of wood" (2:42). The titles of such poems are unambiguous and tell exactly what each poem is about. "Smelost'" ("Bravery," 1941), for example, describes the courage and self-sacrifice of Soviet soldiers who indefatigably and in harsh conditions fight the enemy. The poet expresses his admiration for their heroism in a predictable manner: "Unknown heroes / Of besieged cities, / I will keep you in the depth of my heart, / Your valor is beyond words" (2:43).

Pasternak hardly focuses on his lyrical self in this cycle, and only in the poem "Bobyl'" ("A Lonely Man," 1941) and the already mentioned "The Old Park" can readers detect a trace of his private feelings in the recording of his loneliness and isolation from his family after their evacuation to Chistopol'. "The Old Park" offers a glimpse into the poet's memories of the old house of his friend Dmitrii Samarin, which now serves as a hospital. Pasternak's private world never dominates the cycle and is generally inconspicuous. Thus in "The Old Park" the hero's recognition of the house does not send him on a personal memory journey but rather opens the pages of heroic Russian history with references to the 1812 Napoleonic invasion of Moscow and the Decembrist and Slavophile heritage.[12]

A few lyrics are inspired by Pasternak's trip to the front at Orel and his conversations with soldiers and officers. One of the most characteristic poems is "Smert' sapera" ("Sapper's Death," 1943), based on a real story of three sappers who receive an assignment to penetrate the German line in order to prepare passages for the Soviet offensive through the barbed wire entanglements. During the operation one sapper is wounded, but realizing that screaming and groaning would attract the attention of the enemy, he suffers heroically before his death: "From pain, he would eat mud, / But he did not betray his brothers with groans. / He did not lose his inborn steadfast peasant nature / Even when he fainted" (2:58). Perhaps the most trite poem of the cycle is "Presledovanie" ("Pursuit," 1944). It describes the devastation and atrocities inflicted on Soviet people and land by the Nazis. The poet's outrage about the rape and murder of a young girl by the Germans is part of his high-flung rhetorical description of the Red Army's revenge for the girl's tragic fate: "Broken thunder clouds stretched in the sky, / And we, like thunder clouds ourselves, / With curses and jokes, / Smashed the enemy's viperous nests" (2:61).

Whereas most critics do not see much artistic merit in the cycle, Hingley defends some of its lyrics, pointing to the wide range in quality (Hingley 1983, 147). He singles out the uncompleted long poem "Zarevo" ("Nightglow," 1943)—consisting of an introduction and one chapter divided into six parts—as an example of "Pasternak's finest war poetry" (149) and a symbol of the poet's hope that the victory over Germany will bring some political freedom at home. On the way home from the front the hero of the poem, Volodia, sees a nightglow in the sky created by the intensive artillery fire near Orel. In this light Moscow appears as a symbol of future happiness that the people are earning by fighting for their country: "He thinks: 'I will experience / What I have not even dreamt of before, / What I have bought with blood and victory / And saw through observation slits'" (2:51). Pasternak does not spare exclamation points for his wishful thoughts of freedom and expanding democracy to be granted the Soviet people after the victorious war ("And horizons with broad perspectives! / And the newness of the people's will!," 2:54). The poem also contains a few bold lines targeting the lack of freedom of creative expression: "I think if we did not embellish / Our simple thoughts, / With your permission, we would also write / As Hemingway or Priestley" (1:52). In other words, if Soviet writers did not have to beautify the picture of life under socialism for their readers, they would be true to themselves and write well. While Hingley's assertion about the courage and value of Pasternak's political message in "Nightglow" may be justified, it is hard to find other redeeming qualities in this poem. At its best, it fits the tradition of Russian civil poetry concerned with social injustice in society and preoccupied with its amelioration;[13] at its worst, the poem's artistic quality is weakened by the poet's overflowing emotionalism, and it is awkwardly moralistic in its contrasting of the virtuous young soldier and his adulterous wife who is involved in a relationship with a black marketeer. Nevertheless, during the hard war years the general public needed precisely what the poem con-

133

tained: an optimistic tone and the illusion that a brighter future was ahead. The introduction to the poem was published in the 15 October 1943 issue of the most prestigious party newspaper, *Pravda*. Since Pasternak did not belong to the group of Soviet writers *Pravda* usually favored, the paper's publication of his poetry meant a special honor and personal success for the poet. But it was only due to the extraordinary circumstances of the war that this happened, and the success, moreover, was partial at best since *Pravda* rejected the first chapter of "Nightglow," submitted by Pasternak after the publication of its introduction. After the rejection Pasternak stopped working on the poem, and it remained unfinished.

One other poem, "Pamiati Mariny Tsvetaevoi" ("In Memory of Marina Tsvetaeva," 1943), stands out as unconnected with any of the collection's themes. It was not originally selected by Pasternak for publication in his collected works for reasons of censorship, although he read it at his poetry readings in the 1940s. Only in 1965 did the first five stanzas of this poem appear in the first issue of the literary journal *New World*. In the most recent edition of Pasternak's collected works this poem is included in the cycle *On Early Trains*. Pasternak admired Tsvetaeva's poetic genius throughout his life and was profoundly affected by the "purity and strength" of her talent ("Autobiographical Sketch," 4:359). The two poets' backgrounds were similar: they both grew up in Moscow in highly cultured families; both adored poetry and idolized Rilke throughout their lives; both resisted the politicization of literature; and both had difficulty adjusting to the Soviet regime. Pasternak had always felt a spiritual affinity with Tsvetaeva, but her emigration from the country—initially to Prague in 1922 and then to Paris—made their relationship more distant. However, when Pasternak visited France in 1935, they met and she inquired about her possible return to the Soviet Union. In 1939 Tsvetaeva did return with her teenage son to be reunited with her family, but the reunion was not a happy one. Her husband, Sergei Efron, had left for Russia earlier, at the height of Stalinist purges, and vanished there without a trace. Their daughter followed him and also became a victim of Stalinism, spending sixteen years in prison camps. Tsvetaeva's husband was arrested and shot shortly thereafter. After these horrors Tsvetaeva felt lost and isolated in Soviet Russia. Pasternak did his best to find translation work for her, but that was not enough to rescue her from poverty. Tsvetaeva's emotional state affected her work, and she was unable to write. When the war broke out, she was evacuated to the small provincial town of Elabuga in the Tatar Autonomous Republic, not far from Chistopol where Pasternak was evacuated. Although she petitioned to go to a more urban place, she was not allowed to move. Feeling trapped and driven to complete despair, she hanged herself in

August 1941. Tsvetaeva's death deeply shocked Pasternak, as he felt he had not done enough for her. He also felt guilty about not dissuading her from the return to Russia when they met in Paris, despite his well-founded fear for her in Russia ("Autobiographical Sketch," 4:340). "In Memory of Marina Tsvetaeva" reflects his remorse about his failure to do more for his friend ("There is an unuttered reproach / In the silence of your departure," 2:49), and he feels it is his responsibility to revive her in the memory of her readers: "Marina, it has been a long time, / And it is not much trouble, / To bring your forgotten ashes / From Elabuga" (2:48). There is a strong belief in the last stanza of the poem that Tsvetaeva's poetic heritage will be recognized in the future: "You face God, / And you reach to him from the earth, / During the days when / Noone has yet fully appreciated you" (2:48). In the "Autobiographical Sketch" Pasternak names her as one of the three shadows—the other two are Iashvili and Tabidze—that will always remain with him.

In *On Early Trains* readers see how the strictures of Soviet literary reality imposed on Pasternak's poetry actually helped change it. Pasternak's drive toward simplicity, away from his earlier "baroque of avant-garde," made his later poetry leaner, crisper, simpler, sharper. In an unexpected turn, compliance with the requirements of socialist realism brought out a Pasternak that readers might not otherwise have ever come to know—because he might never have written what he did the way he did in his later years. In a sense then, and just as ambiguously and searchingly as he himself adapted and conformed to Soviet requirements, his style took shapes and forms and went through stages that are not only negative but in fact seem to have produced some remarkable writing. Whether Pasternak would have been a better poet (or perhaps, to rephrase, a refined aesthete of high formalist qualities) without Soviet pressure cannot be determined. But what he did become—pressed from outside but also pushing himself from inside—is, for better or worse, a part of the Soviet legacy in him.

Pasternak's hope that the victorious struggle of the Soviet people against Nazi Germany would ease ideological control in the Soviet Union never came to be. After the war Stalin launched a campaign to rid his country of "antipatriotic" and "cosmopolitan" elements and continued it until his death in 1953. The party attack was especially harsh on science and culture. The main ideological fighter against undesirable trends in literature was Andrei Zhdanov, the secretary of the Central Committee, and his campaign later came to be known as *zhdanovism*. In his speeches of 1946–1948 he vehemently attacked Western literature and demanded that all its influence on Soviet culture be weeded out. He then methodically proceeded to attack the most talented representatives of Soviet culture. His scapegoats in literature became the satirist Mikhail Zoshenko, who implied in his work "Adventures of a Monkey" that the life of a zoo monkey was not much different than that of Soviet citizens, and Anna Akhmatova, who was accused of aestheticism and elitism. By sheer luck Pasternak escaped the fate of these two writers, both of whom were expelled from the Union of Soviet Writers and deprived of their ration cards. But since the obscurantist party campaign to purge the remaining talent from Soviet culture was continuing, Pasternak's work ended up being attacked too. Aleksandr Fadeev, a mediocre writer and obedient servant of the party, who was reappointed as head of the Union of Soviet Writers in 1946, was especially militant in accusing Pasternak of political nonalignment and formalism. Attacks against Pasternak in the Soviet press were numerous and varied in their degree of maliciousness. He well realized his complete fall from grace and expected the worst.[14] Pasternak wrote almost nothing during *zhdanovism,* translations providing his major creative outlet. However, during this period of self-imposed silence he did begin to nourish a large new project that he had dreamed of all his life: a novel. It was to be called *Doctor Zhivago.*

CHAPTER SIX

Doctor Zhivago

On 23 October 1958 Pasternak was awarded the Nobel Prize for Literature for "important achievements both in contemporary lyric poetry and in the field of the great Russian epic tradition" (Conquest 1966, 85). But the award was not altogether a happy event in Pasternak's life because his joy and pride at receiving this high honor were overshadowed by the expectation of imminent trouble with the Soviet authorities and subsequent personal and professional isolation. In his conversation with Max Frankel, the *New York Times* correspondent in Moscow at the time, Pasternak expressed his mixed feelings about the award: "I am extremely happy, but you must understand that I am confident that I will move immediately into this new lonely role, as though it had always been so" (Conquest 1966, 88). Indeed, the Nobel Prize played a double role in Pasternak's literary career: on the one hand, it established his international literary stature, while on the other it made him the target of a slanderous ideological campaign unleashed against him by the Soviet authorities. In order to understand the "Pasternak affair," as it came to be labeled, it is necessary to back up and trace the events that precipitated the new ideological absurdities and excesses triggered against the poet after the recognition of his achievements by the Nobel Committee. Although no Soviet publisher had been willing to publish *Doctor Zhivago,* the Soviet authorities were profoundly irritated by its release in the West and its overwhelming success with the public. It appeared to the party ideologues that the Nobel Prize was awarded to Pasternak solely for his politically provocative interpretation of the revolution in *Doctor Zhivago,* as a part of the West's politics of cold war. The fact that the poet was nominated for the Nobel Prize for his poetry alone first in 1947 and again in 1953 did not seem to bear any significance for the cultural bureaucrats.

Pasternak wrote his novel between 1945 and 1955, but in a sense he had been working on it all his life. Most of his short stories and unfinished fiction in one way or another were geared to culminate in a novel. The first prominent piece that anticipated Pasternak's major project was the short story "Liuvers's Childhood," discussed earlier in this book. The immediate correspondence between *Doctor Zhivago* and this short work lies mainly in the place of the action, the Urals, where Zhenia Liuvers grows up and many of the events of the novel take place. But "Liuvers's Childhood" was also conceived by Pasternak as a chapter of the never-realized novel "Three Names." Important for *Doctor Zhivago*'s genesis is also a prose sketch, "Bezliub'e" ("Without Love"), published in 1918. In this short piece Pasternak outlines one of the essential questions of *Doctor Zhivago* regarding the individual's role in society. The story's two Tatar names, Gimazetdin and Galliula, reappear in the novel. The protagonists of another one of Pasternak's stories, "Aerial Ways," Lelia and Polivanov, anticipate *Doctor Zhivago*'s Lara and Antipov-Strel'nikov. In "Aerial Ways" the theme of the revolution—one of the central themes of the novel—enters Pasternak's fiction for the first time. Both the novella "The Tale" and the novel in verse *Spektorskii* develop around the character Sergei Spektorskii, a writer whose artistic nature and undefined political beliefs make him akin to Iurii Zhivago. By writing "The Tale" Pasternak hoped to develop one of the last chapters of *Spektorskii,* which he tentatively entitled "Revolutsiia" ("Revolution"). He also cherished the dream of using "The Tale" as the beginning of yet another novel. But besides these prose pieces, it is the poet's autobiography *Safe Conduct* that is most profoundly linked with the themes and central issues of *Doctor Zhivago.* The key questions that Pasternak addresses in *Safe Conduct* reappear in the novel. The concept of art as a fresh and original representation of reality, freedom of the artist in society and his role in it, as well as the artist's moral responsibility before himself and others are among the questions that guide both works. There are also the evolution and fate of his own generation that Pasternak is concerned with in both his autobiography and the novel. But whereas *Safe Conduct* spans the period from Pasternak's childhood to 1931, *Doctor Zhivago* expands and diversifies the historical background against which the ideas and ideals of Pasternak's generation are portrayed. The juxtaposition of two poetic types, the more withdrawn and aesthetically distant Pasternak and the politically involved Mayakovsky, anticipates a similar juxtaposition of characters in the novel, represented by Zhivago and Antipov-Strel'nikov. And finally, *Doctor Zhivago,* like *Safe Conduct,* is autobiographical and informed by Pasternak's personal life experiences.

After *Safe Conduct* Pasternak had not altogether given up his hope of writing a novel, and throughout the 1930s he had made further sketches for one, among them "The Notes of Patrick." Although this piece starts with World War I and then jumps back to the events of 1905, other chapters of the novel that Pasternak worked on were supposed to present a wider historical scene than that. Unfortunately, all this material perished in a fire in 1941. What survives is the cover of Pasternak's projected novel with two crossed out titles on it: "Kogda mal'chiki vyrosli" (When the Boys Grew Up) and "Zapiski Zhivul'ta" (The Notes of Zhivul't).[1] It is probably not accidental that the very sound of the name Zhivul't is close to that of Zhivago and that both names are related to the Russian word *zhivoi* (living).[2] This similarity becomes especially meaningful if readers take into account that one of Pasternak's early prose sketches, "Smert' Reliquimini" ("The Death of Reliquimini"), has a variant name, Purvit—for Reliquimini, derived from the distorted French phrase *pour la vie* (for the sake of life, 3:645). The three names, Zhivago, Zhivul't, and Purvit, are then united by their common life-affirming symbolism.

"The Notes of Patrick" contains a range of themes that links it with *Doctor Zhivago*. Its heroine Evgeniia Istomina is reminiscent of Lara. Istomina is married to a teacher of physics and mathematics in the Ural town of Iuriatin, one of the major sights of action in *Doctor Zhivago*. After her husband disappears at the front during World War I, Istomina, like Lara, raises her daughter Katia alone. There are further characters in "The Notes of Patrick" that could be considered models for *Doctor Zhivago*. Among them are Anna Gubertovna (in *Doctor Zhivago* her patronymic is Ivanovna) and Aleksandr Aleksandrovich Gromeko, in whose house Patrick grows up. As in the novel, the Gromekos in "The Notes of Patrick" have a daughter, Tonia, whom Patrick/Zhivago marries. Other similarities that reach beyond the scope of this discussion further enhance the closeness between the two works.

Pasternak began work on *Doctor Zhivago* in the winter of 1945–1946, and his correspondence of that period reflects his intensive work on the novel. On 1 February 1946 he wrote to Olga Freidenberg that he was writing a "large prose" in which he wanted to express things most important to him (5:449). By October 1946 he informed her that he had already written a part of a novel titled "Mal'chiki i devochki" (Boys and Girls), which spans the period 1902–1946 (5:452). The degree of involvement with and excitement about this piece of writing is reflected in a letter to Freidenberg of 13 October 1946, in which Pasternak calls "Boys and Girls" his "first real work" and outlines some issues it was going to address: Christianity, nationalism, and the Jewish question (5:453–54). Despite his intense translation work at that time, Pasternak made progress on his novel, which later was titled *Doctor Zhivago*. In the fall of 1948 he reported to Freidenberg that the first part of the book was finished and he was planning for the second, which would cover the period from 1917 to 1945 (5:471). The letter contains major points of the plot development that indeed later fully materialized in the completed novel: the characters Gordon and Dudorov were to survive their friend Zhivago, who was to die in 1929, leaving behind a notebook filled with poems, which would appear in a separate chapter.

Although the literary-political situation in the Soviet Union continued to be oppressive and Pasternak was systematically attacked in the press despite the fact that he was not publishing new works, on 27 December 1947 he signed a contract with the journal *New World* for the novel with the working title "Innokentii Dudorov," earlier called "Boys and Girls." The work on the novel did not progress as fast as he had hoped because of the bulk of commissioned translations he had to finish first and because of unexpected personal circumstances. In the fall of 1946 he met Olga Ivinskaia, who worked at the publishing house of *New World* and who soon became his new love. His intimate relationship with Ivinskaia lasted for the rest of his life, and once again he was caught in the moral dilemma of making a choice between his wife and his mistress. The problem was never resolved; he was torn between the two women until his death. Ivinskaia began to play a growing role as Pasternak's literary agent during his lifetime, and she also significantly influenced his creation of the image of Lara. Pasternak's liaison with Ivinskaia became known to the secret police, and in the fall of 1949 she was arrested, charged with anti-Soviet activities, and sentenced to five years in prison camps. She served practically the full term and was released in 1953 under the first amnesty for political prisoners. A few months before her return Pasternak suffered a serious heart attack from which it took him months to recover. On 14 March 1953 Stalin died, and a brief relaxation of the political climate, known as the "thaw," followed. In the April 1954 issue of the literary journal *Znamia* (*Banner*), ten poems from Pasternak's novel-in-progress were published with a short authorial introduction, and Iurii Zhivago's name was mentioned as the "author" of the poems for the first time. Also in 1954 Pasternak's *Hamlet* premiered at the Leningrad Pushkin Theater. But liberalism was never a lasting phenomenon in the Soviet Union, and a swift return to the ideological control of culture and literature was inevitable. When *Doctor Zhivago* was finally finished in 1955, Pasternak encountered the usual obstacles of censorship to publishing his novel.

The history of the publication of *Doctor Zhivago* could well serve as the plot for a political thriller. The general controversies have been aptly described by Robert Conquest in his book *Courage of Genius*. A brief review of them may suffice here in order to provide the background of the reception of the novel in the Soviet Union and abroad. Initially Pasternak submitted the manuscript to the journals *Literaturnaia Moskva* (*Literary Moscow*) and *New World,* but both found problems with its ideological overtones and refused to publish it. Despite the "thaw" and signs of some social criticism in newer works of Soviet literature, Pasternak's novel was an oddity because it challenged "the very theoretical basis of Marxism on which the Soviet state was built" and also seemed to demonstrate that Stalinism was the inevitable result of "the nature of the Bolshevik Party and Soviet power" (Fleishman 1990, 278). In addition to its oppositional ideology, the novel was also unacceptable because it contained "no statement of ultimate truths or prescriptions" (Fleishman 1990, 279).

The decision not to publish *Doctor Zhivago* reflected the government line on preventing any political controversy over intellectuals' desire for more freedom. The party also feared an emergence of antigovernment movements that were fermenting in Eastern Europe at the time (the East German uprising in 1953, the Hungarian struggle, and the unrest in Poland in 1956). What precipitated the liberal moods in Eastern Europe and the Soviet Union was the so-called "secret speech" delivered by the new first secretary of the Communist Party, Nikita Khrushchev, at the Twentieth Party Congress in 1956. At a closed session Khrushchev exposed Stalin's crimes and denounced his cult of personality. The content of the speech became widely known and was viewed by Eastern European as well as Soviet intellectuals as a sign of liberalization. But all such hopes were shattered when the political oppositions in Poland and Hungary were quickly suppressed. Especially after the Hungarian rebellion the Soviet government had to make sure that the dangerous spirit of freedom did not infect its own ranks and thereafter its stability. Among the first targets of the Khrushchev government in its preventive campaign to purge literature of the dangerous moods of liberalization were the journals *New World* and *Literary Moscow,* known for their liberal inclinations. Under these circumstances the publication of *Doctor Zhivago* in either of these periodicals or any other Soviet publication was out of the question, and in March 1956 Pasternak gave the manuscript to a visiting Italian journalist, Sergio D'Angelo, a member of the Italian Communist Party who was working in Moscow and visited Pasternak in Peredelkino. With Pasternak's permission, D'Angelo sent the manuscript to an Italian publisher with pro-Communist sympathies, Giangiacomo Feltrinelli, who offered to publish the book in an Italian translation. Pasternak was well aware of the consequences of his acceptance of such an offer, but in view of the near impossibility of publishing *Doctor Zhivago* in the Soviet Union and the urgency with which he wanted to see the manuscript published, he was willing to face the wrath of the authorities after the book's publication in the West (Fleishman 1990, 278). Since Pasternak made no secrets about his plans, the news of the novel's foreign release on 22 November 1957 spread rapidly among the literary circles and alarmed Soviet officials. The entire Soviet press mobilized its forces in a slanderous campaign against him. Pasternak was subject to enormous pressure from the authorities to stop the publication, and the Soviet officials requested that Feltrinelli abandon the book's production. Feltrinelli, however, was determined to publish the novel and pointed out to the Soviets that the English and other editions were already well under way (Conquest 1966, 66).

The rage of the Soviet authorities against *Doctor Zhivago* had been building up even before the novel was published in Italy. What was especially offensive to them was the publication of excerpts from the novel in a Polish literary journal, *Opinie* (*Opinion*), and of a few of Zhivago's Christian poems in the anti-Soviet émigré journal   *Grani* (*Landmarks*). Soviet authors were not allowed to publish abroad without permission from the authorities, and so the fact that Pasternak's writing appeared in print in the West without official approval and on such a forbidden topic as Christianity was seen as a slap in the face of the Soviet literary institutions.

The success of the novel following its publication in Italian was sensational. Its first printing of six thousand copies was sold out on the first day. Over the next two years the novel was translated into twenty-four languages.[3] After Pasternak was awarded the Nobel Prize the Union of Soviet Writers, the Communist Party, and various public organizations began systematic attacks against Pasternak. He was expelled from the Union of Soviet Writers and accused of betraying his country and negatively portraying the socialist revolution and Soviet society—despite the fact that the vast majority of the people participating in the campaign had never even read the novel. Some demanded his expulsion from the country. Privately, however, Pasternak received many letters of support and encouragement from admirers. Yet the psychological pressure on him mounted, and he seriously feared deportation to the West. Compared to other options—prison or labor camps—that dissident Soviet writers had to face, deportation to the West seemed to be a mild punishment. Yet Pasternak did not want to leave Russia. These circumstances forced him first to decline the Nobel Prize and then to write a letter to Khrushchev with a request not to be deported. In this letter he wrote: "I am linked with Russia by my birth, life, and work. I cannot imagine my fate separate from and outside Russia. . . . A departure beyond the borders of my country would for me be equivalent to death . . ." (Conquest 1966, 178). Pasternak was also forced to write to *Pravda* a letter of renunciation of the Nobel Prize. This letter is an interesting document. Despite its generally apologetic tone, it contains lines that can be read as a defense of the views expressed in the novel: "It seems that I assert that any revolution is a historically illegitimate phenomenon, that the October Revolution was one of such illegitimate events, that it brought Russia misfortunes and led the Russian traditional intelligentsia to its destruction. It is clear to me that I cannot accept such assertions carried to absurdity" (Conquest 1966, 181).

Although Pasternak was allowed to stay in Russia and retain both his apartment in Moscow and the house in Peredelkino, the attacks against him never stopped. His last collection of verse, *Kogda razguliaetsia* (*When the Weather Clears*), includes a poem, "Nobelevskaia premiia" ("The Nobel Prize," 1959), that describes his feelings about that hard time: "I am lost like a beast in its bay. / There are people out there, freedom, light, / But behind me there is the noise of the hounds, / There is no escape for me. / . . . How did I dare to write such malicious offense, / I, a murderer and evildoer, / Who make the whole world weep / At the beauty of my native land" (2:128).

Whereas the official Soviet press presented *Doctor Zhivago* as an artistically weak novel noted in the West solely for its political content, the reaction of Western critics, although not unanimous, was for the most part enthusiastic.[4] Particularly favorable reviews came from such distinguished writers as the American Edmund Wilson, the Italian Alberto Moravia, and the French Albert Camus and François Mauriac, to name but a few. But the book was also attacked on both artistic and political grounds in the West. Vladimir Nabokov found it weak, and one American Slavic scholar bluntly called it mediocre in his 1959 review "Courage But Not Excellence" (Cornwell 1986, 11–13). There were also opinions voiced by the European orthodox left agreeing with the official Soviet views on history and politics. These critics presented the novel as ignoring or maliciously distorting facts of Soviet history and life (Conquest 1966, 52–53). There was another reason, beyond politics, however, why the case of Pasternak's novel attracted so much attention in the West. In Fleishman's opinion, Pasternak's frame of mind in *Doctor Zhivago* demonstrated "the organic, indissoluble tie with European culture," a feature that Stalin consistently had tried to destroy in the Soviet intelligentsia during his rule (Fleishman 1990, 286–87). Pasternak appeared to Westerners as a symbol of the old culture that had almost completely vanished in the Soviet Union. His refined education and open-mindedness, resistance to official culture, advocation of humanism, and original interpretation of Christianity—"all this was out of keeping with stereotypical portraits of the Soviet intellectual" (Fleishman 1990, 287). These features of *Doctor Zhivago* go against the grain of ideology and cultural assumptions and present a different, older world of free thinking and originality that the Soviet party apparatus was systematically trying to kill in its writers.

Summary of the Plot and Presentation of Principal Characters

Doctor Zhivago, besides being a great love story, is also a bildungsroman, a historical novel, and a social portrait of pre- and postrevolutionary Russian society. It consists of about 540 pages in the latest Russian collection of Pasternak's works. It is divided into two volumes. Whereas sixteen out of the novel's seventeen parts are written in prose and broken into chapters, the last part presents twenty-five poems purportedly left by Iurii Zhivago after his death. Part 1, "Piatichasovoi Skoryi" ("The Five-O'clock Express"), opens with the funeral of the protagonist's mother. In the same part readers also learn that Iurii's absent father, who has squandered a fortune and left another woman and a son, has committed suicide. Thus orphaned at ten years of age, Iurii stays with his beloved uncle, Nikolai Vedeniapin, a philosopher and religious thinker who poses some of the fundamental questions of the book. In part 1 readers further meet the eleven-year-old Mikhail (Misha) Gordon, a Jewish boy who becomes a witness to the suicide of Iurii's father, and the fourteen-year-old Innokentii (Nika) Dudorov, the son of a revolutionary terrorist and a Georgian princess. These two boys later become Iurii's best friends.

Part 2, "Devochka iz drugogo kruga" ("A Girl from a Different World"), introduces the remaining main characters against the background of the revolutionary events of 1905: a railroad strike, revolutionary meetings, a demonstration, arrests of revolutionary workers, and the fights in the district of Presnia. Pasternak takes the reader into the world of small businesses and revolutionary workers, where the sixteen-year-old schoolgirl Larissa (Lara) Gishar (or Guichard, in the French spelling) lives. Her mother, Emiliia Karlovna Gishar, a widowed Russified Frenchwoman, owns a sewing shop. Emiliia's lover and business adviser, the rich lawyer Viktor Komarovskii, takes an interest in Lara and eventually seduces her. Although tormented by this relationship, Lara also feels flattered by the attention and adoration of the rich and handsome middle-aged man, whose name frequently appears in newspapers, and she enjoys her power over him.

Part 2 also introduces Pavel (Pasha) Antipov, who will play an important role in Lara's life. He is the son of a railroad worker arrested during the upheavals. Pavel lives with the family of Kupriian Tiverzin, his father's coworker and a revolutionary himself. Pasha experiences a strong attraction to Lara and gradually falls deeply in love with her. In part 2 readers also meet Zhivago's foster family, the Gromekos, to whom he is brought by Vedeniapin. Aleksandr Aleksandrovich Gromeko is a university professor, and Anna Ivanovna Gromeko (née Krüger), comes from a family of wealthy industrialists. Iurii and the Gromekos' daughter Tonia grow up together in an atmosphere of high culture and general happiness. Iurii and Lara meet by chance when Iurii, Aleksandr Aleksandrovich, and Misha Gordon accompany a friend of theirs, a doctor, on an urgent call to Madame Gishar. It turns out that Madame Gishar tried to poison herself, but her suicide attempt ends unsuccessfully. Komarovskii is also present there, and Iurii guesses the nature of this man's relationship with Lara and finds it "frightening and attractive" at the same time (3:64). It is obvious that Iurii's world is very different from Lara's, and when he takes a quick glimpse at hers, he is disturbed by its open "vulgarity" (3:64). Nevertheless, thoughts of Lara start to preoccupy him on the way home from the Gishars. He is so deep in his thoughts that even Gordon's revelation that Komarovskii was the man responsible for making Iurii's father drunk before his suicidal leap from a train produces no impression on Iurii.

In part 3, "Elka u Sventitskikh" ("The Sventitskiis' Christmas Party"), readers learn that Iurii has begun to study medicine but is also drawn to writing. Thinking himself too young to produce anything worthwhile in prose, he begins to compose poems instead. The year now is 1911. Iurii learns that in the Siberian town of Omsk he has a half brother, Evgraf Zhivago, the son of his father and Princess Stolbunova-Enritsi. Part 3 also features Lara, who is determined to end her dependence on Komarovskii. She leaves home and moves in with the family of Lavrentii Kologrivov, a rich industrialist, whose daughter Nadezhda (Nadia) is her close friend. Despite her work as a tutor for Kologrivov's other daughter Lipa, Lara manages to graduate from school and takes college courses. A year later she receives a teacher's diploma and decides to leave the Kologrivovs. She has a plan to obtain money from Komarovskii in order to start her independent life, and she has decided she will kill him if he refuses. At the Christmas party at the Sventitskiis', which Komarovskii also attends, in a state of anxiety she shoots him with her brother's revolver. Luckily, the bullet only slightly scratches him. For Iurii, who is also present at the party, this unfortunate incident marks his second encounter with Lara. Part 3 ends with Anna Ivanovna Gromeko's death. As her last wish, she asks her daughter Tonia and Iurii Zhivago to marry each other.

After the introduction of all his principal characters in the first three parts, Pasternak devotes the rest of the novel to their life stories against the background of the turbulent historical events, concentrating primarily on Iurii's and Lara's lives. What happens is that Komarovskii drops all charges against Lara, who has fallen ill after her unsuccessful attempt to kill him. When she recovers, she marries Pasha Antipov. Like Lara, Pasha also has obtained a university degree, and they both leave Moscow to accept teaching positions in the small town of Iuriatin in the Urals. In Iuriatin their daughter, Katia, is born. Iurii indeed marries Tonia and practices medicine in Moscow. The years pass and World War I breaks out. Iurii goes to the front, and his son Aleksandr (Sasha) is born shortly before his departure.

In Iuriatin, Lara and Pasha begin to lose their closeness, tormented by mutual distrust and misunderstanding. In the course of their everyday life and work, Pasha feels discontent because he does not believe in Lara's feelings for him and finds her love self-deceptive. Unable to deal with his insecurity, he decides to join the army and enlists as a volunteer. Dispatched to the front, Lieutenant Antipov is soon captured by the enemy, and rumor reaches Lara that her husband was killed. Driven by her devotion to him and determination to find him, she volunteers as a nurse, is accepted, and is sent to the front. There, in an army hospital, the third encounter between her and Zhivago takes place. They are attracted to each other, but external events caused by the news of the February revolution of 1917 and the fall of the Russian czar separate them. The mood in the army is pessimistic; there is widespread discontent among the soldiers, and Russia is losing the war. It is during this revolutionary time that Iurii returns to Moscow to reunite with his family in Moscow and Lara goes back to Iuriatin with her daughter.

In Moscow, Iurii witnesses the October revolution, which brings the Bolsheviks to power. The revolution both in reality and in the novel is followed by a period of extraordinary hardships for large parts of the Russian population. Working to the point of overexertion at the hospital, Iurii tries to save his family from hunger and cold. Not only is he tired and malnourished, he also falls ill with typhus and spends two weeks in delirium. At this crucial moment Iurii's half brother Evgraf appears; he holds some position of authority and is able to obtain food to help Tonia put Iurii back on his feet. Evgraf also persuades the Zhivagos to leave Moscow for Tonia's former estate of Varykino, not far from Iuriatin, for a year or two until the political climate stabilizes in Russia. Although the Bolsheviks have abolished private property, they have not yet had time to appropriate all of it because of the ongoing war, and Tonia's estate in Varykino is likely to be uninhabited and far from the eyes of the local authorities.

Part 7 is entirely devoted to the Zhivagos' long travel to the Urals in the spring of 1918 and their encounters and conversations with other passengers on the train. Deep in the Urals, Iurii walks away from the train and is arrested by a Red Army guard who delivers him to Strel'nikov, a feared and fearless revolutionary commissar. At this time Iurii does not realize that Strel'nikov is none other than Lara's missing husband, Pasha Antipov. After interrogating Zhivago, Strel'nikov releases him.

From this point up to part 15 the action takes place in the Urals. In Varykino, Iurii, Tonia, her father, and Sasha begin a new life. They grow vegetables in the garden and lead a quiet country life. Iurii's strong desire to write returns, and he starts a journal in which he tries to explain his views on art and literature. One day at the Iuriatin library he meets Lara, and their long-foreshadowed love affair begins. As his love for Lara grows stronger, his sense of guilt before Tonia, now pregnant with their second child, becomes unbearable. Zhivago realizes that he loves and worships Tonia as much as he does Lara and feels incapable of breaking his double bond—not to say double bind. However, his moral dilemma unexpectedly becomes secondary, as on his way home from Lara he is kidnapped at gunpoint by Red partisans and forced to stay with them as the doctor to their group. Zhivago's captivity lasts a year and a half without any outside contact or any possibility to write his family or receive news from them.

Parts 10, 11, and 12 focus on Zhivago's life with the partisans and the realities of the civil war and its atrocities. Zhivago sees how the war turns fathers and sons against each other, how it makes friends into archenemies, and how it drives people to despair and insanity. Unable to bear the cruelties he sees everywhere and on both sides, and under the haunting memory of the recent murder of a whole family by a member of his group, Zhivago attempts his third and this time successful escape.

Part 13 describes his return to Iuriatin, where the new Bolshevik government is now well in control, and his reunion with Lara. In Iuriatin, Zhivago learns that during his absence his daughter Masha was born and Tonia, her father, and the children have gone back to Moscow. Zhivago receives a letter from Tonia with the message that their family is being deported to France. In her letter she conveys her pain of separation from him as well as her feelings of unfulfilled love, and she tells Iurii that she met Lara and found her to be "a good person" although completely opposite in character to herself (3:411).

In part 14 Komarovskii reappears in the narrative to warn Lara and Iurii of the imminent danger for both of them should they stay in Iuriatin. According to Komarovskii, the local Bolshevik authorities are after them and it is only a matter of days before they will be arrested: Iurii for being a partisan deserter and Lara for being Strel'nikov's wife. Strel'nikov, now out of favor with the authorities, is sought by them and hiding somewhere in the Iuriatin area. Although they realize that there is no escape unless they use Komarovskii's help, Zhivago, Lara, and her daughter leave for Varykino to have some peace for at least a short time. They stay in the abandoned snowbound house of Averkii Mikulitsyn, former manager of Tonia's mother's estate and the father of Liverii, the Red partisan commander who held Zhivago as a doctor for his people. Although they have to make great efforts to keep the house warm and wolves begin to draw closer to the house every night, Lara and Iurii are happy there.

Iurii begins to write again. The idyll lasts two weeks before Komarovskii shows up at the house with the news that Strel'nikov has been shot to death by the new authorities and that Iurii and Lara will soon face the same fate. Komarovskii begs them to go with him to the Far East immediately. Knowing that Lara will not leave without him, Zhivago assures her that he will follow them soon and lets Komarovskii rescue her and Katia. Part 14 ends with Zhivago's unexpected visit from Antipov-Strel'nikov, who, it turns out, was not captured by the authorities. For a few hours the two men talk about their experiences of the revolutionary years and also about Lara, who connects them. Strel'nikov admits that everything he did in his life was for Lara and that he would give anything to see her and their daughter for just a moment. During the night after the talk Antipov-Strel'nikov kills himself.

Part 15, "Okonchanie" ("The End"), is a summary account of the last seven or eight years of Zhivago's life. After returning to Moscow on foot in 1922, he finds life and his friends changed. He publishes a few small books on his philosophy of life, history, and religion and prints his medical views about health and sickness, evolution, and his conception of personality. Also among these books are his poems and short stories. But the brief moments of creativity soon end, and Zhivago's life enters a period of steady decline: he stops practicing medicine, is frequently depressed, and develops heart disease. He also starts a new family with Marina, a daughter of a former servant of his, and has two children with her. Marina is a kind woman who puts up with her common-law husband's eccentricities. Eventually the influential Evgraf appears again—and again tries to help his half brother change his life. Evgraf rents an apartment for Iurii and promises to reunite him with his family in France. Iurii takes a job as a doctor and returns to writing but suddenly dies of a heart attack in 1929. At this time Lara comes to Moscow from Irkutsk to enroll Katia at the conservatory. Driven by memory, she goes to see Pasha's place. She finds his building, goes upstairs, and to her surprise discovers Iurii's funeral in Pasha's room. Together with Evgraf she sorts out Iurii's papers and tells the story of her hardships with Komarovskii. Lara also tells Evgraf of her daughter by Iurii, who was born to Lara after her flight from Varykino and who is now lost. Without specifying any time frame the narrator says that Lara disappears, and the narrator suggests that she was arrested and sent to one of the numerous women's gulags.

Part 16, or the "Epilog" ("Epilogue"), opens in 1943 during World War II. Gordon and Dudorov meet at the front and tell each other their experiences of the purges and the war. The epilogue also features Tania, Zhivago and Lara's lost daughter, a linen keeper in the army, who tells Gordon and Dudorov the story of her horrifying childhood. Tania had been found by Evgraf, now an important general, who pledged to take care of her and arrange for her future. The novel concludes with Gordon and Dudorov's meeting "five or ten years later" (3:510) after their encounter at the front. The two friends read Zhivago's books that Evgraf has put together and talk about the present and future of Russia.

Life, Death, and Immortality

The first three parts of *Doctor Zhivago* introduce the principal characters and outline the main issues of the book. One of the central issues of *Doctor Zhivago* is life against death. Related to this is the novel's theme of immortality. The name Zhivago, as has been mentioned earlier, is indicative of the book's orientation toward life-affirmation and the interest in developing a philosophy of life. Early in the novel the following words from the Twenty-third Psalm are pronounced over Iurii's mother's grave: "The earth is the Lord's and the fullness thereof, the world and those who dwell therein." This, one critic noted, could well serve as the motto for the book. Everything comes from the earth, returns to it, and is transformed into life again. "Overcoming death becomes a leitmotif accompanying Iurii" (Livingstone 1989, 50, 52).

Many of the novel's descriptions of nature are symbolic of life and its perpetual transformations. Sudden rain at the end of the funeral scene interrupts Iurii's tears at his mother's grave and reminds him of the continuing life of nature. Transcending a merely realistic description of nature is also the following episode, in which Iurii watches a blizzard covering everything with snow. The blizzard teases Iurii, shows him its power, and enjoys frightening him. Pasternak's universe is not only filled with animated nature, already familiar to the reader from his poetry, but in the novel nature acquires a "definitely pantheistic coloration."[5] Man is viewed as living and bound to the overpowering world of nature, eternally renewing itself. In his Varykino diary Zhivago, in the traditional romantic vein, describes his joy of becoming one with nature through physical work. To "till the soil" and build a house for his family translates for him into a creative power equal only to God's. It is the satisfaction derived from simple physical work in closeness with nature that makes him feel that he continually renews himself (3:275). Zhivago also sees nature as a healer for humans who try to escape the artificiality of their social life. In Zhivago's view, "the silence of nature" is much more meaningful than "the non-stop human babbling" (3:139).

Nature, then, is ever present in *Doctor Zhivago,* and the numerous poetic descriptions of nature scattered throughout the novel begin to acquire a deeper philosophical meaning. Being part of nature and through her immortality, humans gain immortality for themselves. This aspect of Iurii's philosophy of life is revealed in his impromptu speech to the dying Anna Ivanovna, in which he says: "But all the time one and the same immeasurable, unchanging life fills the universe and each hour it renews itself in innumerable combinations and transformations. You are wondering if you will be resurrected or not. But you have already been resurrected when you were born and you did not notice it" (3:69). Iurii's passionate belief in immortality turns the conclusion of his speech into a hymn to life: "There is no death. . . . There will be no death because the past is over. . . . there will be no death because everything that we have already seen is old and is boring, and now we need something new, and this new thing is life eternal" (3:70).

Zhivago's ideas about immortality resonate with the philosophy of life of his uncle, who does not believe that life is terminated by death. Nikolai Vedeniapin arrives at this belief in an interpretation of Christianity that comes surprisingly close to Zhivago's seemingly nonreligious philosophy of life and constitutes the spiritual essence of the novel. Vedeniapin believes that the true value of the Gospel is not in its moral truths as pronounced in the commandments but in the fact that Christ "turns to the parables of everyday life and explains the truth in terms of everyday reality." Wedded to his thinking is the principle that life is eternal and therefore the communion between people is also eternal. For Vedeniapin, the essence of Christ's teaching is that "life is symbolic because it is meaningful" (3:46).

It would be a mistake to treat Zhivago's understanding of life as only romantic and idealistic. Although the idea of life as constant renewal permeates the novel—a concept both romantic and, of course, predating the romantic period—it is contrasted with a different view of life, the view propounded by Marxism and its followers. When the Bolsheviks, under the ideological banner of Marxism, overthrew the old order and established a new one, they hoped for a transformation of life and human relationships. Their goal was to engineer life, to recast it and redirect it into new channels. They also hoped that the new society they projected to build would create a new type of man—Soviet man— a devoted builder of the future communist state. However, the Bolsheviks encountered serious difficulties in realizing their ideals, as their political ideology—totalitarian in its nature—was unacceptable to the vast majority of the population. That was where they had to rely on political coercion, repression, and party dictatorship. Lenin himself advocated terror in the name of building the new society.[6] In *Doctor Zhivago* Strel'nikov and Liverii Mikulitsyn are the major proponents of this point of view. Through Zhivago, Pasternak polemicizes against the Bolshevik drive to reshape the natural order of life. In a conversation with Mikulitsyn, Iurii rebels against the vulgar materialistic understanding of life: "Reshaping life! This is the idea of people who—whatever they have seen—have never known the essence of life or felt its spirit and its soul. For them life is a lump of crude material in need of reshaping and untouched by their noble hands. But life is never simply material, a substance. If you would like to know, it is constantly renewing, transforming, remaking, and transfiguring itself. Life is beyond your and my obtuse theories about it" (3:334). Iurii's words are also at the very heart of Pasternak's philosophy, which conceives of life as "an autonomous and original force, irreducible to categories, be they political, industrial, or economic" (De Mallac, 290). Pasternak's letter to Stephen Spender, written after the Nobel Prize debacle, confirms his fundamental disagreement with theories that try to order or regulate life. He speaks of naturalism as an example, and his opposition to it must be read along the same lines as Zhivago's opposition to Marxism. For Pasternak naturalism fails because it perceives reality "as a substratum, as a common background" governed by "an iron chain of causes and effects, that all appearances of the moral and material world were subordinate to the law of sequels and retributions."[7] In Pasternak's view, in contrast, life is always "original, extraordinary, and inexplicable" ("Three Letters," 5). Along these lines develops Zhivago's argument against Marxism: "I do not know a movement more self-centered and removed from the facts than Marxism. Everyone is worried only about proving himself in practice, and people of power turn away from the truth for the sake of the myth of their infallibility. . . . I do not like people indifferent to the truth" (3:257–58). In a profound way, Zhivago's very system of values is thus threatened by the dry rational theory of Marxism. His response to it is a withdrawal into art, creativity, and contemplation.

And finally, the theme of life, death, and rebirth is connected with the destiny of Russia. Robert Louis Jackson observes that "the death of old Russia and the rebirth of a new Russia, in Pasternak's creative design, essentially are a part of the mystery of all death and birth."[8] Jackson draws attention to Zhivago's contemplation of this mystery after the birth of his son. After the suffering of labor and having faced the threat of death, Tonia is coming back to life: "Raised higher toward the ceiling than ordinary mortals usually are, Tonia lay in the cloud of her spent pain. . . . [Tonia looked] like a barque that had just been unloaded, a barque that makes voyages across the sea of death to the continent of life with new souls immigrating here from nobody knows where. . . . With her lay at rest . . . her oblivion, her vanished memory of where she had been recently, what she had crossed and how she landed" (3:106). Tonia's state, in a sense, becomes symbolic of Russia's.

Art

The contrast between the intrusive regularizing historical force and the alternative free world of art is made explicit in *Doctor Zhivago.* Art for Zhivago is not only a mode of existence, but it is also deeply ingrained in his philosophy of life and immortality. The funeral of Anna Ivanovna suddenly fills Iurii with an urge "to dream, to think, to work on the new form and create beauty" (3:91). Implicit in this desire to be creative is the idea of overcoming death through art, because for Zhivago art is always preoccupied with two concerns: "it constantly meditates about death and thus creates life" (3:91–92). Like Pasternak himself, Zhivago approaches art as he approaches nature and life; in fact for him "nature and art are one" (Terras 1967, 48). Like nature, art transforms finite phenomena into infinite ones. And as in nature, it is the living, creative principle that endows art with meaning. In his diary Zhivago describes art as

something narrow and concentrated, the designation of some principle entering into the work of art, the naming of a force applied in it or of the truth elaborated in it. And art has never seemed to me an object or aspect of form, but rather a mysterious, hidden part of the content. . . . It is a certain idea, a certain statement about life which cannot be broken into separate words because life is so all-encompassing. When a grain of this force enters into a work of a more complex composition, the admixture of art outweighs the meaning of all the rest and becomes the essence, the soul, and the basis of what is depicted. (3:279)

Zhivago's concept of art resonates strongly with Pasternak's own statement in *Safe Conduct* that "art is interested in life at the moment when the ray of power *is passing though* it [life]. . . . in the context of self-awareness, power is called feeling" (4:187). It is through the power of feeling that one is able to look at the world anew, or even discover what one has never known before. When the artist inspires someone by and to feeling, he or she begins to see. Pasternak's theory of art, then, emphasizes perception (MacKinnon 1988, 157). Art as a means of seeing the world is a theme in *Safe Conduct,* and it is emphasized again in *Doctor Zhivago*. It is no coincidence that Iurii, while in medical school, develops a strong interest in the physiology of vision. Pasternak remarks that this interest originated in Zhivago's artistic nature and "his contemplation of the essence of the artistic image and the logical structure of ideas" (3:81).

One of the distinctive features of Pasternak's art in *Doctor Zhivago* is the artistic form that is not connected to social or political functions. In this he remains faithful to the generation of symbolists who influenced his young imagination. Pasternak believes in the primacy of inspiration and feeling in art, and his description of Zhivago working on a poem is a good illustration of Pasternak's own belief. Zhivago is so captivated by writing that he momentarily loses his self-awareness and dissolves into his work. As language acquires primacy, Zhivago feels that he becomes impersonal and as if he is "in the presence of a transformed reality that stands on its own and owes its existence to the medium that makes it possible" (Rudova 1994, 53). Zhivago, like Pasternak, works on the edge of the symbolist tradition in his view of the objectifying power of art: "The relation of things that guide creativity somehow stands on its head. Primacy no longer belongs to man and the state of mind for which he tries to find expression, but to the language in which he wants to express it. Language . . . begins to think and speak for man" (3:431).

But if Pasternak ascribes so much significance to the primacy of language, does it mean that he advocates art outside morality? Does he, in a characteristically modernist manner, separate art and morality and withdraw into his own world? There is certainly some quest for isolation in Zhivago when he lives in Varykino and back in Moscow. He needs isolation in order to perfect his writing. But is perfection the goal of the artist? What is art for? The novel does not shun these questions and addresses them sometimes explicitly and sometimes implicitly in the hidden polemic with socialist realism that predetermines literary forms and emphasizes didacticism. The moral function of art is posited early in the novel in a conversation between Vedeniapin and Vyvolochnov, a follower of Tolstoy. Attacking aestheticism in art, Vyvolochnov ridicules Dostoevsky's idea that beauty will save the world and takes a firm stand against art as a sensual experience. He insists that Russia needs schools and hospitals rather than "fauns and nénuphars" (3:44).[9] Vedeniapin, however, finds the Tolstoyan formulation that "the more a man devotes himself to beauty, the further he moves away from goodness" (3:44) objectionable and argues that above all, people need art rather than preaching. He believes that "what has for centuries raised man above the beast is not the cudgel but music" (3:44) and, therefore, affirms the primacy of art in life, as does Zhivago. Connecting art with Christianity, Vedeniapin sees beauty in its spiritual aspects, and Zhivago's own views point in the same direction. Despite his declaration that "art always serves beauty" (3:448–49), his concept of beauty, although not precisely formulated in the book, clearly goes beyond pure formal characteristics and is endowed with spiritual values. J. W. Dyck rightly says that for Pasternak beauty is not only "a concept" and "a logical substance with intellectual or spiritual characteristics; beauty is also a force." Through his art Pasternak "places beauty into the service of life" (Dyck 1974, 614, 615).

Two other questions that preoccupied Pasternak throughout his life are raised in *Doctor Zhivago:* the moral "I" of the artist in his relationship with official culture; and the artist's quest for simplicity of style. Zhivago's response to these questions is recognizably Pasternak's own. In his Varykino journal Zhivago makes a note that the beginning artist must follow his literary models in order to develop creatively (3:282). Zhivago finds his models in Pushkin, Chekhov, Dostoevsky, and Tolstoy. Unfortunately, the values he cherishes most in these authors have become anachronistic in the new Bolshevik state, and it is not without disdain that he juxtaposes the Soviet and the classical epochs. Tolstoy and Dostoevsky "kept preparing for death, and were worrying and seeking a meaning, summing up their experience" (3:283). Whereas these two great thinkers lived their lives in such a way that their "personal matter . . . was nobody else's business," nowadays this "matter" has become "a general concern" as writers talk more and more about "such loud things as the ultimate goals of mankind and their own salvation" (3:283). Zhivago's words about the bureaucratization of literature, especially its penchant for political rhetoric ("the reigning spirit of noisy phrases" 3:282) that routinely uses such clichés as "the dawn of the future," "the building of a new world," and "torch-bearers of mankind," can be read as a reiteration of ideas that Pasternak expressed in his speech at the third plenary meeting of the Board of the Union of Soviet Writers in Minsk in 1936.[10] Shunning the pomposity and politicization of contemporary literary life, Zhivago remains faithful to the moral ideals of nineteenth-century Russian literature and thus opposes himself to the regime.

Zhivago's deep appreciation of and yearning for simple human values are connected with his drive to achieve simplicity of style. Zhivago clearly thinks Pasternak's thoughts: "All his life he had dreamt about an originality, smooth and discreet, unrecognizable and hidden under the disguise of ordinary and familiar form; all his life he had striven to achieve a style so restrained and unpretentious that it would enable the reader and the listener to grasp fully the meaning without making them realize just how they assimilated it. All his life he had searched for an unostentatious style and felt frightened how far he still was from the ideal" (3:344–45). Time and again Zhivago, together with Pasternak, finds his ideal in Pushkin, who had managed to overcome his period of "mythologism, pomposity, phony epicurianism, and immature faked wisdom" and found his true idiom in objects and events of everyday life and simple poetic forms (3:281). In art, as in life, Zhivago remains faithful to himself: he is a creative artist in search of personal artistic goals, well outside the literary-political standards of the time. His exploration of the domain of art follows the same pattern as his exploration of life: art, as life, is essentially free and cannot follow prescribed external rules. As a moral being, the artist should speak to his public in a language free from dogma and in an accessible style.

Christianity

In his essay "On Pasternak Soberly" Czeslaw Milosz calls *Doctor Zhivago* "a Christian book." Yet he adds promptly that Pasternak's Christianity is far from traditional and in fact "atheological." He further explains that the values that constituted Pasternak's Christianity—"suffering, death, and rebirth"—are also the essence of life, and he declares Pasternak "a man spellbound by reality" (Milosz 1989, 218). Pasternak himself perceived his novel as saturated with Christianity. He wrote to Olga Freidenberg at the beginning of his work on *Doctor Zhivago:* "The atmosphere of the book is my Christianity; in its breadth, it is somewhat different from the Quakers' or Tolstoy's version of Christianity; my Christianity derives not only from the moral aspects of the Gospel, but from other aspects as well."[11]

Pasternak's interest in religion later in his life is by no means accidental. One key to its understanding lies in history itself. In a stimulating analysis of Pasternak's beliefs, Fleishman traces their sources to the ideas of the so-called English "personalists" who caught Pasternak's attention at the time he began writing *Doctor Zhivago*. Thinkers such as Herbert Read, Stefan Schimanski, Paul Bloomfield, and Nikolai Berdiaev emphasized issues around the freedom of man, "the politics of the unpolitical," the unacceptance of fascism and communism, and, finally, the reliance on Christian values (Fleishman 1990, 259). But besides these intellectual sources, the historical circumstances themselves stimulated Pasternak's interest in religion. During World War II the Soviet Union underwent a temporary religious revival. The party understood the importance of strengthening the patriotic sentiment of the Russian people and relaxed its religious policies.[12] As the war awakened a wave of religious feelings, the Russian Church, now tolerated by the Soviet government, used the opportunity to strengthen its power among the believers (*Utopia,* 408). The fact that the Germans allowed religious worship on occupied Soviet territories also played into the hands of the Russian clergy, since the Soviet government could not afford the perception of the Germans as religious liberators in the eyes of the Russian people. In 1943 Stalin met with the Metropolitan Sergii and other church officials, welcomed the patriotic activities of the church, and allowed the election of a "patriarch of Moscow and all Russia" and the gathering of a Holy Synod (*Utopia,* 409). This triggered hope in the hearts of believers that after the end of the war the government would continue its course of religious tolerance. These hopes, however, were shattered when after the war, instead, many churches throughout the country were closed in obedience to the renewed anticlerical government policies. Fleishman points out that this factor—the quiet antireligious war that the government, now no longer in need of the church, began to wage against believers—became decisive in Pasternak's turn toward Christianity. The critic believes that in the political atmosphere of the post–World War II Soviet Union, "the poet found Christianity's universal nature, its transcendence of government and politics, particularly attractive" (Fleishman 1990, 262). However, Pasternak's religious belief should not be exaggerated, since the poet was never baptized and admitted that his religious feelings were "nondogmatic and noncanonical" (Fleishman 1990, 263). It is therefore not surprising that religious views in *Doctor Zhivago* are expressed through such unorthodox exponents of Christianity as the defrocked priest Vedeniapin and the Jew Mikhail Gordon.

Vedeniapin's speech at the beginning of the novel is not only an exposition of his ideas, but it also becomes the means of providing a religious vision in the novel. Much of what Vedeniapin says in this speech foreshadows the evolution of Iurii's own ideas and of his life that remains faithful to these ideals. In fact, Vedeniapin's ideas are echoed throughout the book and "supported by all . . . [its] imagery and structure" (Livingstone 1989, 55). Vedeniapin's philosophy of history is closely connected with the Gospels: "I said one should be faithful to Christize. . . . it is possible to be an atheist, it is possible not to know that God exists and why, and yet to know that man does not live in nature but in history, and that history, as we understand it now, was founded by Christ and that the Gospel is its foundation. And what is history? It is the setting up, through centuries, of consistent work to solve the riddle of death and to overcome it in the future. For the sake of this, mathematical infinity and electromagnetic waves are discovered and symphonies are composed" (3:14). For these discoveries, according to Vedeniapin, man needs "spiritual equipment": "love of one's neighbor," "the idea of free personality," and the "idea of life as sacrifice" (3:14).

All three principles undergo a problematic development in the book and in the final analysis call into question the presence of any "spiritual equipment" in Soviet Russia. To begin with, "love of one's neighbor" remains the quest of a few. With hatred unbridled by the revolutionary class struggle, the confrontation between members of the same community was inevitable. One reads between the lines of Vedeniapin's speech Pasternak's reference to Stalin's dictatorship that created an atmosphere of hostility and suspicion. Although Vedeniapin speaks of pre-Christian history as the "cruelty of pockmarked Caligulas who do not suspect how untalented every oppressor is" (3:14), the image of the bloodthirsty Roman emperor by implication translates into the Soviet dictator Stalin with his pockmarked face. The Christian "future" that Vedeniapin talks about has not come to Russia yet. Vedeniapin contrasts life before and after Christ's birth by alluding to "the boastful dead eternity of bronze monuments and marble columns" of the Romans and the vision of Christ when "man does not die on the road under a fence but at home in history" (3:14). "Bronze monuments and marble columns" are absurd Soviet reproductions of classical models: monuments of Stalin decorated every town square, and marble columns became a standard feature in the monumental structures built under the dictator's rule. The negative parallelism between pre-Christian Rome and the Soviet state is thus established through architectural symbols. It is Christian history, in Vedeniapin's view, that offers comfort in the idea that history is represented as home, as something soothing and sheltering. Soviet reality, on the contrary, personifies a hostile period in a post-Christian state in which the individual can no longer find comfort if he dares to pursue an alternative lifestyle. Symbolically, Zhivago dies in the street, feeling completely alienated from society. What Pasternak suggests in the book is that "love of one's neighbor," or universal love, although not completely stripped of the moral philosophy of individual personalities, is possible only when the state reaches the level of spirituality and freedom that in theory and practice abides by this Christian principle. His hope then is for a world that, at least in its spiritual dimension, would resemble a Christian state. Summing up the Christian orientation of Pasternak's thought, Livingstone writes that much of *Doctor Zhivago*'s concern is with the "return to 'prehistory,' the loss of the sense of home; much is about brief recoveries of it; all is imbued with the hope of re-creating it" (Livingstone 1989, 58).

Closely connected with this discussion is the concept of the free personality. Posited by Vedeniapin as one of the factors defining human happiness, this concept is projected against the background of historical reality. The implication of this projection is that a free personality cannot exist in a totalitarian state. In *Doctor Zhivago* the idea of free personality, instead of being a personification of Christian love, translates into "an extremity of individualism, a self-withdrawal of the *individual* called to the broadening role of the *person,* the citizen, the biblical 'neighbor'" (de Mallac 1981, 313). The whole novel rebels against the restrictions imposed on individual freedom by the Soviet regime, and the destinies of the major characters become symbolic of the destruction of the whole class of the old Russian intelligentsia. The "engineering of human souls" launched by the Bolsheviks went against the most fundamental principle of the Russian intelligentsia—freedom. The weltanschauung of the Russian intelligentsia was above all understood as "free decisions of free men" (Gerschenkron 1961, 198). The intelligentsia was possible only as long as it was free to act and to create. Once freedom disappeared, the intelligentsia was doomed as a class: "decay, disintegration, and finally death became inevitable" (Gerschenkron 1961, 198). Therefore the fate of Iurii Zhivago, as a member of the intelligentsia, stands out as one of the most tragic in the long tradition of "superfluous men" in literature. His complete withdrawal from social life and his gradual social degradation go beyond the limits of individual life and symbolize the death of the whole class of the prerevolutionary Russian intelligentsia. Although Zhivago's best friends, Dudorov and Gordon, are, thanks to the professional status, still living in their world of "good books, good thinkers, good composers . . . good music," they lose their ability "to think freely and lead a conversation according to their will" (3:474). Having conformed to the regime, neither friend is capable of a critical attitude toward political reality any longer. Both now believe in the socialist utopia, and both express themselves in the social-political language of the time. Like Zhivago, both Dudorov and Gordon are the victims of a regime determined to reeducate the old intelligentsia. But unlike Zhivago, the two friends no longer have the will and courage to stick to the principle of the "free personality" that was so dear to them in their youth. With skepticism and irritation, Zhivago listens to their conversations about the positive eye-opening experiences under the Soviet regime. He concludes from talking to them that "an enslaved man always idealizes his slavery" (3:475).

Zhivago feels alienated not only from Gordon and Dudorov, his best friends, but from the whole class of the new Soviet intelligentsia. Indirectly, and in a medical metaphor, he tells Gordon and Dudorov of his feelings about their rejection of freedom. Beginning his speech with the statement that cardiac hemorrhages have become common, he connects the rise of this disease with moral factors, namely with moral compromise, and calls it "a disease of our time": "A great majority of us are required to live a life of constant systematic duplicity.

One cannot, without consequences, day after day, act against what one feels, or lay oneself out before something one does not like and rejoice at something that brings one misfortune." This, concludes Zhivago, is doing violence to one's own soul (3:476).

Zhivago's own quest is to live life fully without abandoning his moral values: "I have an incredible, passionate desire to live, and to live always means to strive to go forward, toward the highest goal, toward perfection, and to achieve it" (3:477). It is in this quest that Zhivago realizes the third aspect of Vedeniapin's "spiritual equipment," "life as sacrifice." Estranged from the regime and society, Zhivago leads a lonely life. His world is purely spiritual; in his pursuit of poetry he ignores material values as well as his social and professional status. From the point of view of society, Zhivago becomes a bum, especially when he gives up practicing medicine and instead does odd jobs in order to get by. Per-Arne Bodin compares him to a "fool in Christ" in the kinetic tradition of Russian Orthodoxy (Bodin 1990, 396). This tradition clings to Christ's "emptying himself" on becoming man, humbling himself even in the face of death. Christ's human qualities become more important than his divine origin, and it is this human aspect of Christianity that allows Sima Tuntseva, a Iuriatin intellectual, to exclaim: "What closeness, what equality between God and life, God and the individual . . ." (3:408).

But the idea of life as sacrifice in *Doctor Zhivago* comes not only from fundamental Christian doctrine; it is also derived from the political atmosphere that surrounded Pasternak, as Bodin points out. His own suffering and the suffering of his friends under the Soviet regime provided Pasternak with the idea of creative life as sacrifice. Arrests, executions, and suicides, as part of the political condition, "turned artists into victims and inevitably marked his own [Pasternak's] creativity" (Bodin 1990, 397). Although there is a tragic element in Zhivago's life, one of the book's important messages is that life, like the life of Christ, is impossible without suffering, and it is only through suffering and death that rebirth is possible. It is on the foundation of the Christian belief in resurrection that Zhivago can make his already quoted statements about immortality: "There will be no death . . . because the past is over . . . and now we need something new . . . life eternal" (3:70).

But Christianity in *Doctor Zhivago* is also intertwined with the condition of the Jewish people. Although Pasternak was aware of his Jewish background, he never made an issue of it and did not leave any writing, except in his novel, about the condition of the Jews in the Soviet Union. Jews certainly formed one group of the population that Stalin hated. After the war anti-Semitic Soviet policies, which were begun in the 1920s, spread rapidly as part of a government campaign to rid the Soviet Union of "antipatriotic" elements.[13] In the postwar Soviet Union all Jews who held high positions in government or the military began to lose them. Attacks against Jewish scientists and cultural and literary figures were also common. It is perhaps in the face of this new anti-Semitic campaign waged by the Soviet government that Pasternak felt the need to reassert his Jewishness and his pride in it. But he does it in fiction only through Misha Gordon's appeal to the Jews: "Do not stick together, disperse. Rejoin. You are the first and best Christians in the world. You are the very thing against which you have been turned by the worst and the weakest among you" (3:125). Fleishman suggests that Pasternak, in view of the anti-Semitic mood in the Soviet Union at the end of the 1940s, may have meant by this appeal that Christianity was "the only practical escape for the Russian Jews"; this may sound like a weak consolation, but it obviously was a better alternative than "assimilation to Soviet communism" (Fleishman 1990, 266). Despite Pasternak's explicitly Christian message in the novel, Judaic traces are not absent from it. De Mallac, referring to the study of Judaic legacy in *Doctor Zhivago* by Judith Stora, names the following Judaic values in it: the "prophetic idea of universal happiness," the celebration of earthly life rather than preparation for an afterlife, the attraction to the prosaic details of everyday life, the union of the body and the soul, and emphasis on action and active life (de Mallac 1981, 331). These Judaic attitudes in *Doctor Zhivago* further emphasize the peculiar nature of Pasternak's Christianity.

History and the Revolution

In *Doctor Zhivago* readers see Russian history from the beginning of the twentieth century to the mid 1950s. Pasternak takes his characters through the turbulent events of the first Russian revolution of 1905, World War I, the February revolution of 1917 that overthrew the monarchy, the October revolution of the same year that installed the Bolshevik regime, and the civil war that followed it. In the conclusion he further, however briefly, treats the first years of building socialism in Russia, and finally, in the epilogue World War II and the postwar situation up to the 1950s are touched upon. This historical sweep and breadth of the novel makes Pasternak's approach to representing history seem problematic for some readers and critics. Isaac Deutscher, for instance, in a highly critical article titled "Pasternak and the Calendar of the Revolution," accuses the author of *Doctor Zhivago* of placing his characters "in the backwoods and backwaters" of history. Deutscher's comparison is to Tolstoy, who, in his celebrated historical epic, *War and Piece,* throws his characters "right onto the stream of history" (Deutscher 1969, 244). Deutscher also points out that whereas in *War and Peace* Tolstoy introduces real historical figures (for example, Czar Aleksandr, Napoleon, and the head of the Russian army, Kutuzov) and describes places of historical significance, Pasternak "has no eye for the historic scene. He runs away from history, just as all the time his chief characters flee from the scourge of revolution" (Deutscher 1969, 245). Deutscher's notion is indeed correct that Pasternak presents his heroes mostly on the periphery of the revolutionary events and introduces no real historical figures into the narrative (the White Army admiral Kolchak fighting in Siberia is perhaps the only historical figure to make a brief appearance in the book). But the critic fails to see that Pasternak was hardly concerned with writing a traditional historical novel or a "political novel *par excellence*" (Deutscher 1969, 241). Pasternak is neither attempting to chronicle history in *Doctor Zhivago,* which is obvious from his somewhat careless use of dates, nor does he intend to write a political indictment of the Soviet regime in a dissident vein à la Solzhenitsyn a short time later. Above all, he is writing "a philosophical novel, a testimony of thought and experience."[14] The focus of Pasternak's exploration is primarily on the individual and, only through the individual and his existential and psychological situation, on history. It is because of this that Pasternak's novel projects a very different sense of history than Tolstoy's—more intimate, personal, and emotionally intense than Tolstoy's, whose philosophical views on the nature of war permeate the novel, and who at the end of *War and Peace* adds an essay on his understanding of the meaning of history. Pasternak approaches history as "an impressionist painter," de Mallac writes: "many strokes create the total impression if one just stands back far enough" (de Mallac 1981, 307).

The impressionistic perception, conceptualization, and projection of history are consistent features of the novel. Although views on history and the revolution are expressed by many characters in the book, the voice that readers hear most prominently is Pasternak's own. Through Iurii, a thinly veiled persona of the author himself, readers follow the evolution of Pasternak's views on Russia's revolutionary history, the view through the eyes of a sophisticated, sensitive, and talented artist, very much like Pasternak himself.

When the provisional government assumes power in Russia after the abdication of the czar, Iurii is at the front, in Meliuzeevo, far away from the events of the revolution. He responds to it with enthusiasm and idealism. The joy of freedom is reflected in his conversation with Lara: "Just think of it, the roof has been torn off Russia and we, with all the people, are out in the open. . . . Freedom! Real freedom . . . out of the blue, beyond our expectation, freedom by accident, through a misunderstanding" (3:145). The language of Zhivago's welcoming of the revolution is significant both for understanding his views as well as the novel's whole meaning. What Iurii's words emphasize is the elemental nature of the events, their accidental occurrence and ambiguity, in fact a possibility of their being a misunderstanding. These aspects stand behind much of the novel's own plot progression. For Zhivago the revolution has a providential quality, and he elevates it almost to divine status in his vision of universal harmony ("mother Russia . . . is talking and she cannot stop. . . . And it is not only people that are talking. Stars and trees got together and are talking, and night flowers are philosophizing, and stone houses hold meetings," 3:145). In his interpretation the revolution acquires an abstract quality. Indeed, with Zhivago on the periphery of the events in Meliuzeevo, readers do feel far removed from the violent historical reality. This feeling is intensified by Zhivago's "double vision" of the revolution: "Everyone has been through two revolutions: first his own, personal as well as another, the general one" (3:145). It is the personal one that readers are mostly exposed to, and the general one reveals itself through the multiplicity of the characters' voices in the novel.

Pasternak does not in any way promote Zhivago's ideas about the revolution as the correct ones. On the contrary, he emphasizes the fact that his protagonist expresses the view of the Russian professional middle class, which constituted the core of the intelligentsia. He makes it clear in the novel that Zhivago's response to the revolution has two sides. The first could be described as the "poetics of home," comfort, stability, "good-heartedness and purity" (3:159). Zhivago is very concerned that this cozy life might vanish and "wanted it safe and whole" (3:159). The second side reveals his naive and romantic attraction to the revolution, identifying it with the freedom-loving ideals of his youth and at the same time being fascinated by its new, unknown drifts. For Zhivago these new elements, while associated with blood and violence (3:160), also symbolize real life and a real change for Russia. With fascination and respect, he describes the Bolsheviks as heroes and "experts of [this] elemental power" of the revolution, guiding the people to the future (3:160).

In part 2 Zhivago's prerevolutionary world of comfort and high values is juxtaposed to the world of the revolutionary railroad workers. Once again it is an individual perception that Pasternak focuses on. Untouched by good fortune, the railroad worker Kupriian Tiverzin lives in a world of injustice, "of ignominy and fraud" (3:34). In his revolutionary dreams, in the name of the workingmen, he rises against his oppressors, among whom Zhivago (by virtue of his class) might very well be placed.

Iurii's initial desire to include himself with the "people" is problematic from the very beginning. The people—like Tiverzin—are not eager to include him in their ranks. Later in the novel the growing polarization of the two worlds after the socialist revolution—the working class on the one hand, professional and industrial bourgeoisie on the other—is explicitly commented on by the author: "Old life and the new order did not correspond to each other. They were not yet openly hostile to each other, as when the civil war broke out a year later, but there was a lack of connection between the two. These were two sides confronting each other . . ." (3:194). The gap between the social classes is tangible even before the October revolution, and therefore, it is not surprising that Zhivago senses it and, while preaching socialism as the road toward an amelioration of society, foresees the imminent death of his class ("he considered himself and his own class doomed," 3:182). This, however, does not change his deep spiritual commitment to the people and their future well-being. A Christian touch of self-sacrifice, reminiscent of *Lieutenant Schmidt,* sounds in his words when he is talking about his fate, which he is willing to accept without resistance in the name of the suffering Russian people: "[He] was ready to sacrifice himself for the general good" (3:182). In these words readers hear an echo of Vedeniapin's revolutionary utopianism ("[it] will lead people toward the light," 3:178) and his total inability to connect theory with real life. In fact, both uncle and nephew preach the radical and complete liberation from the old system but have only a vague idea of the new one. Vedeniapin's metaphor of the complete destruction of the old building (3:178) corresponds in its essence to the medical language of Zhivago's ecstatic welcoming of the October revolution. Zhivago marvels at the Bolsheviks' ability to "cut out the old stinking ulcers" at once (3:193). Vedeniapin's and Zhivago's attitudes toward the revolution are romantic and idealistic. Their political naïveté points to Pasternak's earlier hero Lieutenant Schmidt and even to Pasternak himself at the time of the February revolution.

As the narrative develops, external events are given more attention and gradually influence Zhivago's attitude toward the new regime. As his hardships worsen, the pulse of history is felt more and more strongly and "manifests itself as civil war and domestic strife, in a 'permanent revolution' which is at once material and spiritual warfare, a total struggle without quarter or truce" (Poggioli 1958, 551). Material deprivations, hunger, epidemics, brutality, and the new bureaucracy of the Bolshevik regime all inexorably lead Zhivago to change his views on the revolution. Assuming that he was ready for self-sacrifice and suffering, is his subsequent disappointment with Bolshevism inevitable?

The answer to this question lies in Zhivago's philosophy and his idealistic expectations of new freedoms and enlightened liberalism for all people of Russia. Unfortunately, however, liberalism was scarcely on the Bolsheviks' agenda. Their priorities were the establishment of their dictatorship by means of a victorious class struggle and reshaping the new society according to their uniform ideological pattern. The October revolution that actually took place was not Zhivago's revolution, and he was quick to realize it. During his trip to the Urals he comes in contact with people outside his own social circle for the first time in his life. What he sees in the Russian provinces and hears from people only confirms his view that Marxism, which lies at the foundation of Bolshevism, is an abstract, self-centered teaching, far removed from life (3:257), and as handled by the new regime it becomes not a tool of liberation but an effective means of political suppression. Ordinary people have been fooled by it as much as the intellectuals. As Zhivago's cotraveler, the co-operativist Kostoed observes, the hope of the people for land and freedom was deceived, and instead, "from the fetters of the old government oppression, the people fell under the much harsher yoke of the new revolutionary superstate" (3:223). The omnipresent oppression under the new regime is a major blow to Zhivago's liberal attitudes and leads him to reject the dictatorship of the Bolsheviks as a form of transition to a happier socialist society: "nothing can be gained by brute force. One should be drawn to good by goodness" (3:260).

After the horrors of the civil war, which he experienced during his forced service with the partisans, Zhivago's sense of history and the revolution undergoes a drastic change. Now he clearly sees that his hope for freedom will not materialize in a state based on political dogma and oppression. He cannot expect anything from those "active, limited and fanatical geniuses," as he calls the revolutionaries, who are determined to transform Russia according to their will (3:448). From now on they will perpetually be called "bright heroes," whereas he will be stigmatized as a "petty soul that sides with obscurantism and the oppression of the people" (3:401). This hurts and angers Iurii. But he is not the only one disturbed by the new people in power. Along with Iurii, the author himself responds to the powerful revolutionary force that from now on is going to determine the destiny of the Russian people. And therefore the portraits of the old revolutionaries Tiverzin and Antipov appear in a telling grotesque light: "Counted among gods at whose feet the revolution laid its gifts and sacrifices, they sat silent, as strong idols from whom political conceit annihilated all life and humanity" (3:315).

After the true nature of the Bolsheviks begins to emerge even more clearly, Zhivago justifiably expects that in the process of altering the social order, they will eradicate any hint at individuality in the building of their monolith ideological state. The threat to his humanistic ideal of freedom is real, and he sees only two outlets for himself: art and love. Reality itself forces him to create his own castle, a world within the world of the revolution. To preserve his value system, he must reject the historical context. In that, Zhivago can be perceived as both "the weakest victim" and the most "elusive enemy" (Poggioli 1958, 551) of the Bolshevik regime. Art and love become his islands amid the hostile stormy waters. But despite his proud isolation as an artist without any political cause, he remains a threat to the new regime as long as he speaks his idiom and exists on the margins of the social system. While readers may interpret Zhivago's retreat from the world of socialism into the world of his ideas as a capitulation before the revolution and therefore pronounce the death of his whole class, there is an optimistic message in the novel that must not be ignored. Even under Soviet socialism Zhivago remains spiritually free and faithful to his moral and intellectual principles. It is these principles that Pasternak was interested in presenting in his novel and for the sake of which he avoided the presentation of history through dates, facts, and actual personalities. Instead, he foregrounds the individual perception and experience of history. Pasternak's novel is "a spiritual document of great significance" (Poggioli 1958, 551) in which the self occupies center stage and is elevated above history.

Problems of Characterization

Pasternak has been both praised and criticized for his characters in *Doctor Zhivago*. Whereas some critics perceive them as pale and unbelievable and lacking in psychological motivation for their actions (Livingstone 1989, 59–60), others praise the author's "mastery of depicting the gradual transformation of the inner man" (Dyck 1972, 111). There is a third camp that maintains that *Doctor Zhivago* is a "poet's novel" because it goes beyond traditional novelistic conventions and favors "a language of indirection, association, and symbol to make its statements" (Anderson 1987, 503). Sinyavsky, turning this argument on its positive side, believes that Pasternak deliberately "dematerializes" his characters and leaves them unfinished (Sinyavsky 1989, 363). According to Sinyavsky, individual characters in *Doctor Zhivago* deviate from canonical literary "types" found in nineteenth-century realist novels and "lose defined psychological, social and life-like contours" (Sinyavsky 1989, 363). From a nineteenth-century perspective, the critics' accusations are justified: *Doctor Zhivago* contains little in the way of the detailed portrayal of characters so familiar from nineteenth-century realism. Instead, in his method of narration, Pasternak breaks out of the traditional realist patterns and creates a realism of his own, based on "free subjectivity." In his articles "Pol'-Mari Verlen" ("Paul Verlaine," 1944) and "Shopen" ("Chopin," 1945) Pasternak spells out his own idiosyncratic understanding of realism as an art characterized by the subjective "biographical imprint" of an artist's life, by originality and innovation. Pasternak does not hesitate to call Verlaine a realist because this French symbolist poet grasped the spirit of his epoch through impressionistic "half tones" and "hints."[15] It is this kind of realism of "half-tones" that Pasternak applied to the portrayal of his own characters, thus providing little material solidity for them. Of Zhivago's physical characteristics, for instance, readers know the very basics: Iurii has a snub nose and brown hair. As for Lara, she has gray eyes and light hair and is distinguished by quick movements and a quiet and graceful manner of walking. There is a modernist touch in Pasternak's sketchy character descriptions, familiar from his early prose, in which he is more interested in tone and gesture than a full-fledged character painting. As was discussed it chapter 2, the style of his early fiction was marked by metonymy and gravitated toward the abstract; in *Doctor Zhivago* one can trace similar modernist features. But what becomes really important in the novel is Pasternak's preference to place the power of his characterization into its intellectual aspects rather than in the physical—or even psychological—features of his heroes. Readers, therefore, focused on the intellectual, political, and symbolic aspects will hardly perceive changes in the appearances of characters—for instance, how time etches wrinkles on characters' faces and how their hair turns gray. When readers encounter Gordon and Dudorov in 1929, in 1943, and then in the 1950s, after initially meeting them as children at the beginning of the century, nothing is said about their physical changes. For Pasternak the artistic power of the image lies beyond his characters' physiques; he focuses on the world of their spirituality and intellect.

Antipov-Strel'nikov and Iurii

A special place in *Doctor Zhivago* is occupied with the relationship between Zhivago and Lara's husband, Pasha Antipov, known during the civil war under the name of Strel'nikov. Although the two men belong to two different camps, spiritually they are connected. Both initially are so attached to their visions of the revolution that they miss the signals of its significance and consequences for themselves. As time passes, both Zhivago and Strel'nikov have to pay dearly for their revolutionary idealism despite the fact that different paths had led them there.

On first sight, Zhivago and Strel'nikov have nothing in common except their love for Lara. If Zhivago is a liberal coming from a comfortable bourgeois background, Pasha Antipov is born to a working-class family and has to fight for his position in society. Through hard work he receives a university degree. Unlike Iurii, he negates the mainstream bourgeois existence and after graduation, together with Lara, goes to the provinces of Russia to work as a teacher. He later serves in World War I and reemerges only during the civil war as the revolutionary commissar Strel'nikov. Nothing is more striking than the transformation of the gifted, loving young man Pasha Antipov into a strong-willed, fanatical, and feared Red Army leader. As David Bethea observed, this transformation reduces "the human to the level of machine" (Bethea 1989, 255).[16] The new name, a true nom de guerre, that Antipov chooses for himself is derived from the Russian word *strela* (arrow) and from *streliat'* (to shoot). Strel'nikov's very name thus connotes directness and destruction, unlike Zhivago's life-affirming name.

Although Strel'nikov is among those who set fire to the world and thus embodies the spirit of the revolution, he is no "silent, strict idol" like the old Bolsheviks Antipov and Tiversin. During their first meeting Strel'nikov strikes Zhivago as "entirely a manifestation of the will" and a model of perfection (3:248), but behind Strel'nikov's model revolutionary facade Zhivago perceives a vulnerable human nature. What makes Strel'nikov different from the rest of the revolutionaries is the "presence of his natural talent and unaffected ease" (3:248) amid the all-pervasive spirit of "unrestrained pathos and the most radical views on the revolution" (3:249). Even Strel'nikov's fanaticism is not "an imitation but . . . his own, prepared by all his previous life" (3:249). Strel'nikov, in a sense, is a Bolshevik with a human face, although for doing good he lacks "a heart capable of violating his principles, a heart which does not know of general cases but only of particular, and which is great in little action" (3:250–51). Strel'nikov is determined to remain loyal to the rules of his new profession, as usual trying to achieve perfection in it. When Strel'nikov discovers his misconception about the revolutionary world where no one really cares about moral cleanliness, he feels hurt, but he keeps his pain and grief to himself in the hope that one day he will be able to judge "the dark forces" that distorted his ideals (3:251). Zhivago guesses that Strel'nikov is in a trap because he is obsessed not with the dogma of the revolution, like his revolutionary comrades, but "with the ordeals he has gone through" (3:294). As soon as he is no longer needed by the revolution, he will be "crushed," together with others like him (3:294).

Both Zhivago and Strel'nikov are thus bound by the same fate and doomed from the beginning of the revolution, although they are drawn to it from different places and in different ways. Their revolutions are myth and utopia, and for a while they take this myth for reality. Once their imaginary revolutions clash with the real one, swift disillusionment is bound to follow. In her comparison of Zhivago and Strel'nikov, Livingstone calls Strel'nikov Iurii's "shadow," using Carl Jung's concept of the aspect of one's personality that one rejects in fear of its powers (Livingstone, 78). If readers accept Strel'nikov as Zhivago's shadow, it becomes clear that what Zhivago lacks is Strel'nikov's strong will, discipline, and control. These features constitute the differences between the two men. As Livingstone expresses it, it is "control" that "contains the whole of [Strel'nikov's] 'otherness'" from Zhivago (Livingstone, 78). But Strel'nikov remains a mystery, and the riddle of his otherness for the reader remains unsolved until the end. Even when Zhivago and Strel'nikov meet after Lara's departure, Iurii cannot understand the mystery of Pasha Antipov's transformation into Strel'nikov. And neither can the reader.

Lara

The same concern for internal spiritual development guides Pasternak's portrayal of the main heroine in *Doctor Zhivago,* Lara. Lara becomes Pasternak's rebellious and "non-conformist" character. From the beginning, Lara is a "doomed existence" (Clowes 1990, 326–27), but although her life unfolds as a chain of hardships, her remarkable spirit remains unbroken. In her youth she is seduced by Komarovskii, who from that time on feels responsible for her and resurfaces at crucial points in her life. Even when Lara marries Pasha Antipov and has a child with him, she is unable to free herself from Komarovskii completely. In the end he comes to Iuriatin to take her and her daughter with him to the Far East in order to save them from the Bolsheviks. Reluctantly, Lara leaves Iurii behind, hoping that he will follow her; but she never sees him alive again. After separation from Iurii she gives birth to his daughter, but under Komarovskii's pressure Lara leaves her (for what she thinks will be a short time) with a peasant family in Siberia. Lara never sees her daughter again. At the end of the novel Lara is arrested and perishes. Despite Komarovskii's ominous presence in her life, Lara preserves her spiritual freedom, which from the beginning is her innate characteristic. When Zhivago sees her at the library in Iuriatin, he admires her light and natural manner that he recalls from their brief meeting in Meliuzeevo during World War I: "She does not want to please . . . or be beautiful and fascinating. She despises this aspect of a woman's nature. . . . How well she does everything. She reads as if reading were not the highest human activity, but as if it were the simplest and most accessible thing. . . . As if she were carrying water from a well, or peeling potatoes" (3:289). At times she is domestic, but she is also studying Marxism to educate herself politically, and she is able to comment shrewdly on the war and the revolution in her conversations with Iurii. Whereas Tonia is locked in the world of her family, Lara's world is richer in experience and possibilities. She is a symbol of hope for everyone, and despite her suffering, her inner strength, vitality, and desire to live a full life are always present. Like Iurii and Strel'nikov, she remains faithful to her moral values, and like Iurii, she accepts the concept of life as sacrifice. Together with Zhivago, she becomes a tragic figure, unable to conform to socialist reality; she is marginalized and finally crushed by it.

But regardless of her presence, even prominence, in the novel, Lara remains, in a sense, an elusive figure. Much in her motivations remains unclear (for instance, the reason of her shooting at Komarovskii or her invitation of Komarovskii to her farewell party—after she shot him). But perhaps her image, like Zhivago's, is supposed to break all stereotypical modes of behavior. As Pasternak describes his two major characters: "They both equally disliked everything fatalistically typical of modern man, his admiration learned by rote, shrill excitement, and the deadly triviality" (3:390). For both Lara and Iurii, the pulsation of life is felt in their passions and their love of life. Their eternal quest is for "new discoveries about themselves and life" (3:390). In this ambivalence between emotional, intellectual, and spiritual presence in the novel and her psychological and physical vagueness Lara represents the typical nonrealist—still largely poetic—attitude with which Pasternak approaches his characters. Lara's image constitutes a central part of both the beauty and the weakness of *Doctor Zhivago,* the poetic qualities and the narrative—realistic shortcomings about which critics have complained.

Coincidences

It is because of Pasternak's conception of life as a repository of "new discoveries" and his desire to bring out the "unusualness of the usual" (Pasternak, "Three Letters," 5) that motivation and logical connections in *Doctor Zhivago* may appear artificial. The novel has drawn particularly strong criticism for its use of coincidence and highly improbable connections between events. But what such criticism ignores is that through coincidences Pasternak reshapes the frames of traditional reasoning. For him extraordinary experiences are the commonplaces of everyday life,[17] and so coincidences are a quintessential fact in *Doctor Zhivago.* The most striking examples are as follows: when at the front during World War I Iurii, Lara, Galiullin, and Galiullin's dying father all accidentally appear in one place; on the trip to the Urals, under extraordinary circumstances, Zhivago encounters Strel'nikov, who turns out to be Lara's vanished husband; Zhivago later becomes the last person whom Strel'nikov is to see in his lifetime; Mademoiselle Fleury from Meliuzeevo happens to walk by as Zhivago collapses with a heart attack in the street; and quite by chance Lara comes to Zhivago's funeral. These are only some of the more egregious examples among the novel's numerous coincidences. They are fragments of experience in which the whole life of a character resonates in a spatio-temporal microcosm and suggests "the themes of predestination and of intertwined destinies . . ." (Struve 1970, 236). As plot devices Pasternak makes coincidences into temporal nodes that force the reader to travel back into the past in order to unravel and reexamine the characters' experiences and thus to reconsider events in their lives as extraordinary that initially might have passed for trivialities. Thus his use of coincidences teaches readers that experience is never completed and always remains open-ended.

The Poems of *Doctor Zhivago*

Contrary to the readers' expectations, the novel does not end when the story ends in part 16, with the aging Gordon and Dudorov reading Zhivago's book edited by Evgraf and talking about the ideas it inspires. Pasternak adds one more part to the novel, consisting entirely of Iurii Zhivago's poems. This unusual narrative strategy takes on a special significance because through this cycle Pasternak's and Zhivago's lives join, in a personal quest to transform their poetic style. The poems also acquire a special emphasis because they are closely associated with major themes of *Doctor Zhivago.*

When at some point in the narrative Pasternak comments on Zhivago's aspiration to achieve a simpler, more restrained style, he obviously implies a parallel between the hero and himself (3:434–35). During his second stay in Varykino in part 14 Zhivago is writing a poem, "Skazka," about Saint George— later included in the last chapter under the title "A Fable"—and in the process tries to perfect his style through more distinct imagery and precise vocabulary. Pasternak describes the birth of this new, sparser imagery in detail: "He gave up the pompous meter with the caesura and cut down the lines to four metric feet, as you would do fighting verbosity in prose. After that, it became more difficult to write but more engaging. The work became livelier but useless words still interfered with it. He forced himself to shorten the lines even more. . . .

Objects barely named by words began to acquire concrete shapes" (3:435). The stylistic ideal Zhivago achieves in this poem and in fact in most poems of the Zhivago cycle is a model for Pasternak himself. Pasternak's style in the Zhivago poems is lucid, straightforward, almost devoid of metaphoricity, and the last part of the novel can thus be said to have become Pasternak's realization of his lifelong quest for simplicity of style.

Hiding his authorship behind that of a fictional character, Pasternak gains the advantage, in the opinion of a Russian commentator, that "the removal of the personal, biographical aspect allowed him to enlarge the thematic range of his lyrics and openly to include in his arsenal elements of imagery from the Christian tradition."[18] Despite Pasternak's attribution of the cycle to his fictional protagonist, the poems leave no doubt that they are the work of an accomplished poet. Neither can the reader miss, in fact, that they "represent, in every particular, Pasternak's own responses and attitudes to the worlds around him" (Hingley 1983, 218). The identification of the Zhivago cycle with Pasternak himself has led some critics to discuss it separately from the novel. J. W. Dyck, for example, in a general study on Pasternak, includes the cycle in his chapter on Pasternak's poetry rather than discussing it in the context of the novel. Dyck argues that although the twenty-five poems constitute an indispensable commentary on *Doctor Zhivago* and, if excluded, would make the novel incomplete, they can also be treated apart from the novel, "as an independent artistic structure" (Dyck 1972, 93). In a sense, Dyck is correct in his assessment since all the poems can stand independently and need not be closely and directly connected with the novel. Yet they do enrich readers' understanding of the novel and its protagonist. For these reasons the poems will be discussed here, in the context of the novel. The connection of the two modes of expression seeks "to achieve reconciliation between specific incidents documented in prose and then later . . . [in] poetry, affording a sense of 'dialogue'" between them (Danow 1991, 954). An attempt will be made to establish and analyze this dialogic relationship in discussion of Zhivago's poems.

Pasternak wrote these poems between 1946 and 1953. In the novel they are consecutively numbered, but thematically they break into defined topics that are linked to the narrative of the novel. Dimitri Obolensky, in his seminal essay on *Doctor Zhivago*'s poems, suggests that these topics are nature, love, and "the meaning and purpose of life" (Obolensky 1978, 152), and the last group centers around the ideas of art and Christianity that pervade the whole of *Doctor Zhivago*.

In the opening poem of the cycle the themes of predestination and suffering are sounded with great force. "Gamlet" ("Hamlet") is, as the title suggests, about the eponymous Shakespeare character. Alone on stage, he looks into his own future ("I catch in a far-away echo / What may happen in my future," 3:511). The persona of the actor and the character he plays merge as the poet leaves deliberately vague who is referred to by the pronoun "I." Readers may even suppose that the poet is the hero of this poem. Reconciled with his predicament of suffering and death, the speaker appeals to his father to spare his life. In the speaker's begging his father that "If it is possible, Abba, Father / Take this cup away" (3:511), overtly Christian overtones begin to surface. The speaker and the addressee of these words remain ambiguous, as they could be ascribed to the actor pondering his human destiny, to Hamlet facing the ghost, or to Christ appealing to God. Predestination exists for the actor, Hamlet, and Christ, and neither of them can escape it. The speaker voluntarily accepts the design of his father and agrees to follow it, although he realizes that his life will be full of loneliness and suffering: "Yet the sequence of the acts has been set. / And the end of the path is inevitable. / I am alone. Everything else is drowning in Pharisaism. / To live a life is more than crossing a field" (3:511). The theme of self-sacrifice in Pasternak's "Hamlet" is amplified through the connections with Vedeniapin's philosophy and Zhivago's own ideas on this subject. It also relates to Pasternak and his time. In Sinyavsky's words, "Hamlet" is permeated with Pasternak's "awareness of his own plight as a writer, his possible and imminent death, and in the broad sense, of the lot of each of us." When the secular and the religious planes of the poem interpenetrate, contemporaneity is effectively placed into focus. "Hamlet" "becomes the story of our epoch . . . Christ still lives today" (Sinyavsky 1978, 100). The Christ figure in the poem is closely associated with Zhivago's destiny as a poet and his self-sacrifice in the name of poetry.

"Mart" ("March"), the second poem, may seem just a nature lyric, but in the author's general design it stands first among the poems that follow the progress of nature between the celebration of the Holy Week and Christ's betrayal at Gethsemane. "March" celebrates the awakening of nature and the energy of life that it brings: chattering streams of water from the melting snow, the pigeons cooing and the smells of fresh air and dung. Numerous action verbs charge the atmosphere of the poem with life-affirming dynamism. "March" is significant in two respects. First, it brings together the three forces of the universe important both in the novel and in the first two poems: man, nature, and Christ. Second, as Livingstone points out, this poem fills a temporal gap in the narrative. In part 10 there are several hints that the time is Easter, yet instead of the religious celebration Pasternak describes a meeting full of political speeches glorifying violence (Livingstone, 112). The spiritual world of the poem is thus juxtaposed to the senseless world of violence. The poem also emphasizes the place of the peaceful religious holiday in the natural cycle of life.

The liveliness of "March" is abruptly ended in the following poem, "Na Strastnoi" ("In Holy Week"), by the gloomy mood of people and nature mourning over Christ's death. It is night; everything is cast in darkness, the earth is "naked to the bone," the forest is "unclothed," and the trees resemble "a praying crowd." The sorrow of nature fuses with the sorrow of the procession carrying the cross and Christ's shroud. Man and nature are joined in their grief. There is ritual singing and sobbing of the mourners until midnight, when the expectation of resurrection revives nature and gives people hope that "Death could be overcome / Through the power of the Resurrection" (3:513).

The theme of spring continues in the next two poems, "Belaia noch'" ("White Night") and "Vesenniaia rasputitsa" ("Bad Roads of Spring"), but contains a contrast between urban and rural surroundings. "White Night" is an impressionistic lyric with flashbacks to the white nights in Saint Petersburg, whereas "Bad Roads of Spring" is set in the Urals of the civil war, with an allusion to the partisans. Both poems are united by the singing of a nightingale. If in the first poem the bird's song is reminiscent of youth and romantic love, in the second poem, more concrete in its imagery, the song conveys the complexity of human experience, its "madness, pain, happiness, and torments" (3:515). The first song refers to Iurii's happy youth; the second is about the moods of the more mature Zhivago, returning from one of his trips from Iuriatin to Varykino.

The love theme is introduced in the poem "Ob"iasnenie" ("Explanation"), a veritable hymn to female sexuality ("To be a woman is a great quest, / To drive men mad is true heroism," 3:516). Underlying the passionate lines of the poem are the fictional reality of Zhivago's love for Lara and the biographical reality of Pasternak's love for Olga Ivinskaia. The last line of the poem is fatalistic and points to love's eternal predicament of separation: "The tug to get away pulls yet stronger / And the passion for separation is seductive" (3:517). This was certainly the case in Zhivago's love for Tonia and Lara.

Tension and loneliness permeate the atmosphere of the next poem, "Leto v gorode" ("Summer in the City"), and reflect Pasternak's own fear of spending summers in the city.[19] The poem portrays a sultry summer night; the emptiness of the streets; and the slow, reluctant awakening of the trees at dawn. "Veter" ("Wind") and "Khmel'" (which can be translated into English as "Hops" or "Intoxication") continue the love theme through nature imagery. Both poems are devoted to the poet's feelings for his beloved: the former conveys the poet's sadness on a summer night; the latter describes the intoxicating atmosphere that the physical closeness in a summer rain creates between the poet and his beloved. These two poems are the last "summer" poems in the cycle's progression into fall. The poem "Bab'e leto" ("Indian Summer") marks the change in nature and, as in "March," conveys a sense of dynamism in nature's seasonal transitions. But the emphasis is mainly on the interior now, as all fall activities are organized around the house, where women prepare pickles for the winter. The joys of everyday life are described metonymically, through voices, laughter, and noise. This poem is the poet's somber musings about the imminent end of things. Responding to withering nature, the poet turns to the theme of death. The oncoming fall brings melancholy that also carries into the next poem, "Svad'ba" ("Wedding"). Amid the happy wedding festivities full of music and dance, laughter and noise, the poet observes that "Life is only a moment, / Only the dissolving / Of ourselves in all others, / As is a gift to them" (3:520), and thus reiterates on an existentialist note the topic of self-sacrifice, mentioned above in its Christian variant.

The entire intellectual and emotional context of the poem "Osen'" ("Autumn") is woven around the themes of loneliness, of humility before one's predicament, of self-sacrifice and suffering. Yet toward the end the tone lightens up as the poet turns to nature and love. In the penultimate stanza the imagery of love alternates with that of nature: the forest is shedding its leaves and the beloved loosens her dressing gown, both movements unfolding with graceful, remarkable swiftness before our eyes. The last stanza then, in its celebration of the lightness and joy of true love, reverberates with Pasternak's earlier lyric from the cycle "Second Birth" ("To Love Some Is a Heavy Cross"). For the poet, his beloved appears as a manifestation of beauty and happiness in moments of despair. "Autumn" refers back to Zhivago's second stay in Varykino with Lara.

The poem "Skazka" ("Fable") has already been mentioned in connection with Zhivago's endeavor to polish his poetic style. At the origin of this poem is Zhivago's memory of the wolves howling and drawing close to his and Lara's house in Varykino. He interprets their approach as an omen and wants to protect Lara from danger. His thoughts in the poem take the shape of the legend of Saint George and the dragon, and Zhivago himself can be likened to Saint George and the maiden to Lara. In the dragon, moreover, readers can detect elements of Komarovskii, from whose enslavement Zhivago had always wanted to rescue Lara.[20] But the poem can also be read in a more general context, and it is hard to disagree with Henry Gifford that "Fable" seeks "to transcend individual lives" and symbolizes the struggle for freedom (Gifford 1977, 209). This interpretation gains strength in conjunction with the last poem of the cycle, "Gefsimanskii sad" ("The Garden of Gethsemane"), discussed below.

In "Avgust" ("August"), although its title might suggest so, the poet does not focus on nature but imagines his own death. There is a specific temporal reference: it is the sixth of August, the holiday of Christ's Transfiguration in the Russian Orthodox tradition. On this day in 1903 Pasternak himself had fallen off a horse and only miraculously escaped death. Written in 1953, the poem becomes Pasternak's commemoration of this event. But in the context of the cycle, it resonates with "Hamlet" in the poet's humility in the face of approaching death.

"Zimniaia noch'" ("Winter Night") is arguably Pasternak's most beautiful love lyric. The lovers are portrayed metonymically, through the shadows of crossed arms and legs on the wall and through the sound of shoes falling on the floor. The image of a burning candle on the table appears in four out of eight stanzas of the poem and becomes its refrain: "A candle burned on the table, / A candle burned" (3:526–27). Many critics have commented on the symbolic meaning of this image. Obolensky noticed that a candle appears in those moments of the novel when the destinies of characters unexpectedly intersect (Obolensky 1978, 154). For the first time this motive appears when Iurii sees a candle in a frosted window of a building he is driving past on his way to the Sventitskiis' Christmas party. It is at this moment that the words "The candle burned on the table" come to his mind. Ten years later, during his stay with Lara in Varykino, Iurii finishes the poem. The room with the candle that inspired the lines turns out to be Pasha Antipov's, Lara's future husband. During that Christmas season in 1911, however, Zhivago could not possibly know that he was destined to meet Lara, fall in love with her, lose her, and finally spend the rest of his days in that very room where the candle burned. The candle thus truly illuminates "crossings of destiny" (3:526). The importance of the image of the candle is further emphasized by the fact that "The Candle Burned" was one of the tentative titles of the novel *Doctor Zhivago*.[21]

"Winter Night" is followed by "Razluka" ("Parting") and "Svidanie" ("Meeting"), which close the love theme of the cycle. These poems, respectively, express Zhivago's melancholy upon Lara's departure and a romantic fantasy of the meeting between the poet figure and his beloved. Both poems confirm the poet's reconciliation with the loss of his beloved and sound like a farewell to her.

In the remaining six poems Zhivago turns to religious themes of birth and death, love and suffering. "Rozhdestvenskaia zvezda" ("Star of the Nativity") recounts the events of Christ's birth. With its rich details this longest poem of the cycle becomes a poetic retelling of the biblical story. "Rassvet" ("Dawn") is a more elusive poem that does not explicitly disclose the subject addressed.

When the poet confesses to the unknown stranger that he meant everything in the poet's destiny, readers can only guess that the mysterious "he" is Christ, and the second stanza confirms this assumption by the use of the word *testament*.[22] Gratefully, the poet relates to Christ that, after many years of religious detachment, Christ's words have become the source of spiritual revival for him. Once again the poet yearns for a communion with other people and their love.

"Chudo" ("The Miracle"), like "Star of the Nativity," also follows a biblical story and is a narrative with a rather heavy moralistic ending. The poem relates the incident of Christ's withering of the fig tree on the way from Bethany to Jerusalem. The fruitless tree is portrayed against the parched landscape of the Dead Sea shore, dominated by the desert heat, the still reeds and a prickly scrubwood scorched by the sun. In this arid landscape Christ accuses a fig tree of uselessness and lack of talent. After these words are spoken, the fig tree is "instantly consumed and turned to ashes" (3:534). "The Miracle" returns readers to the cycle of religious holidays, as its central episode marks the Monday of the Holy Week in the Orthodox Church calendar.

"Zemlia" ("Earth") takes readers back to a northern climate again; it is about the return of spring, the awakening of nature: white nights, melting snow, and budding trees are part of its landscape. Everything in the poem alludes to the lot of humans and their suffering. Concrete imagery also appears in "Durnye dni" ("Evil Days"), which is devoted to the first few days of the Holy Week, beginning with Christ's entry into Jerusalem. Anticipating the imminent fulfillment of his fate, Christ recalls major events of his life. The intensification of the dramatic atmosphere occurs in the following two poems, both entitled "Magdalina" ("Magdalene"). In both poems Magdalene prophesies the death of Christ in a highly emotional, personal voice.

Finally, completing the cycle, is the poem "The Garden of Gethsemane." Following the Gospel of Matthew, this account of Christ's betrayal in the garden connects back to the first poem, "Hamlet." If in "Hamlet" the speaker asks his father to take the cup of death away, now the moment has come when he meets his predicament. The prayer to the father is mentioned again. In the last two stanzas of the poem the three voices of Christ, Hamlet, and Zhivago merge in the motif of self-sacrifice. In the last lines Christ appears as the final judge of history ("Like a caravan of sails, out of the dark, / The centuries will come to my judgment," 3:540). And by analogy with Christ and Hamlet, Zhivago becomes the judge of his time. One of the deepest beliefs of the novel is embedded in these last lines: the death of the poet, like Christ's, is not the end. Zhivago will live on in his art.

"The Garden of Gethsemane" sums up the novel with a message both profoundly religious and at the same time universally secular: one must confront the inevitable and accept one's path in life. Within our small personal world, we are all caught in the vast sweep of history and should respond to it without self-deception and with humility. But "The Garden of Gethsemane," taken in a more concrete historical perspective, could also symbolize the resurrection of Russia after World War II and the death of Stalin (Bodin 1990, 398). It is beyond doubt that this last poem, through the related images of Christ-Hamlet-Zhivago and with its glance into the future, endows the novel with the hope of individual, social, and religious resurrection.

CHAPTER SEVEN

The Last Years:
When the Weather Clears
and "People and Situations:
An Autobiographical Sketch"

It is generally accepted that Pasternak's last poetry does not have the linguistic intensity and dazzling brilliance of his early work. Critics sometimes claim that the poet's work after *Doctor Zhivago* shows signs of resignation, even complacency. His tone becomes life affirming, while his view of life seems to lose its depth and abstraction. The content begins to reflect more simple things, and his style turns plainer and loses its earlier ornamental splendor. Angela Livingstone, for example, observes that although Pasternak's ideas, by and large, remain the same, "the immediacy and the tension—the fight—has gone out of [them]. It is more an expounded faith than an urgent experience" (Livingstone 1978, 170). Another critic points out that style in Pasternak's collection of poems *Kogda razguliaetsia* (*When the Weather Clears,* 1956–1959)[1] is characterized by "far less buoyancy" than his early poetry (de Mallac 1981, 251).

When the Weather Clears is Pasternak's most distinct poetic achievement of the last decade of his life. In it he moves toward increasingly contemplative verse and his own final style. Pasternak, in this last collection, which was never published in his lifetime, no longer indulges in the stylistic escapades of his youth, but one should exercise caution in characterizing his late poetry as inferior to his earlier collections, as does Livingstone. During this last stage of his life and career, Pasternak revises his priorities and shifts his attention to a different area—"that of philosophical and metaphysical thought," hardly present in his earlier verse (Sinyavsky 1978, 101). Therefore, rather than approaching his late poetic practice as a pale shadow of his earlier achievements, it is worth taking a look at the broadening of his poetic perspective in its transition from subjective and complex imagery to a more generalized and deliberately laconic expression.

When the Weather Clears is a collection of forty-one poems with familiar themes, often related for Pasternak: nature, the poet and his poetry, praise of women, the fate of his friends, and his relationship to God. The collection opens with an epigraph from Marcel Proust: "A book is a large cemetery where, on most tombstones, the washed-out names can no longer be read." It is hard not to read this epigraph as a commentary on the poetic art in general and its ability to re-create the texture of experience and to restore it through the principle of association around small and commonplace things, around those "washed-out" moments of time that constitute our lives. The poet must illuminate and make meaningful those moments that people tend to lose from sight.

The untitled opening poem outlines this effort: "I want to find / The essence of things, / In work, in seeking out my way, / In my heart's turmoil" (2:72). Pasternak formulates clearly what this collection is concerned with: "I want to grasp the thread / Of great events and destinies, / To live, to think, to feel, to love, / And to make discoveries" (2:72). These concrete human desires, although always pulsating in his art, are now moved to the foreground and named directly. The poet will try to formulate the "law of passion" through its particulars encompassing all its constituents, including sin, the pace of time, blooming trees, the scent of roses, the roar of thunder, and other things associated with sensual experience (2:72–73). His profound quest is to move beyond externalities and fill his poetry with life itself, with less flamboyance than earlier but more insight into the nature of things, into their spiritual unifying principle.

A prominent place is also given to the artist's moral stature and his art, already familiar to readers from earlier work. Pasternak addresses this issue early in the volume in another untitled poem whose first line runs: "To be famous is ugly" (2:74). In Pasternak's view, fame should remain outside the artist's goals and concerns, and he warns the artist against the petty preoccupation of keeping a record of his life or worrying about the manuscripts that can later be used for an official biography (2:74). The most important thing in art, says Pasternak, is to remain human instead of trying to become a literary monument ("But be alive and only alive / Until the end alive," 2:74). Once again he reiterates his old concept of art as a way of seeking personal satisfaction in work and giving oneself to people rather than using art for self-promotion.

A curious example of Pasternak's moral self-criticism can be found in the poem "Peremena" ("Change"). This poem continues the theme "to be famous is ugly," based on the contrast between two stages in the poet's creative life. When he was younger, he was drawn to ordinary people not because of idealistic concepts about them but because only among these people could he find authentic life, "without pomp and bragging" (2:78). However, as the years went by the poet became corrupted by the ideas of his epoch that considered "grief to be shameful" and demanded an optimistic outlook on life (2:78). When he betrayed the trust simple people had in him by flowing with the current of literary politics, he began to feel that he lost them as they "lost him" (2:78). When he chose to follow official cultural decrees, he became detached from the genuine life of real people. This poem is filled with sadness and regret for replacing the voice of his heart and his ideals by political conventions. This reads as a warning to artists who face the choice between official recognition of their art on the one hand and following their own conscience on the other. The image of the "official poet" that emerges in "Change" is contrasted with the image of a true poet committed to his artistic goal in the poem "Veter" ("Wind"), subtitled "Four Excerpts about Blok." "Wind" becomes not only Pasternak's tribute to the memory of one of his most beloved poets, Aleksandr Blok, but also presents a portrait of a genuine artist, who rises above official culture and is loved and known for his true talent rather than through advertisement by the politically correct critics.

The poet's stature in life is illuminated by Pasternak in the poem "Noch'" ("Night"): "Do not sleep, do not sleep, O artist, / Do not give in to sleep. / You are a hostage of eternity, / Captured by time" (2:97). Alive in these lines are Pasternak's thoughts of the self-sacrifice and immortality of the artist, who has to give himself completely to the service of art and unconditionally accept his predicament. There is a sacral quality to being a poet: the poetic vocation is a vow, comparable to a vow taken in religious orders. Regardless of the consequences, it is the artist's responsibility to be truthful in his portrayal of life. Pasternak repeatedly says in his last collection that the true aim of art is to understand the essence of life through a free creative process, not connected to any social or political functions.

In *When the Weather Clears* Pasternak succeeds in revealing his inner thoughts through the external forms of the natural world. As before, man and nature are inseparable in his poetic universe, but now, as in the Zhivago cycle, this connection is deepened by the transitoriness of life. The sight of the falling snow in "Sneg idet" ("Snow is Falling") becomes a reminder of life's eternal cycle and time's unrelenting progression from one snow to the other, from one season to the next, and from year to year. Predictably, the poet ponders his own predestination. Without illusion and with remarkable control he faces his future, his end. Although he can see the end of his life journey, his mood is consistently optimistic. In two poems, "Za povorotom" ("Around the Turning") and "Vse sbylos'" ("Everything Has Come True"), the poet strolls in the forest, pondering his life and the future. It is not thoughts of sadness about the imminent death that overcome him but rather the joy of realization that all his dreams and hopes will come true after he is gone (2:120). This life-affirming attitude, also shared by Zhivago, follows from Pasternak's belief in rebirth. There is no reason to have a tragic view of life if one sees the future in bright colors. And therefore, even his most melancholy poem in *When the Weather Clears,* "Dusha" ("Soul"), presents a rational outlook on death and suffering. "Soul" is about the poet's friends who suffered and died under Stalinism. The poet compares his soul to a crypt, an urn, and a cemetery where the memories of his friends are buried forever. His soul, like a mill, grinds his memories of hardships and mixes them with his happy memories. The poem ends on an optimistic note: "Go on grinding / Everything that happened to me / Into funereal decay, / As you have been doing for nearly forty years" (2:75). Thus although pity for his friends will always remain with the poet, the loss of them will be balanced by the joys of his life and art.

It is in a few undeniably religious poems, however, that the quintessence of the late Pasternak comes through. His emphasis throughout *When the Weather Clears* is on the joy of existence and should be treated as part of his Christian views (Hughes 1973, 160). The autobiographical poem "V bol'nitse" ("In the Hospital") is based on Pasternak's hospitalization for a heart attack in 1952. The sick poet arrives at the hospital in a life-threatening condition. There, for lack of space, he is placed on a bed in the hall. He looks out of the window and marvels at the view. Suddenly the ordeal of his present situation and his fear of death give way to an overpowering joy of having experienced the world (2:102–3). The poet humbly thanks God for his marvelous deeds, as well as for the gift of life that he received from him. In his letter to Nina Tabidze, Pasternak describes this moment at the hospital almost in the same words used in the poem: "'Lord, I whispered, thank Thee for having laid the colors so thickly and for making life and death such that Thy language is majesty and music, for making me an artist, and for creativity, which is Thy school and for preparing me all my life for this night. And I rejoiced and wept from happiness."[2] Pasternak's religious effusion in this poem has an epiphanic quality not only for himself but also for the reader. Nowhere before has Pasternak been revealing so directly his Christian feelings as in "In the Hospital." This poem provides the most direct access to the old poet's view of the universe and shows how "everyday detail serves as attestation of eternity; both landscape and human soul are illuminated here by the touch of God . . ." (Sinyavsky 1978, 108).

Stylistically "In the Hospital" is direct and precise in its diction and, in fact, borders on prose. "In the Hospital" is an excellent example of how Pasternak attains simplicity and restraint without losing his commitment to revealing the "unusualness of the usual." In this poem life continues to manifest itself in all its richness and conveys a sense of the vastness and diversity of the world in which there is something for everybody. Pasternak tries to place himself everywhere, as if he were a guide for rediscovering the world. For example, in the poem "Bozhii mir" ("God's World"), in one stanza, he imagines the infinite immensity of the universe symbolized by the letters he receives from his correspondents: "Mountains, countries, frontiers, and lakes; / Island and continents appear; / Discussions, reports, and reviews, / Children, adolescents and old people" (2:129). In the Russian original this stanza has no verb, and the feeling thus created is that the poet wants to catch the simultaneity and vivacity of existence in one moment. Contrary to Livingstone's criticism that enumeration of objects is a weakness in the late Pasternak, the poet's commitment to detail allows him to create images of complex intensity. Pasternak's use of "nouns in lists" (Livingstone 1978, 173) is an associative and juxtapositional generation of meaning, implicit rather than explicit, free rather than guided by the structures of a predicate. What he says by these "lists" is that eternity resonates in every fragment of reality. The leanness of his imagery in comparison with his early poetic practice is no indication of his declining mastery but rather asserts the freedom and naturalness of his new idiom.

Several of the poems in *When the Weather Clears* are written in praise of women. Pasternak has always shown a great respect for and veneration of women, and many of his lyrics are devoted to them. But in his last collection Pasternak's subject is no longer attainment or rejection of love nor a meditation on the world transformed by love. There is only one poem, "Bez nazvaniia" ("Without a Title"), that is still explicitly about love and feminine beauty ("Let me lock up your beauty / In my dark chamber of verse," 2:77). Rather, the woman's attraction now lies in her inspirational power for the poet's verses. In "Eva" ("Eve") the poet confirms his attitude toward women as material for his poetic inspiration. With eroticism increasingly marginalized in *When the Weather Clears,* woman personifies warmth, the emotional security of childhood, and life itself. In the poem "Zhenshiny v detstve" ("Women in My Childhood") Pasternak thanks all women, as he would thank God, for filling his life with wonder and declares his indebtedness to them. And in "God's World" he lavishes all his power of adoration on women: "Precious letters of women! / I too have fallen from the sky. / I swear before you now and forever / I shall remain yours in all eternity" (2:129).

A more rational attitude toward love is expressed in the long poem "Vakkhanaliia" ("Bacchanalia"). Although the title promises a drunken feast and a celebration of passion, Pasternak's focus is on a trivial fling between the lonely "someone," in whom the poet himself is recognizable, and a bored young dancer who meets him at a party.[3] Their love lasts one night, and in the morning "Their sport and jokes are forgotten, / The dishes are washed in the kitchen. / No one remembers anything" (2:118). These lines, in the general spirit of the book, are, again, about the transitoriness of life and time's propensity to transform experience into fleeting memories. Love no longer sets the poet's heart aflame but rather fills him with gratitude for the joyous moments. Once they are over, he must return to his art. The ending of "Bacchanalia" is hardly a surprise in its matter-of-factness. Love can no longer dominate the whole of the poet's life that is now drawn to the world of nature and spiritual experience. Increasingly only these latter aspects of existence evoke a truly passionate response. The title poem of the volume provides a perfect illustration of this shift of poetic focus: "O Nature, O world, O Universe's Essence, / With tears of happiness / And with joyous trembling, / I will be in your long service" (2:86).

In 1956 Pasternak prepared an autobiographical essay titled "People and Situations: An Autobiographical Sketch" for a collection of his poetry. This work has already been referred to on several occasions in this study, but a few more words should be said about its affinity with *When the Weather Clears.* As in his last verses, Pasternak assumes in this essay a more distant and philosophical view of his past and present than in his earlier works. Although the essay deals largely with the same topics as *Safe Conduct* and describes, with a few alterations, the same events, gone is the immediacy of experience and the complexity of the stylistic texture characteristic of his earlier autobiographical sketch. Pasternak's last poetry collection as well as the autobiographical essay can be and indeed have been called "Tolstoyan in their nakedness," because in both the poet demonstrates an unprecedented moral discipline in his attempt to clarify his vision of life (Milosz 1989, 218). Within the limits of this late contemplative approach to the self and the world, what really matters to the older Pasternak is that his imagery becomes a true reflection of his state of mind and grasp of reality and that it expresses the spiritual harmony and control he has been trying to achieve since his early poetic experiments.

To the end of his career Pasternak, remarkably, preserves his artistic vitality, looking into the future in a never ending search for his artistic ideal. It seems that readers' response to his late work should be like his own response to life and art as expressed in the conclusion of his autobiographical essay and in the last poem of *When the Weather Clears,* "Edinstvennye dni" ("Unique Days"). In both instances he steps back from what he has gone through and contemplates his life as an "experience out of time" (Gifford 1977, 222). He insists that the memorable days of love, as the whole of life, are unique, and it is this uniqueness that he has always tried to capture in his poetry. The difference is that now the right language does not come to him as spontaneously as when he was young. This thought is well conveyed in the last lines of the autobiographical essay: "Now this unique and unrepeatable world has receded into the distance and is seen on the horizon like mountains are seen from the plain or as a faraway big city emerges in the night glow. One would have to write about it in a way to make the heart stop and the hair stand on end. To write about it in a manner less stunning and vivid than Gogol and Dostoevsky have depicted Petersburg, is not only senseless and aimless; to write like that would be both low and dishonest. We are still far from that ideal" (4:345).

CHAPTER EIGHT

Conclusion

Pasternak's work unfolded over a period of fundamental changes in Russian cultural, social, and political history. He lived through three revolutions—the one of 1905, the February revolution of 1917, and the October revolution of the same year—and his life spanned three wars: World War I, the Russian civil war, and World War II. He witnessed both the rise of Stalin and his death and in between the terrors of Stalinism when many of his friends vanished in prisons or camps, were executed, or committed suicide. Pasternak himself went through years of political pressure and persecution, and when *Doctor Zhivago* was published abroad, he faced the threat of exile from Russia. Before he died in 1960, only one great literary figure of his generation, Anna Akhmatova, was still alive. But her work was more intimate and more oriented toward her own sensibilities and the realm of the personal than his. She had remained quiet during the years of oppression, whereas Pasternak had never quite left the literary scene. Of these two survivors, therefore, Pasternak was the more public figure, and his works continued to be published throughout his career. In his writings Pasternak reached beyond the purely lyrical world and, especially in *Doctor Zhivago,* expanded into the realm of history, relating its effect on the lives, thoughts, and preoccupations of his contemporaries. Of his entire literary generation, he was the only one who "revealed a capacity to grow with the times, and yet remain essentially himself" (Gifford 1977, 237).

When his literary career began in the second decade of the twentieth century, he associated with the artistic avant-garde, and his modern sensibility rang out loud and clear in his two volumes of poetry, *My Sister-Life* and *Themes and Variations.* In these collections Pasternak invested language with dazzling metaphorical power and magic and demonstrated his authentic talent for capturing the grandeur of life in its every small manifestation. In Marina Tsvetaeva's words, "his is the eye which sees the hidden but aspires to become an eye which sees the obvious."[1] When the Soviet ideologues began to forge their own literary tradition and certain types of artistic experience became difficult to express and publish, Pasternak managed to adjust to the change. He succeeded as much as it was possible, never allowing the new literary policies to alienate him completely from the reading public and trying his artistic potential in the genre of the epic poem, a form favored by the literary authorities. He strove toward greater linguistic clarity and restraint in the last three decades of his literary career, thus moving from avant-garde mannerism through some faux realist-romantic attempts to classical lucidity. Despite the changes in his style, he remained faithful to his principle of artistic representation of reality as constantly changing and original. There is a sense of continuity in his entire work, in which the world of Soviet Russia meets the world of the author's modernist past. This is particularly evident in *Doctor Zhivago,* the work that takes the mature Pasternak's artistic aspirations to their culmination.

Pasternak still stands as the most powerful figure of his literary generation. The poet Vladimir Mayakovsky tried to merge with the revolution and put his avant-garde ardor at its service, only to be devoured by the ideological machine hostile to his rebellious spirit and innovations; Osip Mandelstam remained critical and unaccepting of the transformations in Russian society brought on by the new regime and was thus marginalized on the literary scene and eventually destroyed in the horrors of Stalinism; Marina Tsvetaeva, by virtue of her refined sensitivities, was unable to embrace Soviet Russia and took her own life; and Anna Akhmatova was isolated and relegated to oblivion. Unlike these other great contemporaries, Pasternak was artistically active throughout the most brutal periods of Soviet history. It is fair to say that his was the most resilient and hopeful voice of this entire poetic generation. It should also be emphasized that he paid a price, both artistic and personal, for having his voice heard, but he never really caved in to the regime and preserved his moral and artistic integrity throughout his life.

In his works Pasternak continues the best traditions of Russian literature: devotion to individual freedom and moral and spiritual values; intolerance of oppressive government; and concern with the present and the future of Russia. But what makes Pasternak's contribution to Russian literature especially valuable is the life-affirming nature of his works and their magnificent ability to breathe life into gray everyday reality and invigorate it through a unique and vibrant vision. It is this vision that makes Pasternak, especially the mature Pasternak, a true "poet of hope" (Gifford 1977, 237).

Notes

Introduction

1. Pasternak worked on his play *Slepaia krasavitsa* (*Blind Beauty*) during the last year of his life but never completed it. It was published in the unfinished version in the journal *Prostor* (*Spacious Land*) in 1969.

2. Ironically, this was the journal that rejected the publication of *Doctor Zhivago* in 1956.

3. Victor Erlich, "Boris Pasternak and Russian Poetic Culture of His Time," in *Boris Pasternak and His Times: Selected Papers from the Second International Symposium on Pasternak,* ed. Lazar Fleishman (Berkeley: Berkeley Slavic Specialties, 1989), p. 45.

4. Basil Dmytryshyn, *A History of Russia* (Englewood Cliffs, N.J.: Prentice-Hall, 1977), p. 442.

5. Pasternak's views about the Jewish question in Russia are discussed in chapter 6 of this book.

6. The original—in Pasternak's own German—is quoted from *Rainer Maria Rilke, Maria Tsvetaeva, Boris Pasternak: Briefwechsel,* ed. Jevgeniy Pasternak, Jelena Pasternak, and Konstantin M. Asadovskiy (Frankfurt am Main: Insel, 1983), pp. 75–76. All translations from German are mine unless indicated otherwise.

7. Valerii Briusov, "Kliuchi tain" ["The Keys to the Mysteries"], in *Literaturnye manifesty* [*Literary Manifestoes*], ed. Karl Eiermacher, vol. 1 (Munich: Wilhelm Fink, 1969), p. 29.

8. A. Bely, "Simvolizm kak miroponimanie " ["Symbolism as a World View"], in *Literaturnye manifesty,* p. 31.

9. Pasternak's knowledge of German was exceptional: he began studying German with a private tutor and later continued it at school. He also excelled at French and English as a student.

10. Viacheslav Vsevolodovich Ivanov, "Pasternak i OPOIAZ," ["Pasternak and OPOIAZ"], in *Tynianovskii sbornik: Tret'i Tynianovskie chteniia* (Riga: Zinatne, 1988), p. 72.

11. Boris Pasternak, "Simvolizm i bessmertie" ["Symbolism and Immortality"], in Lazar Fleishman, *Stat'i o Pasternake* (Bremen: K-Presse, 1977), p. 116.

12. Cubo-futurism was the Russian precursor of Western Dadaism. Cubo-futurist

experiments with painting and *zaum'* are similar to the abstract art of the dadaists. Although there was no connection between dadaism—founded largely as an artistic and literary movement in Zurich in 1916—and cubo-futurism— which gained recognition in Russia as early as 1912 after the publication of the first 1912 Cubo-futurist manifesto, "A Slap in the Face of the Public Taste"—their artistic goals were similar. In Roman Jakobson's words, both movements "finished once and for all with the principle of the legendary coalition of form and content, through a realization of the violence of artistic form, the toning down of pictorial and poetic semantics, through the color and texture *as such* of the nonobjective picture, through the fanatic word of transrational verses *as such*" (see Jakobson, "Dada," in *Language in Literature,* ed. Krystyna Pomorska and Stephen Rudy [Cambridge, Mass.: Belknap and Harvard Univ. Press, 1987], p. 39). Cubo-futurists anticipated such dada experiments as, for example, a simultaneous recitation of poetry and the creation of illustrations almost entirely out of letters.

13. Vladimir Markov, *Russian Futurism: A History* (Berkeley: Univ. of California Press, 1968), p. 229.

14. Nikolay Khardzhiev, "Poetry and Painting," in *The Russian Avant-Garde* (Stockholm: Hylaea Prints, 1976), p. 23.

15. Vladimir Mayakovsky, "O noveishei russkoi poezii i zhivopisi" ["About the Newest Russian Poetry and Painting"], in *Polnoe sobranie sochinenii [Complete Collection of Works],* vol. 1 (Moscow: Gosizdat khudozhestvennoi literatury, 1955–1961), p. 365.

16. Aliksei Kruchenykh and Velemir Khlebnikov, "Slovo kak takovoe" ["The Word as Such"], in *Manifesty i programmy russkikh futuristov,* ed. Vladimir Markov (1913; rpt. Munich: Wilhelm Fink, 1967), p. 53.

Chapter 1: Early Poetry

1. Pasternak's letter to Mandelstam of 24 September 1928, in *Sobranie sochinenii v piati tomakh,* vol. 5, p. 249.

2. Ibid.

3. Pasternak's religious views are discussed in more detail in chapter 7.

4. Miroslav Drozda, "Pasternak i levoe isskustvo," *Ceskoslovenska rusistika* 12, no. 4 (1967): 224.

5. Boris Pasternak, *Poems,* trans. Eugene M. Kayden (Yellow Springs, Ohio: Antioch Press, 1964), p. xx.

6. Yury Tynyanov, "Words and Things in Pasternak," in *Pasternak: A Collection of Critical Essays,* ed. Victor Erlich (Englewood Cliffs, N.J.: Prentice-Hall, 1978), p. 32.

7. Efim Etkind, "Pasternak, novator poeticheskoi rechi," in *Boris Pasternak 1890–1960: Colloque de Cérisy-la-Salle (11–14 septembre 1975),* ed. Michel Aucouturier (Paris: Institut d'Etudes Slaves, 1979), pp. 118–41.

Chapter 2: Early Prose

1. The editors' notes to Pasternak's short fiction in volume 4 of his *Sobranie sochinenii v piati tomakh* provide a valuable commentary on the history of the writing and publication of his short prose.

2. Wladimir Weidlé, "Boris Pasternak i modernizm" [intro.], in Boris Pasternak, *Sochineniia* [*Works*], vol. 1, p. xxxv.

3. Boris Pasternak, "Neskol'ko polozhenii" ["Some Propositions"], *Sobranie sochinenii v piati tomakh,* vol. 4, p. 369.

4. Jakobson also addresses this subject in "The Contours of *The Safe Conduct,*" in *Semiotics of Art,* ed. Ladislav Matejka and Irwin R. Titunik (Cambridge, Mass.: MIT Press, 1984), p. 192.

5. See Larissa Rudova, *Pasternak's Short Fiction and the Cultural Vanguard,* Middlebury Studies in Russian Language and Literature (New York: Peter Lang, 1994), pp. 113–48.

6. Boris Pasternak, "O predmete i metode psikhologii" ["About the Object and Method of Psychology"], *Slavica Hierosolymitana* 4 (1979): 274–85.

7. See Chrystina Pomorska, "Mayakovsky i vremia" ["Mayakovsky and Time"], *Slavica Hierosolymitana* 5–6 (1981): 341.

8. The resemblance of the relationship between the two poets in the story and that of Mayakovsky and Pasternak is so apparent that a number of critics have commented on it. See, for example, the commentary on the story in vol. 4 of *Sobranie sochinenii v piati tomakh,* p. 806; Christopher Barnes, *Boris Pasternak: A Literary Biography,* vol. 1 (Cambridge: Cambridge Univ. Press, 1989),p. 195; and Lazar Fleishman, *Boris Pasternak: The Poet and His Politics* (Cambridge, Mass.: Harvard Univ. Press, 1990), p. 78.

9. These references are provided by B. M. Borisov and E. B. Pasternak in the commentaries to "The Apelles Mark" in vol. 4 of his *Sobranie sochinenii v piati tomakh,* pp. 805–6.

10. As quoted in Leonore Scheffler, *Evgeniy Zamyatin: Sein Weltbild und seine literarische Thematik* (*Grani* 32 [1956]; Cologne: Böhlau, 1984), p. 94.

11. All quotations from "Liuvers' Childhood" are from Boris Pasternak, *The Voice of Prose,* ed. Christopher Barnes (New York: Grove Press, 1986), p. 158.

12. The theme of Zhenia Liuvers's poetic apprehension of the world is discussed in detail in Susan Layton's article, "Poetic Vision in Pasternak's 'The Childhood of Liuvers,'" *Slavic and East European Journal* 2, no. 22 (1978): 163–74.

13. Boris Pasternak, "Three Letters," *Encounter* 83 (August 1960): 5. Pasternak's written English and German had a slightly idiosyncratic nature, probably due to his primarily academic knowledge of them and his limited experience with the actual spoken languages.

14. See, for example, Isaac Deutscher, "Pasternak and the Calendar of the Revolution," *Partisan Review* 26 (Spring 1959): 251.

15. Sheila Fitzpatrick, *The Cultural Front: Power and Culture in Revolutionary Russia* (Ithaca: Cornell Univ. Press, 1990), p. 112.

16. Shiv K. Kumar, *Bergson and Stream of Consciousness Novel* (London: Blackie and Son, 1962), p. 20.

17. Michel Aucouturier, "Pasternak and Proust," *Forum for Modern Language Studies* 26, no. 4 (1990): 345.

18. Ibid., 343, 346.

19. Yury Sheglov, "O nekotorykh spornykh chertakh poetiki pozdnego Pasternaka" ["About Some Arguable Features of the Late Pasternak"], in *Boris Pasternak: 1890–1990,* ed. Lev Loseff (Northfield, Vt.: Russian School of Norwich Univ., 1991), p. 191.

20. Boris Gasparov, "Vremennoi kontrapunkt kak formoobrazuiushii printsip romana Pasternaka *Doktor Zhivago*" ["Temporal Counterpoint as a Formal Principle in Pasternak's novel *Doctor Zhivago*"], in *Boris Pasternak and His Times: Selected Papers from the Second International Symposium on Pasternak,* ed. Lazar Fleishman (Berkeley: Berkeley Slavic Specialties, 1989), p. 345.

21. Victor Erlich, *Modernism and Revolution: Russian Literature in Transition* (Cambridge: Cambridge Univ. Press, 1994), p. 218.

22. Sergei Tret'iakov, "Happy New Year! Happy New Lef!," in *Russian Futurism through Its Manifestoes. 1912–1928,* ed. Anna Lawton, trans. Anna Lawton and Herbert Eagle (Ithaca: Cornell Univ. Press, 1998), p. 267.

23. I use the concept of the autobiographical "self" of the narrator as it follows from Elizabeth Bruss's formulation, which emphasizes its dual role. The autobiographical self is both an object of study and, simultaneously, the creation of the text about itself. See Bruss's *Autobiographical Acts: The Changing Situation of a Literary Genre* (Baltimore: Johns Hopkins Univ. Press, 1976), pp. 10–11.

24. John Paul Eakin, *Fictions in Autobiography: Studies in the Art of Self-Invention* (Princeton: Princeton Univ. Press, 1994), pp. 3–4.

25. The concept "literariness" was formulated by Roman Jakobson in his article "New Russian Poetry" and widely used by the Russian formalist critics. "Literariness" describes those properties of texts that make them an aesthetic object, for example, their narrative-linguistic features and tropes. See Roman Jakobson, *New Russian Poetry* (Prague: Republika, 1921), p. 11.

Chapter 3: Epic Poems

1. "Pisateli o sebe" ["Writers about Themselves"], in *Sobranie sochinenii v piati tomakh,* vol. 4, p. 621. Originally this short statement appeared in the journal *Na literaturnom postu* 4 (1927).

2. "Otvet na anketu *Leningradskoi pravdy*" ["Answer to a Questionnaire in the *Leningrad Truth*"], *Sobranie sochinenii v piati tomakh,* vol. 4, p. 619.

3. "Chto govoriat pisateli o postanovlenii TsK RKP(b)" ["What Writers Say about the Resolution of the Central Committee of the Workers' and Peasants' Party"], *Sobranie sochinenii v piati tomakh,* vol. 4, p. 618.

4. "Otvet na anketu *Vechernei Moskvy:* 'Moia pervaia vesh'" ["Answer to a Questionnaire in the *Evening Moscow:* 'My First Work'"]), *Sobranie sochinenii v piati tomakh,* vol. 4, pp. 626–27.

5. *Princeton Encyclopedia of Poetry and Poetics,* ed. Alex Preminger (Princeton: Princeton Univ. Press, 1974), p. 246.

6. *Sublime Malady,* p. 89. Quotations from this poem are from Boris Pasternak, *Poems,* trans. Eugene M. Kayden (Yellow Springs, Ohio: Antioch Press, 1964).

7. All quotations from this poem are from the bilingual edition of Pasternak's poem *The Year Nineteen-Five,* trans. Richard Chappell (London: Spenser Books, 1989). This line is from p. 9.

8. Nicholas V. Riasanovsky, *A History of Russia* (New York: Oxford Univ. Press, 1984), p. 383.

9. As quoted in Lazar Fleishman, *Boris Pasternak v dvadtsatye gody* (Munich: Wilhelm Fink, 1981), p. 83.

10. See, for example, Lazar Fleishman, *Boris Pasternak: The Poet and His Politics* (Cambridge, Mass.: Harvard Univ. Press, 1990), p. 136; Christopher Barnes, *Boris Pasternak: A Literary Biography,* vol. 1 (Cambridge: Cambridge Univ. Press, 1989), p. 362; Henry Gifford, *Pasternak: A Critical Study* (Cambridge: Cambridge Univ. Press, 1977), p. 112; and Ronald Hingley, *Boris Pasternak: A Biography* (New York: Alfred A. Knopf, 1983), p. 85.

11. See commentary on *Lieutenant Schmidt* in the Russian collection of Pasternak's selected works, *Boris Pasternak, Izbrannoe v dvukh tomakh,* vol. 1 (Moscow: Khudozhestvennaia literatura, 1985), p. 575. For a more detailed analysis of Pasternak's use of documentary material in the poem see also Yurii Levin, "Zametki o 'Leitenante Shmidte' B. L. Pasternaka," in *Boris Pasternak: Essays,* ed. Nils Ake Nilsson (Stockholm: Almquist and Wiksell International, 1976), pp. 85–161.

12. See Pasternak's letter to Medvedev of 28 November 1929, *Sobranie sochinenii v piati tomakh,* vol. 5, p. 285.

13. In 1922 Pasternak married a painter, Evgeniia Lur'e, and in the following year their son Evgenii was born. The couple lived in strained housing and financial conditions throughout their marriage, which ended in 1931.

Chapter 4: *Second Birth* and Translations

1. As quoted in Mikhail Heller and Aleksandr Nekrich, *Utopia in Power: The History of the Soviet Union from 1917 to the Present,* trans. Phyllis B. Carlos (New York: Simon and Schuster, 1992), pp. 244–45.

2. In 1903 the Marxist-oriented Russian Social Democratic Party, formed in 1898, split into the Bolshevik fraction, led by Lenin, who wanted to turn the party into an organization of professional revolutionaries, and the Mensheviks, who desired a less structured and radicalized organization. After the October revolution took place, the

Mensheviks opposed the new regime and were gradually suppressed as counterrevolutionaries and eliminated.

3. *Pervyi vsesouiznyi s''ezd sovetskikh pisatelei* (Moscow: Khudozhestvennaia literatura, 1934; Moscow: Sovetskii pisatel', 1990), p. 154.

4. As quoted in the annotations to *Sobranie sochinenii v piati tomakh,* vol. 1, p. 718.

5. Robert Conquest's seminal book *The Great Terror: A Reassessment* (New York: Oxford Univ. Press, 1990) remains the most complete and comprehensive history of Stalinism in the 1930s. It has been updated since its initial publication in 1970.

6. Boris Pasternak, "Neskol'ko slov o novoi gruzinskoi poezii" ["A Few Words about New Georgian Poetry"], in *Sobranie sochinenii v piati tomakh,* vol. 4, p. 412.

7. In a letter to his cousin, Olga Freidenberg, Pasternak wrote that he was afraid that some "accident" might prevent him from completing the translation. He never mentions Meyerkhold by name in this letter but refers to him several times indirectly and mentions that the director's wife was stabbed to death in her apartment, probably on the orders of the secret police. Pasternak's letter to Freidenberg of 14 February 1940, in *Sobranie sochinenii v piati tomakh,* vol. 5, pp. 380–81.

8. Letter to Freidenberg of 14 February 1940, in *Collected Works,* vol. 5, p. 381.

9. Vladimir Markov, "An Unnoticed Aspect of Pasternak's Translations," *Slavic Review* 20 (October 1961): 503–8.

Chapter 5: *On Early Trains*

1. Quoted from *Sobranie sochinenii v piati tomakh,* vol. 5, p. 427.

2. Although Pasternak welcomed publication of his selected fiction in *The Collected Prose Works,* arranged by the young critic Stefan Schimansky in London in 1945, he complained in a December 1945 letter to his parents that the collection included "the horrible 'Apelles Mark,' 'Letters from Tula,' and 'Aerial Ways,'" works no longer compatible with his new aesthetic orientation. See *Sobranie sochinenii v piati tomakh,* vol. 5, p. 444.

3. See "Vystupleniie na III Plenume Pravleniia Soiuza pisatelei SSSR v Minske," in *Sobranie sochinenii v piati tomakh,* vol. 4, pp. 633–39.

4. The poems Pasternak refers to are "Mne po dushe stroptivyi norov" ("I Like the Stubborn Temper," 1936), later included in the collection *On Early Trains* as part of the opening poem "Khudozhnik" ("The Artist"), and "Ia ponial: vse zhivo" ("I Have Realized: Everything Is Alive," 1935), a clichéd tribute to Stalin and happy new life under socialism. The latter poem has not been included in any collections.

5. Pasternak's situation is comparable to that of some German writers who decided to stay in Germany even after the Nazi takeover. They called their situation the "inner emigration," and they had of course to steer a very careful course between maintaining some freedom and at least official acknowledgment of the state norms. Some stopped

writing altogether; others wrote for the masses; and yet others, such as Erich Kästner and Hans Fallada, did some "official" cultural work for the Nazis (or at least in their service) and kept their own work to themselves.

6. See a letter to Freidenberg of 5 November 1943, in *Sobranie sochinenii v piati tomakh,* vol. 5, pp. 422–23.

7. In a letter to Danin of 31 December 1943, in *Sobranie sochinenii v piati tomakh,* vol. 5, p. 424.

8. Pasternak's letter to Freidenberg of 1 July 1932, in *Sobranie sochinenii v piati tomakh,* vol. 5, p. 322.

9. Vladimir Weidlé, "The End of the Journey," in *Pasternak: A Collection of Critical Essays,* p. 178. Henry Gifford also adduces this poem as an illustration of Pasternak's new style and acknowledges Weidlé for selecting it as an example. Henry Gifford, *Pasternak: A Critical Study* (Cambridge: Cambridge University Press, 1977), p. 168.

10. See commentary on the cycle *On Early Trains,* in *Sobranie sochinenii v piati tomakh,* vol. 2, p. 627.

11. A letter to V. D. Avdeev from 21 October 1943, in *Sobranie sochinenii v piati tomakh,* vol. 4, p. 890.

12. The Decembrists were mostly aristocratic liberal army officers who staged a rebellion under Nicholas I in December 1825. They fought for the establishment of constitutionalism and basic freedoms in Russia. The Slavophiles were a group of intellectuals who believed in Russia's unique historical and religious missions. Among the many questions the Slavophile movement addressed in the 1840s and 1850s was the emancipation of the serfs, in which the Slavophile ancestor of Pasternak's friend George Samarin was to play an important role.

13. The most notable representative of Russian civil poetry is Nikolai Nekrasov (1821–1877). For his poems against social inequality and his penchant for imitating folk poetry he was especially praised by Soviet critics.

14. In a letter to Freidenberg of 26 March 1947 Pasternak mentions the intensifying attacks against him in the press and writes that he is "always prepared for anything" (5:461).

Chapter 6: *Doctor Zhivago*

1. Commentaries to *Doctor Zhivago* in *Sobranie sochinenii v piati tomakh,* vol. 3, p. 645.

2. The name Zhivago is a Church Slavonic form of the genitive case of the adjective *zhivoi.* Church Slavonic is the oldest ecclesiastical and literary language among Slavic languages. It is still used in the liturgy of the Eastern Church.

3. Olga Ivinskaia, *V plenu vremeni: Gody s Borisom Pasternakom (A Captive of Time: My Years with Boris Pasternak)* (Paris: Arthéme Fayard, 1978), pp. 232–33.

4. A review of critical opinions following the publication of Pasternak's novel is presented in Conquest, *Courage of Genius,* pp. 49–58. A meticulous study of critical perspectives on *Doctor Zhivago* was accomplished by Neil Cornwell in *Pasternak's Novel: Perspectives on Doctor Zhivago, Essays in Poetics Publications,* no. 2 (Keele: Keele Univ., 1986).

5. The pantheistic dimension in Pasternak's representation of nature has been discussed in Guy de Mallac, *Boris Pasternak: His Life and Art* (Norman: Univ. of Oklahoma Press, 1981), pp. 289–95. De Mallac also draws attention to the closeness between Pasternak's view of nature and that of eighteenth-century vitalism, the doctrine that life is self-determining and cannot be explained solely by science.

6. See, for instance, a recent account of Lenin's ruthlessness in the yearly postrevolutionary years in Robert Conquest's review article "The Somber Monster," *The New York Review of Books* 42 (8 June 1995): 8–12.

7. Boris Pasternak, "Three Letters," *Encounter* 83 (August 1960): 4.

8. Robert Louis Jackson, "*Doctor Zhivago: Liebestod* of the Russian Intelligentsia," in *Pasternak: A Collection of Critical Essays,* ed. Victor Erlich (Englewood Cliffs, N.J.: Prentice-Hall, 1978), p. 149.

9. Vyvolochnov refers here to the Symbolists and their popular imagery. *Nénuphar* is the French word for a water lily. Water lilies often appeared on the designs of Symbolist books and in Symbolist works.

10. This speech is discussed in chapter 5 of this book.

11. A letter to Freidenberg of 13 October 1946, in *Sobranie sochinenii v piati tomakh,* vol. 5, p. 454.

12. Mikhail Heller and Aleksandr Nekrich, *Utopia in Power: The History of the Soviet Union from 1917 to the Present,* trans. Phyllis B. Carlos (New York: Simon and Schuster, 1986), pp. 407–10.

13. For an excellent documented account of the fate of Jews in the Soviet Union after WW II see Benjamin Pinkus, *The Soviet Government and the Jews 1948–1967: A Documentary Study* (Cambridge: Cambridge Univ. Press, 1984), pp. 147–92; see also Yeshua A. Gilboa, *The Black Years of Soviet Jewry: 1939–1953,* trans. from the Hebrew by Yosef Shachter and Dov Ben-Abba (Boston: Little, Brown, 1971), pp. 146–86; or Benjamin Pinkus, *The Jews of the Soviet Union: The History of a National Minority,* vol. 3 (Cambridge: Cambridge Univ. Press, 1988), pp. 139–208.

14. Stuart Hampshire, "*Doctor Zhivago:* As from a Lost Culture," in *Pasternak: A Collection of Critical Essays,* p. 128.

15. Pasternak, *Sobranie sochinenii v piati tomakh,* vol. 4, p. 396.

16. In his analysis of the character of Antipov-Strel'nikov, Bethea convincingly demonstrates the self-destructive implications of this transformation (pp. 254–55).

17. For the use of coincidences in Pasternak's fiction see chapter 2.

18. See editorial commentaries after the novel in *Sobranie sochinenii v piati tomakh,* vol. 3, p. 713.

19. Toward the end of his life, Pasternak explained his uneasiness about living

in the city in the summer by the dramatic element in the city atmosphere as opposed to the charm of nature in the country. See commentaries to the poem in *Sobranie sochinenii v piati tomakh,* vol. 3, p. 719–20.

20. This interpretation is suggested by Olga R. Hughes in *The Poetic World of Boris Pasternak* (Princeton: Princeton Univ. Press, 1973), pp. 74–75.

21. The deeper meaning of the phrase "the candle burned" refers to Christ's words to the apostles that their deeds, like a candle, should illuminate life and thus glorify the Lord (Matthew, 5:14–16). See the comments in the Russian edition of *Doctor Zhivago,* in *Sobranie sochinenii v piati tomakh,* vol. 3, p. 726.

22. Hughes, in *The Poetic World of Boris Pasternak,* p. 70, points to this word as the key to understanding the religious dimension of the poem.

Chapter 7: The Last Years

1. This collection has also been translated into English under the titles *When the Skies Clear* and *When It Clears Up.*

2. A letter to Nina Tabidze of 17 January 1953, in *Sobranie sochinenii v piati tomakh,* vol. 5, p. 504.

3. "Bacchanalia" has an autobiographical background and is connected with the production of Schiller's drama *Maria Stuart* (in Pasternak's translation) in Moscow in 1957.

Chapter 8: Conclusion

1. Marina Tsvetaeva, "Epos i lirika sovremennoi epokhi (Vladimir Mayakovsky i Boris Pasternak)" ("Epic and Lyric In Contemporary Russia: Mayakovsky and Pasternak"), in *Izbrannaia proza v dvukh tomakh* [*Selected Prose in Two Volumes*], vol. 2 (New York: Russica Publishers, 1979), p. 24.

Select Bibliography

Works by Boris Pasternak

Sochineniia. Ed. Gleb Struve and Boris Filippov. 3 vols. Ann Arbor: University of Michigan Press, 1961.

Doktor Zhivago. Ann Arbor: University of Michigan Press, 1976.

"Iz rannikh prozaicheskikh opytov B. Pasternaka." *Slavica Hierosolymitana* 4 (1979): 286–93.

"O predmete i metode psikhologii." Ed. S. G. Gellershtein. *Slavica Hierosolymitana* 4 (1979): 274–85.

Izbrannoe v dvukh tomakh. Ed. E. V. Pasternak and E. B. Pasternak. Moscow: Khudozhestvennaia literatura, 1985.

Sobranie sochinenii v piati tomakh. Ed. E. V. Pasternak and K. M. Polivanov. Moscow: Khudozhestvennaia literatura, 1989–1992.

English Translations

Safe Conduct: An Autobiography and Other Writings. Trans. C. M. Bowra, Babette Deutsch, and Robert Payne. New York: New Directions, 1958.

The Poetry of Boris Pasternak, 1914–1960. Trans. George Reavey. New York: Putnam's, Capricorn, 1959.

Poems, 1955–1959. Trans. Michael Harari. London: Collins and Harvill, 1960.

Poems. Trans. Eugene M. Kayden. 2nd ed. Yellow Springs, Ohio: Antioch Press, 1964. The most complete collection of translations of Pasternak's poetry in English.

The Poems of Dr. Zhivago. Trans. Donald Davie. New York: Barnes and Noble, 1965.

Collected Short Prose. Ed. and intro. Christopher Barnes. New York: Praeger, 1977.

The Correspondence of Boris Pasternak and Olga Freidenberg, 1910–1954. Ed. Elliott Mossman. Trans. Mossman and Margaret Wettlin. New York: Harcourt, Brace, 1982.

I Remember: Sketch for an Autobiography. Trans. and ed. David Magarshack; includes "Translating Shakespeare," trans. Manya Harari. Cambridge, Mass.: Harvard University Press, 1983.

My Sister-Life and A Sublime Malady. Trans. Mark Rudman with Bohdan Boychuk. Ann Arbor: Ardis, 1983.

Selected Poems. Trans. Jon Stallworthy and Peter France. London: Allen Lane, 1983. Selected translations from Pasternak's major collections of poetry, *Nineteen Hundred and Five,* and some poems from *Doctor Zhivago.*

Poems of Boris Pasternak. Trans. Lydia Pasternak Slater. London: Unwin Paperbacks, 1984. Translated by Pasternak's sister.

Pasternak on Art and Creativity. Ed. Angela Livingstone. Cambridge: Cambridge University Press, 1985. A useful collection of Pasternak's literary and critical works and excerpts from his works on art. Insightful editorial comments.

The Voice of Prose: Early Prose and Autobiography. Trans. Christopher Barnes et al. Ed. Christopher Barnes. New York: Grove Press, 1986.

The Zhivago Poems. Trans. Barbara Everest. Huntington, W.V.: Aegina Press, 1988.

Doctor Zhivago. Trans. Max Hayward and Manya Harari; includes "The Poems of Iurii Zhivago," trans. Bernard Guilbert Guerney. New York: Ballantine Books, 1989.

The Year Nineteen-Five (Deviat'sot piatyi god). Trans. Richard Chappell. Bilingual ed. London: Spenser Books, 1989.

Second Nature: Forty-Six Poems by Boris Pasternak. Trans. Andrei Navrozov. London: Peter Owen, 1990.

Leitenant Shmidt=Lieutenant Schmidt. Trans. Richard Chappell. London: Spenser Books, 1992.

My Sister-Life. Trans. Mark Rudman and Bohdan Boychuk. Evanston, Ill.: Northwestern University Press, 1992.

Critical Works about Boris Pasternak

Anderson, Roger B. "The Railroad in *Doktor Zhivago.*" *Slavic and East European Journal* 31, no. 4 (1987): 503–19.

Aucouturier, Michel, ed. *Boris Pasternak, 1890–1960: Colloque de Cerisy-la-Salle (11–14 septembre 1975).* Paris: Institut D'Etudes Slaves, 1979. Useful collection of scholarly articles on different aspects of Pasternak's work.

Barnes, Christopher. *Boris Pasternak: A Literary Biography.* Vol. 1. Cambridge: Cambridge University Press, 1989. The best study of Pasternak's life and works from 1890 to 1928. The second volume is forthcoming. Excellent documentation. Superb index.

———. "Boris Pasternak and Rainer Maria Rilke: Some Missing Links." *Forum for Modern Language Studies* 7, no. 1 (1972): 61–78.

———. "Pasternak as Composer and Scriabin-Disciple." *Tempo: Quarterly Review of Modern Music* 121 (1977): 17.

Berlin, Isaiah. "The Energy of Pasternak." *Partisan Review* 17 (September–October 1950): 748–51.

Bethea, David M. *The Shape of Apocalypse in Modern Russian Fiction.* Princeton: Princeton University Press, 1989. A chapter devoted to *Doctor Zhivago* provides an interesting analysis of the novel's apocalyptic symbolism.

Bodin, Per-Arne. "Boris Pasternak and the Christian Tradition." *Forum for Modern Language Studies* 26, no. 4 (1990): 382–401.

———. *Nine Poems from Doktor Zhivago: A Study of Christian Motifs in Boris Pasternak's Poetry.* Stockholm Studies in Russian Literature, no. 6. Stockholm: Almqvist and Wiksell, 1976.

———. "The Sleeping Demiurge: An Analysis of Boris Pasternak's Poem 'Durnoi son.'" In *Text and Context: Essays to Honor Nils Ake Nilsson,* edited by Peter Alberg Jense, Barbara Lönnqvist, Fiona Björling, Lars Kleberg, and Anders Sjöberg. Stockholm: Almqvist and Wiksell, 1987.

Clowes, Edith W. "Characterization in *Doktor Zhivago:* Lara and Tonia." *Slavic and East European Journal* 34, no. 3 (1990): 322–31.

———, ed. *Doctor Zhivago: A Critical Companion.* Evanston: Northwestern University Press, 1995.

Conquest, Robert. *Courage of Genius: The Pasternak Affair.* London: Collins and Harvill, 1966. An excellent study of events surrounding Pasternak's Nobel Prize.

Cornwell, Neil. *Pasternak's Novel: Perspectives on Doctor Zhivago.* Essays in Poetics Publications, no. 3. Keele: Keele University, 1986. Provides a useful classification and summary of critical views on Pasternak's works.

Danow, David K. "Dialogic Poetics: *Doktor Zhivago.*" *Slavic Review* 50 (Winter 1991): 954–64.

Davie, Donald, and Angela Livingstone, eds. *Pasternak: Modern Judgements.* London: Macmillan, 1969.

Deutscher, Isaac. "Pasternak and the Calendar of the Revolution." In *Pasternak: Modern Judgements,* edited by Donald Davie and Angela Livingstone. London: Macmillan, 1969.

Dyck, J. W. *Boris Pasternak.* New York: Twayne, 1972. A basic introductory survey of Pasternak's major works. Sketchy on poetry but a good guide to *Doctor Zhivago.*

———. "Boris Pasternak: The Caprice of Beauty." *Canadian Slavonic Papers* 16 (1974): 612–26.

Erlich, Victor. "Boris Pasternak and Russian Poetic Culture of His Time." In *Boris Pasternak and His Times: Selected Papers from the Second International Symposium on Pasternak,* edited by Lazar Fleishman. Berkeley: Berkeley Slavic Specialties, 1989.

Faryno, Jerzy. *Poetika Pasternaka ("Putevye zapiski"—"Okhrannaia gramota").* Wiener Slawistischer Almanach. Sonderband 22. Vienna: Gesellschaft zur Förderung Slawistischer Studien, 1989. Good for its erudite structural and intertextual analysis of *Safe Conduct.*

Fleishman, Lazar. *Boris Pasternak: The Poet and His Politics.* Cambridge, Mass.: Harvard University Press, 1990. Establishes connections between Pasternak's literary works and the political climate in which they were produced. In-depth analysis of the cultural-political climate in Soviet Russia during Pasternak's lifetime.

————. *Boris Pasternak v dvadtsatye gody.* Munich: Wilhelm Fink, 1981. Examines Pasternak's work in relation to the literary policies of the 1920s in the Soviet Union. Impressive documentation.

————. *Boris Pasternak v tridtsatye gody.* Jerusalem: Magnes Press, 1984. In-depth study of Pasternak's work in the context of the political climate in the Soviet Union in the 1930s. Excellent documentation.

————. "Fragmenty futuristicheskoi biografii Pasternaka." *Slavica Hierosolymitana* 4 (1979): 79–113. Explores aspects of Pasternak's Futurist period.

————. "Problems in the Poetics of Pasternak." *PTL: A Journal for Descriptive Poetics and Theory of Literature* 4 (1979): 43–61.

————. *Stat'i o Pasternake.* Bremen: K-Presse, 1977. A collection of articles on Pasternak.

Folejewski, Zbignew. "Some Problems of Semantics in Painting and in Poetry: Mayakovsky, Pasternak, and the Italian Manifesto of Futurist Painting." *Canadian Slavonic Papers* 25, no. 1 (1983): 108–16.

Frank, Victor S. "A Russian Hamlet: Boris Pasternak's Novel." *Dublin Review* 477 (1958): 212–20.

Gerschenkron, Alexander. "Notes on *Doctor Zhivago*." *Modern Philology* 58 (February 1961): 194–200.

Gifford, Henry. *Pasternak: A Critical Study.* London: Cambridge University Press, 1977. A sensitive and beautifully written book on Pasternak's literary work. Particularly strong in poetic analysis.

————. "Pasternak and European Modernism." *Forum for Modern Language Studies* 24 (October 1990): 301–14.

————. "Pasternak and His Western Contemporaries." In *Boris Pasternak and His Time,* edited by Lazar Fleishman. Berkeley: Berkeley Slavic Specialties, 1989.

Harris, Jane Gary. "Pasternak's Vision of Life: The History of a Feminine Image." *Russian Literature Triquarterly* 9 (1974): 389–421.

Hingley, Ronald. *Boris Pasternak: A Biography.* New York: Alfred A. Knopf, 1983. A study of Pasternak's work in the context of his life. Useful historical references.

Hughes, Olga R. *The Poetic World of Boris Pasternak.* Princeton: Princeton University Press, 1974. A sensitive study of major aspects of Pasternak's poetics.

Ivinskaia, Olga. *V plenu vremeni: Gody s Borisom Pasternakom.* Paris: Arthàme Fayard, 1978. Memoirs of Pasternak's lover, Olga Ivinskaia. Rich in personal detail.

Jackson, Robert L. "*Doktor Zhivago* and the Living Tradition." *Slavic and East European Journal* 4 (1960): 103–18.

Jakobson, Roman. "The Contours of *The Safe Conduct*." In *Semiotics of Art,* edited by Ladislav Matejka and Irwin R. Titunik. Cambridge, Mass.: MIT Press, 1976.

————. "Marginal Notes on the Prose of the Poet Pasternak." In *Language in Literature,* edited by Krystyna Pomorska and Stephen Rudy. Cambridge, Mass.: Belknap Press of Harvard University Press, 1987.

Layton, Susan. "Poetic Vision in Pasternak's 'The Childhood of Luvers.'" *Slavic and*

East European Journal 22, no. 2 (1978): 163–74.

Livingstone, Angela. *Boris Pasternak: Doctor Zhivago.* Cambridge: Cambridge University Press, 1989. A useful comprehensive introduction to Pasternak's novel. Textbook format. Detailed chronology.

———. "Pasternak and Faust." *Forum for Modern Language Studies* 26, no. 4 (1990): 353–69.

———. "Pasternak's Last Poetry." In *Pasternak: A Collection of Critical Essays,* edited by Victor Erlich. Englewood Cliffs, N.J.: Prentice-Hall, 1978.

———. "Some Affinities in the Prose of the Poets Rilke and Pasternak." *Forum for Modern Language Studies* 19, no. 3 (1983): 274–84.

Ljunggren, Anna. *Juvenilia Borisa Pasternaka: 6 fragmentov o Relinkvimini.* Stockholm: Almqvist and Wiksell, 1984. A study devoted to Pasternak's earliest prose sketches.

Loseff, Lev, ed. *Boris Pasternak: 1890–1990.* Northfield, Vt.: Russian School of Norwich University, 1991. Useful collection of essays.

MacKinnon, John Edward. "From Cold Axles to Hot: Boris Pasternak's Theory of Art." *British Journal of Aesthetics* 28 (Spring 1988): 145–61.

Mallac, Guy de. *Boris Pasternak: His Life and Art.* Norman: University of Oklahoma Press, 1981. Extremely useful discussion of *Doctor Zhivago* within the context of modern philosophical ideas. Excellent chronology.

Malmstad, John E. "Boris Pasternak—The Painter's Eye." *Russian Review* 51 (July 1992): 301–18.

Markov, Vladimir. *Russian Futurism.* Berkeley: University of California Press, 1968.

Milosz, Czeslaw. "On Pasternak Soberly [1970]." *World Literature Today* 63 (Spring 1989): 215–20.

Mossman, Elliott. "Pasternak's Prose Style: Some Observations." *Russian Literature Triquarterly* 1 (1969): 386–98.

———. "Pasternak's Short Fiction." *Russian Literature Triquarterly* 3 (1972): 279–302.

Nilsson, Nils Ake, ed. *Boris Pasternak: Essays.* Stockholm: Almqvist and Wiksell, 1976.

Obolensky, Dimitri. "The Poems in Doctor Zhivago." In Pasternak: A Collection of Critical Essays, edited by Victor Erlich. Englewood Cliffs, N.J.: Prentice-Hall, 1978.

O'Connor, Katherine Tiernan. *Boris Pasternak's My Sister-Life: The Illusion of Narrative.* Ann Arbor: Ardis, 1988. Explores the narrative continuity of the cycle.

Pasternak, Evgenii Borisovitch. *The Tragic Years: 1930–60.* Trans. Michael Duncan; poetry trans. Ann Pasternak Slater and Craig Raine. London: Collins Harvill, 1990.

Payne, Robert. *The Three Worlds of Boris Pasternak.* Bloomington: Indiana University Press, 1963. Impressionistic overview of Pasternak's selected poetry and prose.

Plank, Dale L. *Pasternak's Lyric: A Study of Sound and Imagery.* The Hague: Mouton, 1966. A good analysis of Pasternak's poetic language. Many examples.

Poggioli, Renato. "Boris Pasternak." *Partisan Review* 25 (1958): 541–54.

Pomorska, Krystyna. *Themes and Variations in Pasternak's Poetics.* Lisse: Peter de Ridde Press, 1975. A basic study of major themes of Pasternak's poetry and prose.

Rowland, Mary F., and Paul Rowland. *Pasternak's Doctor Zhivago.* Carbondale: Southern Illinois University Press, 1967. A thorough analysis of *Doctor Zhivago*'s symbolism.

Rudova, Larissa. "On Pasternak's 'Aerial Ways.'" *Canadian American Slavic Studies* 24 (Spring 1990): 33–46.

———. "Parameters of the Self in Pasternak's *Safe Conduct.*" *A/b: Auto/Biography Studies* 9 (September 1995): 1–16.

———. *Pasternak's Short Fiction and the Cultural Vanguard.* Middlebury Studies in Russian Language and Literature. Vol. 6. New York: Peter Lang, 1994.

Sendich, Munir. *Boris Pasternak: A Reference Guide.* New York: G. K. Hall, 1994.

Sinyavsky, Andrey. "Pasternak's Poetry." In *Pasternak: A Collection of Critical Essays,* edited by Victor Erlich. Englewood Cliffs, N.J.: Prentice-Hall, 1978.

Struve, Gleb. "The Hippodrome of Life: The Problem of Coincidences in *Doctor Zhivago.*" *World Literature Today* 44 (Spring 1977): 231–36.

Terras, Victor. "Boris Pasternak and Romantic Aesthetics." *Papers on Language and Literature* 3 (1967): 42–56.

———. "Boris Pasternak and Time." *Canadian Slavic Studies* 2, no. 2 (1968): 264–70. Discusses Pasternak's understanding of time and its manifestations in the poet's works.

General Index

Index of Works by Boris Pasternak